The Modern Girl's Guide to Motherhood

Also by Jane Buckingham

The Modern Girl's Guide to Life

The Modern Girl's Guide to Motherhood

Jane Buckingham

With Jen Furmaniak

ReganBooks

An Imprint of HarperCollins*Publishers*

THE MODERN GIRL'S GUIDE TO MOTHERHOOD. Copyright © 2006 by Jane Buckingham. All rights reserved. Printed in the United States of America. No part of this book may be used or re-produced in any manner whatsoever without written permission except in the case of brief quotations embodied in critical articles and reviews. For information, address Harper-Collins Publishers Inc., 10 East 53rd Street, New York, NY 10022.
HarperCollins books may be purchased for educational, business, or sales promotional use. For information please write: Special Markets Department, HarperCollins Publishers Inc., 10 East 53rd Street, New York, NY 10022.

FIRST EDITION

Designed by Judith Stagnitto Abbate / Abbate Design

Printed on acid-free paper
Library of Congress Cataloging-in-Publication Data has been applied for.

ISBN-13: 978-0-06-088534-2
ISBN-10: 0-06-088534-3

06 07 08 09 10 9 8 7 6 5 4 3 2 1

To Marcus: Without you, none of this would matter. I love you.

 To Jack and Lilia: I love you. Thank you for giving me meaning.

Contents

Introduction   1

1. The Mother of All Shopping Sprees   5

The Nursery
Decorating Themes · Gear Guide: What You Need,
What You Don't · Cribs, Beds, and Planning Ahead ·
Linens and Things · Moses Baskets, Cosleepers
and Basinettes · Changing Table Basics · Changing
Table Essentials · Monitors · Other Nursery
Essentials   6

Beyond the Bedroom
Infant Seats and Swings · Playmats · Exersaucers ·
Walkers · Jumpers · Toys · High Chairs · Infant Tubs ·
Bath Products · Humidifiers   20

Heading Out the Door
Car Seats · Infant Carriers · Strollers · Playpen/
Travel Crib · Packing It In: Diaper Bag   25

The Home Medicine Cabinet   33

Creating a Layette
Buying Guide · Washing Your Baby's Clothes ·
The Modern Mom's Guide to Stain Removal   35

**2. Experts, Epidurals, and Everything
   Else Before Baby   43**
Choosing a Pediatrician   44

Bracing for Delivery Day
Some Great Books on Labor and Delivery ·
Birthing Methods and Ways to Ease the Pain   45

While You Still Have Some Time on Your Hands
Ordering Announcements · Preserving Memories ·
Writing a Will · Appointing a Legal Guardian ·
A Living Trust · Dollars and Sense: Planning for
Your Child's Financial Future · Compiling a Call List ·
Packing for the Hospital   50

Eight Unpleasant Things You Need to Know About
Pooing on the Table · Tears and Episiotomies ·
Peeing and Pooing Post Pushing · Pain Pain
Pain!#@%#$*^%!!!!! · Hemorrhoids · Bizarre Side
Effects · Sex · Postpartum Depression   63

Deciding About Cord Blood Banking   71

Help Is on the Way!
Choosing a Nanny · Choosing Day Care   74

**3. The Babymoon: The First Few Weeks Home
   from the Hospital   78**
Introducing Your Bundle of Joy (and Screams)
New Siblings · Furry Friends   79

Dealing with Wanted (and Unwanted) Visitors
Drop-by Visitors: At the Hospital and at Home ·
Friends with Toddlers · Overnight Houseguests   84

Babyproofing   88

*Reality Check: Everything Has Changed, but Your
Life Will Come Back*   90

4. Food for Thought (And Little Tummies)   **92**

Your New Bosom Buddy
Advantages of Breast-feeding · How Long Should
You Breast-feed? · Latching and Learning the Ropes ·
Feeding on Demand · Problem Eaters · Your Baby
Is What You Eat · Ouch! Sore Nipples · Pumping   93

Hitting the Bottle
Choosing a Formula · How Much? · Bottle
Do's and Don'ts   104

Burping, Colic, and Crying
Spit Happens · Burping Your Baby · Colic   107

Everybody Stay Calm! Making the Most of Pacifiers   111

Introducing Solid Foods
Six to Ten Months · Great Foods · How Much? · Foods
to Avoid · Gas in Children · Making Your Own Food ·
Drinks and Things · Ten to Twelve Months · How Much? ·
Food Safety   113

One Year and Beyond
Healthy Eating Habits · Treats and Desserts ·
Dealing with a Fussy Eater · Healthful Snack Alternatives
to Sweets · How Much? · Vitamins   123

Family Dinners: You Mean Carryout Doesn't Count?
Table Manners   129

Dining Out with Kids in Tow   131

5. Wake Up! We Need to Talk About Sleep   **134**

Birth to Three Months: From A to Zzz's
What If He Screams? · Getting on a Schedule ·
Response Time · If All Else Fails · SIDS and Flat Heads   136

Three to Nine Months: Sleep Is on the Way
Possible Hiccups · Bedtimes   145

Nine to Twelve Months: Too Good to Be True
Possible Hiccups   148

One-Year-Old Sleep Patterns
Possible Hiccups   149

Big Boy/Girl Beds
Staying Until They Sleep   151

Terrible Twos at Night
Lights Out! · The Party's Over   153

What the Experts Say   156

6. Baby Care 101 (Because Dressing Them in Cute Outfits Isn't Enough)   **160**

Bath Time
Sponge Baths · Bathtub Baths · Best Bath Time ·
Switching to a Big Tub · Little Kid Bath Activities ·
If Your Child Is Terrified of the Bath   160

Caring for Those Other 1001 Small Parts
Eyes · Umbilical Stump · Cradle Cap · Hair ·
Penis · Ears · Nose · Nails · Teeth   166

Teething
Relieving Teething Pain   172

That Doesn't Look/Feel/Sound Right!
Get Help STAT! · Get Help When It's Practical ·
Temperatures · Ear Infections · Sore Throat ·
Congestion · Diarrhea · Cuts · Blisters · Burns ·
Bumps and Bruises · Nosebleeds · Bee Stings ·
Splinters · Hiccups   174

Vaccinations
What the Heck Are All These Shots For? ·
Vaccinations Month by Month · Preparing Your
Child for Shots   187

Many Mini-Milestones
What to Expect Developmentally and When   193

7. Teach Your Children Well . . . Or Else It's Hell   **206**

Hi, My Name Is Mommy, and You Are . . . ?
Birth to Fifteen Months · Fifteen to Twenty-one
Months · Twenty-two to Twenty-seven Months ·
Twenty-eight to Thirty-six Months   207

Communicating with Your Child
Creating Independence   210

Discipline
Saying "Yes" Instead of "No" · Teaching That
Actions Have Consequences · Time-Outs · Disciplining
Your Child's Friends · Other People Disciplining
Your Child · Praise When Praise Is Due   214

The Bad and the Ugly: Dealing With . . .
Tantrums · Physical Aggression · Pulling Hair ·
Spitting Food · Banging Heads · Whining · Bad Words ·
"I Don't Like You" · Baby Talk/Play · Tattling   219

Mind Your Manners
Saying You're Sorry · Excuse Me · Please and
Thank You · Hello and Goodbye · Sharing ·
Eating Behavior · Responsibilities · Nose Picking,
Farting, and Burping   225

Dealing with the Hard Stuff
Separation Issues · Death   232

Ask the Experts
The RIE Method · The Happiest Toddler on
the Block · Books by Louise Bates Ames · Dr. Spock ·
The *What to Expect . . .* Series   235

**8. Breaking Up* Is Hard to Do
(*With Old Habits, That Is)**   **241**

Breaking Old Habits
The Mommy Store Is Closed · Buh-Bye
Bottle · Pitching the Pacifier · Thumb
Sucking · Security Blankets and Other
Comfort Items   241

Have a Seat: The Fine Art of Potty Training
Are We There Yet? Signs Your Child Might Be Ready ·
Ready, Aim, Pee · At Night · Bathroom Hygiene   254

9. The Play Dating Game and Beyond   261

Best Toys and Activities at Any Age
Birth to Three Months · Baby Massage · Four to
Twelve Months · Twelve to Eighteen Months ·
Eighteen to Twenty-four Months · Twenty-four to
Thirty-six Months · To TV or Not TV   262

Play: Is It All It's Cracked Up to Be?
Picking the Right Playgroup and Classes ·
Play Dating · Observational Play · Parallel Play ·
Imaginary Play · Cooperative Play · Play Date Ideas ·
Nannies Versus Mommies   275

Birthday Parties
Party Ideas · Some Fun Party Activities ·
Goodie Bags · Gift Tips   281

Picking a Preschool
Getting Your Child Ready for Preschool   289

Bibliography   295
Acknowledgments   298
Index   303

The Modern Girl's Guide to Motherhood

Introduction

Okay, just when I started thinking that I could cook (hey, one meal counts), clean (if the queen were coming), and seduce a man (well, long enough to get married), I discovered that my previous ineptitude in life paled in comparison to the task that was awaiting me. With one simple extra line on a pregnancy test, I realized how little I knew about the world of motherhood. From when to tell my boss I was pregnant to covering up leaking shirts, to how to take a pacifier away from a two-year-old who has the grip of a pit bull, it was all beyond a mystery.

Without a mom (man, do I miss her) and as one of the first of my friends to enter the childbearing stage, I felt a bit rudderless. And while it's fine to be indecisive when, say, picking out cribs, it's less advised when figuring out what to do with the baby inside the third crib you finally landed upon. Oh sure, there are books on these topics—dozens, in fact. But that's the problem. For every piece of advice there seems to be a conflicting one. And every book requires you to wade through endless babble before getting to the good stuff (or warning you about the really really bad stuff). So enter *The Modern Girl's Guide to Motherhood*. From giving birth to raising a toddler, I'm hoping to cut through the clutter to offer the best advice out there, the best-kept secrets, and multiple solutions for the hardest-to-deal-with problems. Like my first book, *The Modern Girl's Guide to Life*, this book will offer simple information and practical advice—how to get your child to sleep, how to wean, how to get them off the pacifier, how to get them to stop throwing a tantrum, and so on. My goal is to help you feel in the know and in control.

But don't get me wrong. I am not a perfect parent. My children aren't perfect. You won't get a perfect child by reading this book (and anyone who tells you they can get you that is either lying or delusional and definitely not to be trusted). I'm not an "expert," but I have done a heck of a lot of research in trying to compile the best information out there. And while I'd like to tell you I've covered every situation in this book, I haven't. Otherwise, this would be a daunting zillion-page edition that was too expensive to buy and too intimidating to read. But I've tried to cover the essentials and the toughest issues out there.

To that end, this book was not written alone—and please read the Acknowledgments, 'cause this ain't them, but they are important. I want to mention in particular three incredible women without whom this book wouldn't exist.

Jen Furmaniak, my coauthor, is a new mom who truly knows more than the other mommies on the block ('cause she's read every darn book and interviewed all kinds of experts). Her voice, her stories, her issues, like mine, are within. She is a friend, a pro, and if this had gone any better we'd have to get married. Betsy Brown Braun is a child development specialist, parent educator, and multiple-birth parenting consultant. She has a master's degree in human development and teaching credentials from all kinds of fancy places. She offered the sound advice only an expert and mother of triplets could provide. She knows her stuff. She tells me things, I try them, and they work. She gave 120 percent at a time when she could have given 50. Rebecca Whitney, MD, is the essence of a Modern Girl—a pediatrician with degrees from Harvard and Tulane who not only dispenses the best medical advice, but does so while looking fabulous. She's like a *CSI* character, but she is a real live person whom little children love and who knows everything about everything. Between their wise counsel, the dozens of books I've read, the hundreds of moms I've spoken to, and my own day-to-day life, this book is a compilation of what I truly feel is the best advice out there.

There are people who will disagree adamantly with certain tips or ideas, and others who will send hate mail for advocating a toy or technique, and to those people, I am sorry. But that's one of the biggest lessons I have learned: that you will make mistakes, and you will have regrets, but that's just part of being a parent.

And finally, I wanted to pass on the two best pieces of advice I ever received. The first came from Nancy Schulman. Nancy is a teacher, friend, mom, and preschool director who told me, as I frenetically listed all of the things I was sure I had done wrong, that children need only two things:

1. Unconditional love

2. Clear limits

And while you'll tell yourself that that's easy, you'll soon find out that while number one is no problem, number two is a bit of a challenge. So as I tell you about strollers, as you curse me for not answering a pressing question, try to remember the above advice, take a deep breath, and remember what matters.

The second piece of advice came from my friend Andrea Stanford, a model of motherhood (and fashion, but I suppose that's less relevant here), who has three daughters we'd all kill to have. Hers was that there are no bad habits you can't break in three painful days. And while experts will tell you to avoid the bad habits, they'll happen. So as you grit your teeth bracing for sleep training, getting rid of the pacifier, or whatever it is, know that there is always an end in sight (even if three turns into five, but it usually doesn't), and you haven't "ruined" your child if something "bad" develops. Life is long, and there will be many things to deal with.

I hope you love this book as much as I enjoyed putting it together. Here's to modern mothering!

CHAPTER 1

The Mother of All Shopping Sprees

Face it, half the reason you *got* pregnant was the too-cute comforters and the to-die-for diaper cozies you saw at your girlfriend's house and needed a reason to buy. Okay, maybe it's not *half* the reason, but decorating a whole new room in supercute baby stuff can make a bad meeting with the doctor's scale a little better. The problem is that some of the cutest stuff out there is the least practical (and the most expensive). I had sterilizers, warmers, things that bounced, things that vibrated, and every gadget available. If someone had told me that buying the Brooklyn Bridge might help me get a baby who slept better, I would probably have handed over a check. I wasted a lot of money and time on unnecessary stuff.

The reality is there are things you *need* to have, things that are *nice* to have, and those that are *not necessary*. And chances are, if you are reading this book in chronological order, you've already stocked up on quite a bit. I can't blame you; I clearly didn't resist the urge either. But the truth is, you don't need to buy up the store before the baby comes. Many things you won't use for several months and you can swap out if space is tight. Now while I've sorted the list into three, you may feel differently about some items. That's your choice; I'm a modern mom, not *your* mom. So I've included thoughts on just about everything (other than feeding-related products, which you'll find in chapter 4).

The Nursery

Decorating Themes

Now before you run out to buy everything, you should figure out where you will be keeping the baby and when. Someone once told me (as I stressed about where we would put a baby in our cramped apartment) that for the first few months a baby could easily sleep in a dresser drawer. Yes, and women have babies in fields and go right back to work, but that isn't my scene either. But the truth is that until your baby is crawling around, she doesn't need the space as much as you do. You may even find it more convenient to have the baby in your room for the first few months in a bassinet or (as I preferred) a cosleeper, and discover you barely use the nursery for several months. But assuming you are going to have a separate room or space, here are a few things to keep in mind.

MODERN MOM (MM) TIP:
I was (and still am) a big fan of sites like Babystyle.com, Target.com, and Amazon.com for big purchases so that I don't have to lug them home myself. And I've set up an account on Drugstore.com for all my supplies (such as diapers, wipes, and so on) so that I'm not stuck juggling a baby in one hand and an economy-size fifty diapers in the other.

- Make sure the room is well ventilated, with windows and a ceiling fan or air conditioning for the summer, and good insulation and heat for the winter. While my son's room was perfect most of the time, it was an icebox in the winter. We had to move his crib, get insulation, and basically have him spend his first winter sleeping in a snowsuit.

- You'll be spending a lot of time going back and forth to this room in the beginning, so it is helpful if it is near to your room, preferably on the same floor. Climbing the stairs—while a great way to get back in shape—isn't much fun bleary-eyed at 4 A.M.

- Invest in a nice, glowing night-light. You can use it to maneuver in the middle of the night while not taking your baby out of "night-time" mode by switching on overhead lights (and here you thought a night-light was for the *baby*).

- Go with fabrics that are washable. You won't believe how much laundry you'll be doing. If it's dry clean only, regift it to your biggest enemy.

GEAR GUIDE: WHAT YOU NEED, WHAT YOU DON'T

I've provided a timeline because I expected that once I had a baby, I would never leave my house again. Not only is that not true, but I also didn't need to have everything piling up in my living room, as I didn't use much of it for many months.

NEED TO HAVE

Before They Arrive
- Changing table
- Diapers
- Cotton squares
- Diaper pail
- Changing pad
- Blanket for the crib or stroller (*avoid using with babies under six months old due to suffocation risks*)
- Receiving blankets—*smaller blankets used for swaddling (ideal for newborns and young babies)*
- Baby audio monitor
- Nail clippers
- Bulb syringe
- Night-light
- Thermometer
- Hairbrush and/or comb
- Infant car seat
- Diaper bag
- Laundry detergent

By One Month
- Baby shampoo and body wash
- Diaper rash ointment

(continued)

- Infant bathtub
- Wipes
- Stroller

By Two Months
- Crib/mattress
- Bedding
- Mattress pads

By Six Months
- High chair
- Toddler car seat

MM TIP:
Hold off on buying items you don't need right away until *after* you've received all of your gifts. When the presents stop coming, recalculate your needs and *then* go shopping.

NICE TO HAVE

Before They Arrive
- Cosleeper, Moses basket, or bassinette
- Baby carrier/sling
- Video monitor
- Rocking chair/glider
- Mobile
- Wipe warmer
- Electric clock with CD player
- Activity mat
- Bouncer/swing
- Bottle warmer
- Nipple ointment or cream
- Pacifiers
- Premeasured formula container

By One Month
- Portable crib
- Stroller weather shield
- Stroller toys

By Three Months
- Sleep sacks
- Jogging stroller

By Six Months
- Exersaucer/walker

NOT NECESSARY

- Footrest/ottoman
- Hooded towels
- Humidifier
- Privacy blanket
- Bottle sterilizer
- Baby powder
- Baby oil
- Baby lotion
- Disposable diaper sacks

MM TIP:
Although there was a study that freaked this particular parent out saying night-lights contributed to nearsightedness, subsequently the original authors backed off of the finding and another study didn't find any relationship.

MM TIP:
Babies aren't afraid of the dark until about age two or three, when cognitive development enables them to understand the concept of fear. Until then, your baby will sleep better in the dark; the night-light is more for you.

Avoid hanging anything above your baby's crib that could fall and hurt him, such as picture frames, a shelf with knickknacks, or large pictures. Instead, paint a mural or hang something soft, like a quilt.

To save money on wallpaper, paint instead, and then add a wallpaper border to the top of the wall.

Have someone *else* paint well in advance of the baby's arriving. You should avoid the fumes when you're pregnant, and the smell can linger for up to five days, so this is *not* the activity for the night before the baby arrives.

Avoid too much stimulation in the contents of the crib, as it could affect his sleep. Instead, opt for it in other areas. My son loved to

MM TIP:
When choosing colors, if you want something relaxing, go for greens, soft blues, and creams. Reds, oranges, and bright yellows are stimulating. Although you may want to avoid too much red in the room, it is great for toys, as red has been shown to stimulate a baby's brain. Lime green and bright orange can also help stimulate the senses and imagination.

stare at the striped curtains above his changing table. This made changes *much* easier in the first six months.

- If you don't want to go with a traditional nursery theme, consider:

  - Blowing up photos of your family and framing them in inexpensive frames. It's a cheap way to cover the walls and make the room immediately feel like home.

  - Opt for an astrological theme based on your child's birthday or the solar system.

  - Cover one wall with corkboard (which can be painted so you don't have to leave it brown) and then attach mementos on the wall—clippings of hair from a first cut, fun family pictures, and postcards.

  - Paint the wall with giant number and alphabet stencils.

  - Use chalk paint on one wall and let your child doodle with chalk when she's old enough.

  - Create a family tree with natural materials such as leaves and branches.

  - Use a travel theme based on places that are important to your family, or post a giant map with pins pointing out where certain family members have visited.

  - Paint a mural with favorite children's book characters.

MM TIP:
The Consumer Product Safety Commission discourages the use of used cribs, as current crib safety regulations weren't in place before 1990. So that means that any crib built before 1990 needs to have its rail bars/slats measured, and any crib built before 1978 could have lead-based paint on it and needs to be professionally stripped and refinished.

Cribs, Beds, and Planning Ahead

We tortured ourselves over which crib to buy for our son's room. For some reason we got stuck on the notion that this had to be a functional bed that would last him for years, so we ended up buying the crib that converted into a toddler bed, and then eventually becomes the head and footboard to a twin bed. In reality, we passed the crib to my daughter and bought my son a different bed when he outgrew the crib anyway. To make matters worse, we bought my son twin bunk beds.

Now, every time he's sick, he wants me to sleep with him, and the two of us end up crammed in one twin bed and neither of us gets much sleep. In the end, I would have been better off to buy a simple crib and then a double or queen bed when he moved on to the next stage. I live, you learn.

But there are some things to look for when buying a crib. This is not an area to skimp, as your child will spend a great deal of time there, and there is potential for danger if you don't look out for the right things. Having said that, you don't need to spend more than a few hundred dollars.

- The mattress or the rails should be adjustable, so when your child starts standing, she can't easily climb out of the crib.

- Rails should be vertical, and no more than two and three-eighths inch apart.

- The mattress should fit snugly into the crib with no extra spaces.

- The mattress needs to be firm.

- Buy a bumper that is soft but not too thick. It should also attach in at least six places and fit very snugly.

- Cover the mattress with a fitted mattress pad, followed by a sheet, and then a lap pad (trust me on this—a pad is much easier to change in the middle of the night than the entire sheet). You should have at least three sets of all of these.

- Avoid putting pillows or stuffed animals in the crib with an infant, as he could suffocate.

Linens and Things

Here's the lowdown on what you'll need in terms of linens in and around the crib and changing table:

- Ten cloth diapers

- One mattress pad

MM TIP:
Go for a safe but basic crib and spend the extra money on fun bedding. People tend to notice the fabrics you choose more than the piece itself—unless you were planning on spending $30,000 for the Cinderella-like coach crib. No? Me neither.

MM FAVE:
Forever Mine crib by Forever Mine. They're attractive, absorbent, and last forever!

MM TIP:
Sometimes cribs can take up to two months to be delivered, so plan ahead. *Do not* panic if your delivery date is sooner than that. There are many sleeping options you can use before a crib.

MM TIP:
It's easier to change sheets in cribs with bars on all sides than a solid headboard and footboard.

MM TIP:
Even if you are going with disposable diapers, the cloth ones make the best burp cloths around. Skip the fancy ones with satin on the back; they slip right off your shoulder. And like socks, you'll lose at least one a week.

MM FAVE:
I found virtually all of the listed baby goods at Target.

MM TIP:
If space is tight, consider a futon instead of a bed (for you) so that in emergencies you can spread it out without having a bed in the room all the time.

MM TIP:
Make sure the handles are firm and well connected and the basket sides high and firm. One day, during my first nap since giving birth to Lilia two weeks prior, my husband was carrying her outside in the Moses basket and the handle ripped and she rolled out onto the brick patio. She was fine. I haven't napped since.

- Three to four fitted sheets
- Two mattress pad covers
- Two or three changing pad covers
- Five lap pads
- Two bassinette, Moses basket, or cosleeper sheets (if you are using one)
- Three washable cotton receiving blankets that stretch nicely for swaddling
- Three blankets for covering the baby in the stroller
- Skip the fancy sheets. Babies spit up and diapers leak, and you will freak out all the more if your linens are pricey.
- If the size of the room allows, consider putting in a queen, full, or at least a twin bed. Although not scientifically proven, I think it helps your baby prepare for a big kid bed. They see you sleeping in it (which will inevitably happen) and figure it *must* be good.

Moses Baskets, Cosleepers, and Bassinets

You may think you'll want to hold your precious bundle every moment, but this isn't great for him or you. Many people like to use alternate options to a crib for the first few months, as they are smaller, cozier, and more portable. Although you can certainly get away without having these, I loved my Moses basket and cosleeper.

Moses Baskets

No, I'm not suggesting you wrap up your baby and float him down the river, but you've got the right look. These baskets are great for newborns up to about four to six months, depending upon how big and active your baby is. They are great, as you can move them from room to room (or house to house) and keep your baby near you. They are also fairly small, so they may help your baby feel more "womb-like" and tucked in. Once your baby starts rolling over or sitting up, these will no longer work, as they are not hugely supportive. Also, I would often find one of our cats cuddled up in the corner with the baby if I had left him for two seconds to go put in a load of laundry. Although I trusted our cats, this might make some people uncomfortable.

Cosleeper

These are mini-cribs that attach to one side of your bed and allow the baby to be at your level, but not *in* your bed (which is dangerous). They are great because when your baby wakes up, you just slide him over to you for a feeding and don't have to get out of bed. These work to varying degrees, depending on your baby. Jack was a screamer, and by the fifth night we moved him into his room so that at least one of us could get sleep. Lilia was an eater but quiet, and would peep, eat, and go back to sleep, so it worked out great. These can't be used once your baby starts sitting up or pulling up or is over thirty pounds. They also take up a lot of room and make it harder for the person who is getting out of bed on that side to maneuver. But I *loved* mine and wouldn't have traded it.

> MM TIP: Some people say using a cosleeper may make it harder for the baby to transition to his crib after being so close to you. I did not find that to be true, but wanted you to be forewarned.

Freestanding Bassinets

In my opinion, the best thing about these is how they look. Nothing screams BABY more than a wicker bassinet with gingham fabric. But I found that having to get out of bed to reach in and get Jack was far more intrusive than using the cosleeper. Recently, I've seen some models that are basically a Moses basket with a stand or base, and this seems nifty, but the Moses baskets in these tend to be a bit heavier than a traditional Moses basket.

MM TIP: If you are using your Moses basket frequently but will be moving your baby to the crib, put the Moses basket with the baby in the crib. It's a great way for him to get used to his new environment while remaining familiar with his old one.

MM TIP: Don't want to splurge on a Moses basket? One friend used a plastic laundry basket lined with soft towels. Go figure!

MM FAVE: Moses basket from Babystyle.

MM TIP: If you plan on using a cosleeper, have it set up before you get home from the hospital. It's not hard, but not something you want to be doing right before the baby's first nap.

MM FAVE: Armsreach cosleeper bedside bassinet by Armsreach. It fits well against the bed and is a good size.

MM TIP:
It's also okay to use an infant seat as a temporary crib/portable sleeping site, but babies need rest for a good portion of the day flat on their backs, so limit this use.

MM FAVE:
Bassinet by Pottery Barn Kids. It's cute, inexpensive and can convert to a Moses basket.

MM FAVE:
Waterproof lap and burp pads by Continental Burping.

MM TIP:
It's important to keep track of when your baby eats, sleeps, and goes to the bathroom. The changing table is a great place to keep a notepad to jot down the vital stats. Attach a pen to the changing table with a string to ensure it doesn't walk away with you.

Changing Table Basics

Sure, you *think* you can skimp and use the bench at the foot of your bed, a chair, or even the floor as your changing table, but *don't!* After about two weeks of bending over to change your baby's diapers—not to mention having to do stain control every time your baby decides to pee during a changing—you'll wish you had a proper one.

It doesn't need to be a traditional changing table, just simply the right height to ease the strain of your back when changing the baby. For example, you can use the top of a dresser, but be sure to buy a nice pad and attach it to the dresser somehow so that it doesn't slide off when your baby starts to wiggle. A good strap on the pad is also great for when your baby begins to roll over.

- Cover your changing pad with a terrycloth or cotton cover, and then put down a lap pad. Again, switching out a lap pad is easier than switching the cover.

- Remember to always keep a hand on your baby when he's on the changing table. I know for the first few months it seems like there is no way he could possibly move, let alone roll off the table. But it never ceases to amaze me how many times—to the surprise of their parents—babies first roll over on (or should I say off) the changing table.

- Set up the room so that all the essentials are well organized and within arm's reach of the changing table. Personally, I'm a big fan of partitioned baskets that hold the essentials but can still be easily

MM SAFETY TIP: A two-inch guardrail around all four sides of the changing table is recommended; a baby's taking a header off the changing table really is one of the most common calls a pediatrician gets! If you are converting furniture, you'll need to be extra careful! And this sounds crazy, but a quick reminder: never, ever put a changing table, crib, or bed against a window.

transported to another room when needed. There is nothing worse than desperately hunting for Desitin at 2 A.M., only to find it across the room and unreachable. Keep the baby essentials in a drawer or on a high shelf if you have other children who may get into them.

Changing Table Essentials

Make sure you have the following close to your changing table. I'd also suggest having a spare of each in a closet. You'll find that you run out at the least convenient time to go for a drugstore run. The essentials include:

- *Diapers:* I'm a Pampers Premium girl, but other friends swear by Huggies. It's best to experiment with what works for you; but if you have a boy, be brave. I would say that every other night until about age one, Jack's diaper leaked. I was convinced I was doing something wrong. Truth is, it's more about anatomy. My daughter used the same diapers, and it was like a desert in the crib.

- *Wipes and cotton squares:* For the first two weeks to month of your baby's life, your doctor may tell you to wipe your baby with water and cotton, not wipes. You'll do it, but you'll resent it. You're constantly getting bowls of water, throwing away shreds of cotton with poo, and watching your newborn shiver because the water has settled to a cold room temperature. With Jack, I wouldn't let a wipe touch his bottom for the first month and he had diaper rash the whole time. With Lilia (bad mother alert), I used wipes from the moment she was born, and never a blemish. Look, listen to your doctor, use the water, but if you just can't take it and try *gentle* wipes and you're okay, I won't tell.

- *Wipes warmer.* As for a wipes warmer, I know, why spend $19.99 on a warmer when there are hungry people in the world? Okay, I'm a bad person, but for those first few months I promise your baby will appreciate the even room temperature or warm wipes over a cold wet rag on his behind.

MM FAVE:
Baskets with partitioned inserts from Pottery Barn Kids.

MM TIP:
If you have a boy, remember to point his penis down so he doesn't pee out. Won't stop it, but it will help.

MM TIP:
Don't be afraid to go up a size in diapers even if his weight doesn't seem to reflect the need. The minute you think the diapers are too tight, they are, and a bigger one will make you and your baby a lot happier.

MM TIP:
Use cotton squares, not balls to wipe. And go for 100 percent cotton, *not* the synthetic type (geez, if you're going to go through the hassle, do it right). They're bigger, easier to handle, and you won't get grossed out when you're using the cotton balls to take off your makeup.

MM FAVE:
Wipes Warmer by Prince Lionheart.

MM FAVE:
I love Huggies Supreme Care wipes. They are pricier, but I've found that cheaper versions are too thin, require more to get the job done, and often get stuck together so that you run out even faster.

MM TIP:
Go for a tube with a flip top, not a screw-on lid or basic cap. You want to keep one hand on your baby, not have to use both to open and close the darn cream.

MM FAVE:
I like Aquaphor and Desitin Creamy diaper rash creams. Right tube, easy to spread, and smells good.

> **MM TIP:** Look for wipes that are unscented and alcohol free. And consider keeping a bowl of water nearby. You can dip the wipes in to squeeze out some of the extra cleanser that it's loaded with. It will be gentler for your baby but still effective.

- *Petroleum jelly.* This is essential if your baby boy has been circumcised. Once you've been told to stop using the antibiotic ointment, you can put a dab on under the gauze or diaper to keep the diaper from sticking.

- *Diaper rash cream and/or ointment.* Some lucky babies don't need any diaper cream, but other more sensitive bottoms need cream with each new diaper. There are two basic types to use:

  - *Petroleum ointment (original A&D ointment):* This is an excellent, preventative everyday ointment, especially if your baby is prone to rashes or dry, cracked skin. It's less sticky and less messy and is clear. Use it after each bowel movement is cleaned off.

  - *White zinc oxide (such as Desitin):* A thicker product that may be better for babies who are more prone to rashes. Use on all babies after diarrhea.

  - Avoid the kind with steroids such as cortisone or hydrocortisone.

- *Cornstarch.* Although you may think you're supposed to use baby powder to powder your baby, rethink that. It can get into your baby's lungs, causing swelling and irritation and even breathing problems, such as pneumonia. It can also exacerbate diaper rash. I never actually used cornstarch and could skip it, but some people prefer it over diaper cream.

- *Cotton swabs and tissues.*

- *Baby nose aspirator.* I hope you never need this. I didn't. My coauthor Jen did (Sam came out so fast, all the liquid wasn't squeezed out completely, so she began using this from day one). Should your baby have trouble breathing or get a runny nose, you want this on hand, not deep in a drawer where you have to dig for it. And re-member: squeeze the ball first, and while holding it in, insert it into your child's nostril to suck out what's blocking the airway.

- Baby nail clippers and file.

- Comb or brush.

- A clean onesie or pajamas (for middle-of-the-night bottom blowouts).

Monitors

Hard as it is to believe, your baby *will* sleep. And if you're like me, the only way to resist going in to check on him every twenty minutes (okay, ten) is to have a monitor that will pick up any and every sound to ensure that some bad fairy hasn't snuck in to bestow a dark curse. (Sorry, I've been watching a lot of Disney movies lately.) If your house or apartment is small, you may not want or even need a monitor. But if you're out of ear's range, you may find the monitor lets you travel more freely throughout your home.

There are several different types of monitors:

- *900-MHz long-range monitors.* Okay, people swear by these. They love them. They use them. Me? I couldn't find a single one that didn't pick up every cell phone conversation in my neighborhood. They cost a lot of money, and the interference and static may well wake up your baby as it did mine. Both Jen and I had better luck with the cheaper, more pared-down 600-MHz version. Far less static and a lot less money. Go figure.

> **MM TIP:** After you've decided which type of monitor you want, look for one with two receivers. Whether your house has two rooms or ten, you'll find the spare comes in handy.

MM TIP: Trim your baby's nails while he's sleeping or drinking a bottle. He'll be far less squirmy.

MM TIP: Some clippers have a magnifying glass so you can see up close. They don't work that well, so save your money.

MM TIP: To avoid ingrown nails, cut straight across and then file the edges so they are not sharp.

MM TIP: I'm a big fan of the infant gown, as they're easy to put on and take off, especially in the middle of the night. They are basically long shirts with an elasticized bottom that your baby's feet sort of tuck into.

MM FAVE: Infant gown by Carter's.

MM FAVE: Safe Glow 2 Receiver Monitor by Safety First.

MM FAVE:
Sweet Dreams Monitor by Fisher Price. Not only can you talk to your baby, but also this one has a lullaby and light show you can activate remotely.

MM FAVE:
Angelcare Movement Sensor with Sound Monitor by Bebe Sounds. This one is supersensitive and reliable.

MM FAVE:
Baby's Quiet Sounds Video Monitor by Summer Infant. At under $100, this was a great buy for the money. Be warned, though, the light from the camera may make your baby feel like she's under surveillance. Oh, wait, she is!

MM TIP:
Skip the ottoman. It may look nice, but there really aren't that many times when you find yourself perfectly balanced, lounging around. Even if you have it, I promise your baby will finally get in the right comfortable position right when you realize the ottoman is *just* out of foot's reach.

- *Two-way monitors.* Two-way monitors let you talk to the baby. They're great if you tend to be a long way from the baby and want to reassure her that you are on your way. Some mothers have warned, however, that this became tricky, as their baby would become hysterical if the mom didn't respond quickly enough. Another mother felt she sometimes responded too quickly, waking a baby who was just stirring.

- *Movement monitors:* These monitors detect small movements and can even detect breathing. Some have monitors for breathing that will sound an alarm if it doesn't detect breathing for twenty seconds. If your baby is a tummy sleeper or you are really nervous, these are great. I had one but I sort of sat there waiting in panic for the alarm to go off (which it never did). So, up to you.

- *Video monitors.* These tend to be the most expensive but are great if you want to watch, not just listen to your baby. My friend swore by them because it helped her figure out at night whether her baby was crying and really awake or just making nighttime noises. It also showed her that her baby was a bit of a Houdini and was able to crawl out of her crib at twelve months, prompting her to get a toddler bed. The trickiest part of these is figuring out where to put the camera eye. Mine wouldn't fit on the crib, and the shelf I ultimately put it on could only cover half of the crib (but I had a lot of fun checking his feet for signs of distress). If money is no object or you know you're a worrywart, go for it. Otherwise, you can probably skip it.

Other Nursery Essentials

- *Chair.* After lying in bed and nursing my son for several days—and thus keeping my husband awake—I realized that a nice, comfy chair in the nursery was essential. Not only did it provide me with a cozy place to sit for late-night feedings, it also meant that when it was my turn to sleep through the shift, my husband was out of the bed with our son, too! Whether that chair is a rocker, a glider, or just a great armchair is really up to you—and you should look for one with comfy arms. But whatever you do, never buy a nursery chair without sitting in it first. You will likely spend more time in it than any other chair you've ever owned.

- *Curtains.* Here's something that seems counterintuitive, but trust me. Your curtains shouldn't block out the sunlight. It is very important for your baby to distinguish between daytime and nighttime sleep (more on that in chapter 5), so don't stress if you fall in love with adorable sheer panels with butterflies sewn on that let light stream in. Go for it.

- *Diaper pail.* This is one of those things that your mother probably *won't* understand. You will no doubt get the speech about how she had to rinse out your poopy cloth diapers in the toilet and then keep them in a nasty bucket until the diaper service came around. Well, guess what, welcome to the twenty-first century!

- *Electric clock with a CD player.* Skip the baby versions of these. Sure they may be cute, but I had separate versions of both and they broke before I had barely used them. You may spend twice as much for the baby versions and get half the performance. And trust me, bleary-eyed as you'll be, you'll want to know what time your baby woke up, and electric clocks are far easier to see. The CD player will come in handy for nighttime lullabies and fun sing-alongs during the day.

- *Mobile.* This is a great way to stimulate and captivate an infant. Many suggest that for newborns you use a black, white, and red one (colors they can see) and move to a more elaborate one as they get older. But here's the problem: you'll probably want to take it down at around five months—once your child can sit up—so that he doesn't pull it down on his head (owww). So I say skip the first one and go for a musical spinning one that he may not see as well but can hear and watch move.

MM TIP:
For the long summer months when it is light until 9 P.M., you may want to have the option of making the room dark for nighttime sleep. Your best bet is roll-down blackout shades.

MM FAVE:
Invest in a Diaper Genie. It individually seals each disposable diaper and contains the smell. Gotta love modern science.

MM TIP:
While this is a great solution, don't be alarmed if your Diaper Genie starts to smell after about a year. The plastic does soak up the odors, and you'll likely need to buy a new one.

MM TIP:
Another option is to hang something (securely) from the ceiling out of the baby's reach. My friend Julie put stuffed fish on strings. It's colorful and fun but totally safe.

MM FAVE:
Symphony-in-Motion geometric shapes by Tiny Love. At $49 it's pricey, but both of my children were captivated by it. I also tried the Deluxe Zoo Mobile version, but the elephant terrified both my children.

Beyond the Bedroom

If you've ever spent an afternoon wandering around Babies 'R Us (and if you haven't, I'm thoroughly impressed by your restraint), you're well aware that there is pretty much a piece of equipment out there for absolutely everything you could possibly imagine a baby would need. And while it is fun to imagine your little one bouncing away in a jumpy seat, or strolling through your kitchen in a walker, try to resist the urge to buy it all like I did. Not only will your living room look like Gymboree, but also you'll have wasted money, space, and valuable assembly time you'll need your husband to be storing up for future shipments.

Infant Seats and Swings

These are great for the first few months, as they will literally give you your hands back. Infant seats typically rock or vibrate, and most babies will lie contentedly in the seat and even sleep in it at times. Swings offer a little more motion and typically take up more space, but some children like them better. Jack hated his swing but could stay for thirty minutes (an eternity) in his bouncy chair. Lilia hated the bouncy seat but thought the swing was the best invention ever. It simply comes down to preference of the baby (or you).

MM TIP:
Bouncy seats and swings can double as a place to feed your baby for the first few months of feeding. While they won't replace a booster or high chair, it's a great transitional item if you're short of space. And by the time your baby *really* needs the high chair, chances are the bouncy/swing will have outgrown its use.

MM TIP:
If you had asked my husband, he would have said the baby swing was the devil. It was one big piece of equipment and interfered with our living room's Mediterranean decor. If you don't have a lot of space, try the bouncy seat first and resort to the swing only as a backup.

> **MM TIP:** *Never* put a bouncy seat on top of a high surface. My friend's mother-in-law did, with the baby in it. The seat basically vibrated its way off the table and the baby wound up with a concussion. The baby is fine. The relationship between my friend and her mother-in-law has yet to heal. Also, never rest a bouncy seat on a soft or uneven surface, no matter how big and stable the couch, chair, or bed looks.

Here are a few things to look for:

- Make sure the seat or swing has a strap to secure your child.
- Look for rubber feet on the bottom to prevent sliding.
- Cloth-covered seats should be removable for washing.

Playmats

Look, you *can* just put out a blanket with toys. Absolutely. That's what you *should* do. But you won't. Because you'll hope, pray, beg, that *something* will occupy your infant for a few minutes a day so you don't have to. Enter the playmats. They are really for infants who have yet to roll over and have toys dangling from the top. What I liked most was that if the baby spit up, it was on the playmat, not my carpet. And I have to say that while Jack seemed bored, Lilia would play happily on hers for a good twenty minutes.

> **MM TIP:** Make sure your playmat allows you to adjust how high or low the toys are, so that you can place them based on your child's age/ability to grab, and put the ones he's most interested in closer to his reach.

Exersaucers

The exersaucer is useful only after your baby can sit up on his own. These have become very elaborate over the past few years, with built-in toys, music boxes, and other stimuli. I liked the exersaucer because

> **MM TIP:** Adjust the height so that your baby's toes just hit the floor, *not* so that he is fully standing, as this can be too much pressure on his growing legs.

MM FAVE:
Swing: Link-a-doos Top Take-along Swing by Fisher Price. Not only is this swing small, portable, and sturdy, but also you can change out the "toy" at the top as your baby gets bored. I wish they'd had this when Jack was a baby!

Bouncy seat: Ocean Wonders Aquarium Bouncer by Fisher Price: It has a little aquarium with fish that move around and bubbles that will keep your baby entertained. And the vibrations seemed enough to calm but not so rigorous he'd think he was off-roading.

MM FAVE:
Gymini 3D Activity Gym by Tiny Love. While this one doesn't have fancy lights and sounds, it's got a lot of bang for the buck. Lilia had the one with sounds and lights, and frankly, they often seemed to startle her.

MM TIP:
While these are great, their use can be short lived. My son liked it for a month (and what a month) but quickly tired of it. I was then stuck with a *big* piece of equipment until I could pawn it off on an unsuspecting friend who still hasn't figured out how to unload hers. (Sorry, Jen!)

MM FAVE:
ExerSaucer Active
Learning Center by
Evenflo. If I had this many
bells and whistles on me,
I'd be having a lot more
"active learning" with my
husband. :)

MM TIP:
Do not use a walker
anywhere near stairs if you
do not have a gate. I can't
even think about it. Just
don't do it.

it rotated around a stationary leg, so while he felt as if he were moving, I knew he was stuck in one place.

Walkers

The walker, on the other hand, allows your baby to move around the house with assistance "walking." These days you can actually get a combined walker/exersaucer that adjusts with height, but I have yet to find one that I love. Also, some books have claimed that, ironically, walkers can make your child walk a bit later, as they have less motivation to do so on their own. But I found that it allowed our son to explore different things that he wouldn't otherwise see (like the handles on all the kitchen cabinets—hours of fun!), thus causing him to be more interested in moving on his own. Nonetheless, we used the walker only until he began pulling himself up on his own.

> **MM SAFETY TIP:** The American Academy of Pediatrics doesn't recommend the use of walkers; they cite the number of injuries associated with their use (28,000 per year). If absolutely necessary, the walker needs at least six wheels, and a child in a walker should never, ever be left unattended.

MM FAVE:
Bumper Jumper by Graco:
I liked the bumper that
kept Jack from crashing
into the door when his
jumps got overly
enthusiastic.

Jumpers

Jumpers are more of a short-lived whim. They attach to a door frame and let your child bounce up and down ad nauseam. Once that novelty wears off, so does the bouncer. I personally think we could have saved this $40.

Toys

I'm going to address actual toys in chapter 9, when I talk about socializing your child. But suffice it to say, you probably already have too many, as most infants can be quite happy with a scarf and a wiffle ball. But I've found few parents (or grandparents) who consider that enough.

High Chairs

High chairs are a bit of a personal preference in terms of size, color, and décor. The most important things to look for are:

- A removable, washable tray. Eventually, you will put food directly on the tray like a plate, so make sure you can sterilize it.

- A tray with a lip helps keep spills intact.

- A padded seat, all the way up to the head. Babies do this weird thing in which they bang their head against the chair sometimes, and it's better to have it padded.

- A strap with a clip to keep them in.

Infant Tubs

Okay, this is a tricky one. Some people swear that the infant tub made them feel more secure and safer when bathing their newborn. And when it comes to confidence, about $20 seems okay to pay. But for me, after my first use with Jack (picture me bending over the tub, groping for a towel by my knees, trying to stop what seemed like a squirming octopus), my mother-in-law kindly suggested that I try using the sink. Now that's easy. He could be seated, I could stand less like a Cro-Magnon man, and the supplies were laid out right near me. And I *hated* the look of that tub. I couldn't fit it anywhere other than in my bathtub (his bathroom had a shower stall) and even if I did take a bath, the heinous plastic beast was a reminder that soon my bubbles would be burst by a bout of baby crying (sorry, too much alliteration, but you get my point).

That said, there are now baby bathtubs that have a notches in

MM TIP:
Go for a cover/fabric that has a pattern. No matter how much you scrub and clean, the plain fabrics seem to show more grunge and dirt.

MM FAVE:
Prima Pappa by Peg Perego. It's a high chair, not a piece of art, but compared to others I found this more attractive, functional, and easy to clean.

MM TIP:
Some people skip the high chair and get a booster seat they can use at the table. Many can be used at young ages and some people feel this helps make your child feel more included, get used to the routine of sitting at the table and it takes up less room.

MM FAVE:
Healthy Care Booster Seat by Fisher Price.

MM FAVE:
If you go for it, I like the Sure Comfort Deluxe Newborn-to-Toddler Tub by Fisher Price.

MM TIP:
Your baby doesn't get as dirty as you do. And while a daily bath is a nice routine, washing his hair and most of his body once or twice a week is plenty. You only need to do daily washing of his hands and diaper area.

MM TIP:
Hooded towels are cute but an unnecessary expense. Just be sure to dry your baby's head first to keep him from getting cold. The hoods tend to be huge on an infant, and many babies don't like them. And I can almost guarantee you'll receive one as a baby gift. It's like the fondue pot of baby showers.

MM TIP:
Go for a dispenser that has a pump so that you can keep a hand on the baby at all times.

MM TIP:
You can start using most adult bath products on your baby by the age of three, but stick with products with short, simple lists of ingredients.

MM FAVE:
Head-to-Toe baby wash by Johnson's.

them so that they fit nicely in a kitchen sink. This way, you're not bent over trying to bathe your child. It is also helpful for when they can't sit up yet on their own, as sometimes they get a little slippery when wet. In the end, the choice is yours.

Bath Products

Infant Wash

You're not supposed to use soap for the first few weeks of your baby's life. And until your baby's umbilical cord stump falls off and the area heals, you should give only a gentle sponge bath. And when you first do, you'll fear that your baby will break into hives, develop a rash, or cry like a banshee because you've gotten some in his eyes. So you'll spend half of what you've saved for college tuition on overpriced and well-packaged grooming products. Don't. They're lovely, but they're truly unnecessary. Go for a gentle baby product and call it a day.

> MM TIP: The way baby shampoo is made gentler on the eyes is that it is more alkaline and less acidic than regular shampoos. But while gentle on the eyes, it is actually harsher on your baby's hair. So don't wash every night (every second or third is fine), and don't think you're being all earth motherly by using his products for your own. If you have color-treated hair, it will fade it much faster.

Lotion

Although you may think you *should* coat your baby's skin in lotion, chances are you don't need to. Because they are no longer surrounded by amniotic fluid, many newborns have dry, peeling skin. But over-the-counter lotions typically won't cure that. In most cases, after a few sponge baths the dryness disappears. Lotion can offer a great scent or a nice feel when you are massaging your baby, but stick with basic lotions; in the summer, you may want to avoid using lotion as it can clog pores and sweat glands.

Humidifiers

Although previous generations seemed to think that a humidifier was the cure to all that ails you, unless your baby has irritated nasal passages, you probably don't need it. Germs thrive wherever there is water, so you have to keep them very, very clean and change the water every day. Otherwise, the humidifier can harbor bacteria and molds, and when you turn on the humidifier they'll disperse in the air.

> **MM TIP:** To clean a humidifier, run the unit with a mixture of half water and half white kitchen vinegar. This should be done every third day.

MM TIP:
If your baby's skin is dry, it *may* be due to too many baths and too much soap.

MM TIP:
When using a humidifier, point it away from your child's crib to prevent the bedding from getting damp.

MM TIP:
Although it's pricey, consider using distilled water in your humidifier to avoid impurities.

Heading Out the Door

Sooner or later (er, later) you'll leave your house with the baby, and suddenly, you'll think that getting a man to the moon required less preparation than taking your infant to the doctor for his first checkup. But no need to fret—with a little gear and a little good cheer, you'll be on your way. Unlike me, whose first appointment was on a rainy day. I didn't have the stroller cover and couldn't get a cab to go the three blocks. I hobbled with an umbrella over the stroller and nothing over me. We both showed up looking wet, homeless, and pathetic. On the upside, we didn't have to wait in the waiting room, as they whisked us into an exam room to get us out of sight.

Car Seats

Infant Car Seats

This is the most important piece of equipment you will buy, and most hospitals won't let you leave with your baby until they've checked to see that you have a car seat that is properly installed. Here's what you need to know:

- Make sure your car seat meets the Federal Motor Vehicle Safety Standards. The tag will be labeled as such.

- Look for a five-point harness system, which secures your child best.

- Make sure the car seats have sides that come around a bit to protect your child's head in case of a side collision.

- Car seats should be rear-facing for infants until they are at least twenty pounds *and* one year old. After one year, you can turn the car seats to face forward until they are forty pounds or up to four years. At that point, you can switch to a booster seat.

- Go to your local fire station to have your car seat checked for proper installation.

Toddler Car Seats

While you've probably heard the phrase "small kids, small problems; big kids, bigger problems," you probably missed "small baby, small car seat; bigger baby, ridiculously big and annoying car seat." These things are big, bulky, and with you for several years, but you must use them *every* time your child is in the car. Here's what to look for:

- One that can eventually be converted from rear-facing to forward-facing.

- A five-point harness system.

- A good safety rating.

- One that has enough padding to cradle your toddler while she sleeps.

- One that you can put a cover on so that you can clean it without having to dismantle the whole thing.

Booster Seats

Look, I'd like to tell you to keep your kid in the Britax Marathon until he gets to college; but the minute he sees his friend in a backless booster he's going to want one. And given the ease of portability and small amount of space a backless booster takes up, you may want to switch around age three or four, or when your child weighs forty pounds or more or has outgrown her car seat. The good news is these tend to be less expensive and less varied than the previous two you've had to deal with. However, car seats are the safest option so you may want to use yours as long as it fits.

Infant Carriers

Strollers are great, but you may find that up until your baby is about twenty pounds (or twenty-five if you've been working out), a carrier is far easier. Not only do you know exactly where your baby is and what he's doing, but he may feel happier cuddled up against you or your partner's chest. The bonus is that you have both hands free—

MM TIP: My husband was quick to move Lilia into a seat that fit her age but not really her body. When she's awake she's fine, but when she falls asleep there is nowhere for her to rest her head, and she winds up doubled over like a pretzel. So don't get a bigger seat until your child is not only the right age, but also the right size.

MM TIP: Even if you keep your kid in the Marathon, consider buying a backless booster if you ever carpool or will be sending your child in someone else's car as they are far easier to move.

MM TIP: If you really want brownie points with the other moms and tend to be the carpooler, buy an extra backless booster so no one needs to bring one when an extra child is coming home with you.

MM FAVE: Turbobooster by Graco. This one is inexpensive, can go from backed to backless, and is pretty comfortable.

MM TIP: The first day I took Jack out in the Baby Bjorn I figured everyone was staring at my precious child. Only later when I got home did I realize that I had his leg through the armhole and his arm out the shoulder. Practice with your baby, a doll, or someone else around until you can master the process with one hand.

MM TIP:
Go for the extra-large size infant carrier. No one likes to think they're going to have an extra-large baby, but this just means it will last you longer.

MM TIP:
Do not get suckered by the suede or shearling carriers. Unless you live in Alaska, you will find these too hot for you and your baby most of the time.

MM FAVE:
Baby Carrier Original in XL by Baby Bjorn.

MM TIP:
If you live in the city or do lots of walking, look for a stroller with rugged wheels.

MM TIP:
Make sure you can do at least a little steering with only one hand. There will be many times when you wind up holding your child in one arm and steering with the other.

particularly valuable when Lilia was a newborn but Jack was still in the stroller.

While many people like the sling, and while I *know* they're safe, I just didn't like carrying my baby like a messenger bag (heck, I graze too many doors for that). I preferred the Baby Bjorn because it was easy to use, totally safe, and lasted me through both kids.

Strollers

I truly thought that my inadequacy in picking a stroller was a clear sign of my failure as a parent. By the time Jack was three I think I had gone through four different strollers (but to be fair, I'm also the person who always gets the supermarket cart with the bum wheel). Every other mother seemed perfectly happy with her choice, while I wondered how I could have (continually) chosen so badly. But I soon discovered that just as there are no perfect babies, there is no perfect stroller.

> **MM TIP:** Per the above, *don't* do what I did and take your child out of the stroller every time he protests. I did with Jack and he soon realized that being with me was preferable to being on his own and would throw a fit when I buckled it. Not wanting to make the same mistake with Lilia, I put up with a few crying fits at first, and now she's pretty content even during long strolls (pretty, mind you, not perfectly).

The Snap-and-Go

This is basically a car seat that snaps into a base in your car, and then just as easily snaps into either a full-size stroller or a stroller frame. This allows you to take your child from car to stroller without waking him. I loved this thing. If my baby fell asleep in the car, I could transport him into the snap-and-go without waking him up, and shop or run errands to my heart's content. It's also great as many strollers are not meant for infants and can't really support them until they are about four months old. This way, you save the expense of a pram. Unfortunately, all good things must come to an end, and most children outgrow the weight and length of the snap-and-go by six months. It was a very sad day in our household.

The Umbrella Stroller

This is a light, compact, and very maneuverable stroller that will make going shopping a breeze (works great in the shoe section). Maclaren makes a terrific one that I bought. However, I made the mistake of buying one that didn't recline and I found those all-day shopping outings (what can I say, my feet grew a size in pregnancy, I had to replenish my shoe collection!) would have been that much better if my son could have napped as I went. So I went back and bought the more pimped-up version of the same stroller so that it would also have the ability to recline.

The Jogger

This is great if you are superactive, go to the beach a lot, or like to hike on trails (and if you truly are this person, I hate you. Kidding). The bigger the wheels, the better it will be able to absorb the shock and maneuver over tough terrain. But keep in mind that it's not a good everyday stroller. They are typically wider than your normal stroller, don't maneuver well, and may not fit into the trunk of a smaller car. So buy this with your specific need in mind and don't be disappointed if you need another stroller for every day. Or do what I did, and forget the jogging and take a nice stroll to Starbucks for a pastry.

> **MM FAVE:** Mac 3 by Maclaren. Active mommies will appreciate the twelve-inch wheels and conveniently placed pouches (for holding keys, a wallet, and a cell phone) on this jogger.

MM TIP:
If you're going to buy the snap-and-go, make sure the infant car seat you choose is compatible.

MM TIP:
If you do want to use a "regular" stroller for the first few months, look for one that reclines completely.

MM FAVE:
Universal Car Seat Carrier by Kolcraft. Easy to fold, easy to use, and has a nice basket to store any sleepytime purchases.

MM TIP:
Just as I've noticed that virtually everyone east of Chicago seems to use Balmex and the west prefers Desitin, with strollers the east takes Maclaren while the west likes Combi. I'm a New Yorker, so I'm a Maclaren girl, but I did covet the easy maneuvering and cup holder on the Combi.

MM FAVE:
Techno XT by Maclaren. This light but durable stroller turns well, folds easily, and is very comfortable for your child.

The Bugaboo

This isn't a category, it's a brand. But it's a brand that not only deserves its own category but also almost caused me to have a third child just so that I could get one. (I said *almost.*) The Bugaboo is the Bentley of strollers. It can pretty much be used from birth until they're driving, with a separate "bassinet," a seat for toddler stage, and a reversible handlebar that allows your child to face you or (as most strollers do) look away from you. (Hello! How come no one else thought of *that*?) And while I live vicariously through my friends' Bugaboos and covet my own, be warned. This is not a light stroller, and not as easy to fold up or put away as others. It's a lot of money, and at the end of the day, I'd say worth it, but experiment, lift, test, and take apart before you fall head over heels in love. It might be perfect for you, and if not, you can come covet some with me.

The Double Stroller

MM FAVE:
DuoGlider Stroller (front to back) by Graco. It's light, turns well, and is affordable.

Whether you have twins or two children who both happen to be of stroller age at the same time, you may find yourself investing in a double stroller so that you can manage both kids at once. Of course, the debate is side-by-side (thus giving wide load a whole new meaning) or front-to-back (leaving one child with a view of the other child's head all day). And while the front-to-back seems to be the more popular choice among moms who buy these strollers, take your lifestyle into account when you are choosing (*hint:* the side-by-side will *not* maneuver through department stores, but the front-to-back is a bit long for making sharp turns). The great thing is that most of the strollers I've talked about above (snap-and-go and jogging strollers) come in the double form. The other thing you may want to consider if one of your kids is slightly older is a kiddy stand. These are cool platforms that attach onto the back of most strollers so that your older child can ride along.

Playpen/Travel Crib

These are great, safe places for kids to play, and they fold up well for travel to convert to a portable bed. Many now come with added extras like night-lights, music boxes, and mobiles. In the end, unless you will be using this as a bed (which I wouldn't recommend because it's not good for their backs), skip the frills and go with a basic model. It's much more important to find one that folds up easily for trips.

MM FAVE:
Pack N Play Playard by Graco. It's easy-to-assemble, extremely mobile, and comes with a removable bassinet and other convertible components.

Packing It In: The Diaper Bag

Like the stroller, I thought that if I could find the perfect diaper bag, I would then be the perfectly organized mother who, like Mary Poppins, could produce the right toy, bottle, or snack at the right moment to ensure my baby never wanted for anything—or worse, cried in public. Well, in my mind the only thing worse than most of the diaper bags out there are T-shirts that say "Baby on Board" and point to your tummy. Come on, just because you've got a baby, do you really need to be forced to carry something that looks like it was made from Aunt Esther's plastic-covered couch?

Your needs from your diaper bag will change as your baby (and your confidence) grows. With Jack I might have been visiting a neighbor two doors down but was sure to have a change of clothes, sweater, bottle and extra formula, four favorite toys, and so on. I think my husband assumed each time that I was actually leaving him, not just going for a visit. By the time Lilia came along I had narrowed supplies down enough to fit into most of my favorite handbags. Live, lug, and learn.

Here's what you want to look for:

* A lightweight and easily washable (and wipeable) fabric.

* Extra *sealed* pockets for when (not if) your bottle leaks.

* A place you can put your keys. It doesn't have to *be* a place for keys, but you *must* designate it a place for keys or you will find yourself in the mall parking lot unloading all of your supplies to find the keys you then realize you have locked in the car.

MM FAVE:
Diaper Bag Essentials from Mommy's Helper have all the things you need (changing pad, bottle holder, etc.), and you can then transfer into any bag you like. Available on Babystyle.com.

- A pattern your husband will carry. You'll want to be carrying the baby; let him carry this load.

- Consider a messenger bag style. Shoulder straps slip off too easily, and these things do get heavy.

> **MM TIP:** Consider non-diaper bags as diaper bags. I used a black Le Sportsac for both kids and loved it. It was lightweight, durable, and easy to clean, and now that I don't need a diaper bag it's a great overnight bag. Gym bags are also great options. The matching diaper pads and bottle holders that come with expensive bags will lure you, I understand. But chances are that after a few months you won't use the changing pad, and you'll have ruined the bottle holder.

Stocking the Diaper Bag

Here's what you should stock your diaper bag with—depending, of course, on how long you'll be gone. Always anticipate running an extra errand on the way home, so make sure you've planned the next meal/bottle accordingly.

MM FAVE:
I love the portable refillable Huggies holder. It came free with some wipes that I bought, and I haven't stopped using it since. You can buy them separately.

MM FAVE:
Try the powdered formula dispenser by Right Start. It has three compartments in which you can premeasure formula. It's great for the diaper bag and late-night feedings. Just pour it into the baby bottle when you're ready to feed.

- *Two to three diapers.* **Bring two more than you think you'll need.**

- *Diaper wipes.* **Store them in a Ziploc bag or portable case.**

- *Burp cloth.* **Good for spit-ups and burping, and can also be used to change your baby on in a pinch.**

- *Baby bottle.* **Fill it with the amount of water you'll need for feeding (unless you're breast-feeding).**

- *Premeasured formula.*

- *Change of clothes.*

- *Blanket or jacket* **if it's cold,** *sun hat and sunscreen* **if it's warm.**

- *Small toy on a ribbon.*

- *Pacifier* (if you use one) pinned to the bag so you don't have to search.

- *Infant Tylenol and/or Benadryl.*

MM TIP: Keep an extra set of the following in your car trunk in a Ziploc bag for emergencies:

- Two diapers

- Portable wipes

- Portable cream

- Baby bottle

- Bottle of water

- Change of clothes

- Extra sweater

- Full-size towel (can double as a blanket or changing area)

- Two single-serve boxes of Cheerios (so that after you eat the first one, you still have one left for him)

- Sunscreen (I like the Banana Boat spray-on variety in the yellow bottle)

MM TIP: Although it would seem like a good idea to keep formula and infant Tylenol in there too (heck, you're talking to a girl who has more shoes in her trunk than her closet), the heat in your trunk can help make them expire before their time.

MM TIP:
I always have a ribbon or yarn in the diaper bag so that I can tie my son's toy to the stroller. That way, when he throws it out of the stroller, it doesn't get dirty and he can pull it up himself.

MM TIP:
If you're like me, this will soon feel like too much. So what I did was buy a twelve-by-twelve see-through bag. In it I kept three diapers, portable wipes, small-size cream, two children's Band-Aids, and infant Tylenol. Not only did I have essential supplies ready, but if I was in a restaurant, plane, or friend's house, I could toss that mini-bag into any bag I was carrying and know I had the basics.

MM TIP:
Consider storing your baby's bottle in a Ziploc bag and in a separate pocket. Not only will it prevent spills, but in an emergency you can use the plastic bag to store a stinky diaper or wet set of clothes.

The Home Medicine Cabinet

It's always best to err on the side of having everything you need in advance. You'll know what I mean the first time you try find a twenty-four-hour pharmacy in the middle of the night when your child has a fever. Or you'll do what I did and give your infant the child's medi-

MM TIP:
Go for the dye-free versions. Your child will undoubtedly spit some out (deliberately or not) and it will get on their clothes, the crib, and maybe you, too. A dye-free product won't make it look like your child has started coughing up blood.

MM TIP:
Although many moms will say to give a dose of Benadryl to guarantee some sleep on a plane ride, Benadryl can make some kids more energetic. So definitely do an experiment before a trip! Also, remember to check with a pediatrician if your child is under the age of two.

MM TIP:
It may seem mean, but I promise, shooting it down the back of their throat with a syringe is faster and easier than trying to get them to sip out of the medicine cup.

MM TIP:
Infant Tylenol is the medicine of choice for babies between 2 months and 6 months of age. After that, either acetaminophen or ibuprofen are safe to use. At that point, it is probably less expensive to buy the children's rather than the infant.

cine, but just a small dose of it. Turns out that the infant drops are more concentrated, so a smaller amount of the children's may not be as much as they need to do the job. And, of course, always check with your doctor before administering medicine to an infant. Here's what you'll need:

- Liquid acetaminophen (Tylenol) (see TIP, bottom left)
- Liquid ibuprofen (Motrin) (not for use in babies under six months)
- Liquid or chewable Benadryl. Benadryl stops allergic reactions and can be given safely to kids over the age of two (and sometimes babies, under the advisement of a doctor).
- Antibiotic ointment or cream (Neosporin)
- Hydrogen peroxide
- Calamine lotion or hydrocortisone cream (0.5%)
- Pedialyte to rehydrate your child

> **MM TIP:** Grab Pedialyte pops and stick them in your freezer. While I could never get my daughter to drink Pedialyte, I convinced her that the pops were a dessert and she couldn't get enough of them. Also, they last longer in the freezer so you'll always have them on hand.

- Oral syringe to give medicine
- Bandages and gauze with adhesive tape
- Tweezers

> **MM TIP:** If you're going after a splinter, try removing it with a piece of Scotch tape first. It won't work on really deep ones, but will work on those close to the surface.

Digital thermometer for the rectum or ear. For babies under two months old, a fever can be very serious, so for the first few months you should have a digital thermometer on hand (the kind that looks like a stick with a window on the end). These can be used rectally for the most accurate readings.

Sunscreen. If your baby is younger than six months old, he shouldn't be out in the sun at all. After six months, he should wear sunscreen.

Band-Aids. Go for a variety of shapes and sizes. Don't forget fingertip ones (as toddlers seem drawn to paper cuts like moths to flames) and butterfly ones. You'll never have enough of them.

MM TIP:
Although digital thermometers could be the best invention after the epidural (our parents put glass ones with mercury *where*?) they can be off by as much as a few degrees. So take a reading two or three times to make sure you have an accurate temp.

MM FAVE:
For babies over six months old, I love the Banana Boat spray kids' sunscreen at SPF 35. It's easy to spray, fun to use, and won't spill.

> MM TIP: Most people use too little sunscreen—on themselves and their children. No matter what kind of sunscreen you use, lay it on thick and make sure that every part of her body has a good coating—especially areas most likely to get burned, such as the ears, nose, back of the neck, and shoulders. You'll need to reapply every two hours. Waterproof sunscreens may be slightly hardier, but don't trust an eight-hour protection claim. Reapply after two hours with these, too.

Creating a Layette

Unlike Barbie dolls who don't move, spit up, or fuss when you try to put their clothes (and tiaras) on, infants are a bit trickier to dress. But as adorable as those little outfits for newborns are, avoid the urge to buy more than one (okay, *maybe* two). First of all, many babies are born bigger than newborn size, so you'll be packing up outfits that have never been worn. Second, everyone loves to give gifts of teeny-tiny outfits. Perhaps they think your baby will never grow. And everyone wants their outfit to be the one you take the baby home in. (Remember this when you buy baby presents for other moms!)

News flash! You will be far too busy checking your car seat, having the hospital hurry you out the door, and wondering why the perfect

MM TIP:
If you feel the need to buy, go for the six-to-nine-month sizes. Your baby will outgrow the little sizes quickly, and it is much easier to roll up sleeves on the larger items if need be.

MM TIP:
Pace yourself. Remember, you will have to clothe this child for at least another decade or two, so don't feel you should buy everything now. In fact, I really felt I didn't get the real "cute" effect of the expensive clothes until Jack and Lilia could stand and walk on their own, a bit after a year.

MM TIP:
I found the best onesies were the kind that wrapped around the baby and either snapped or tied on the side. It saved me the trouble of trying to put something over my baby's head (which all babies hate), and it also helps to not have a row of snaps rubbing against his belly button as it is healing.

angel who hadn't cried for the last two days has turned into babyzilla to care what he's wearing. Also, he will probably be swaddled most of the time. And most important, you won't want to deal with anything that is fussy or difficult to put on: tiny buttons, too many snaps, and multiple layers.

Buying Guide

Clothes for Your New Doll (Oops, I Mean Baby)

Here's what you'll need for newborns:

- *Five side-fasten onesies.*
- *Three to six rompers.* These are great for summer babies. They are all one piece and snap between the legs.
- *Two two-piece outfits.* These are pretty impractical, but you'll want a few for cute photo ops. Just know you'll never choose to put these on your baby on a normal day, so try to limit the urge (I know, it's hard).
- *Four to six footie PJs* in either terrycloth or cotton, weight depending on the season your baby is born.
- *Three to six nightgowns* with elastic at the base, sometimes known as infant gowns. These keep your baby snug and secure at night. The sleep sack is especially great for winter babies, as it keeps them warm without having loose blankets for them to get tangled up in.
- *One to three sweaters,* depending on the season.

MM TIP: I loved infant gowns and had both of my children wear them every night for the first six months. They were the easiest for changing diapers in the middle of the night, as you just need to lift them up. No snaps, buckles, or anything. But if they're sleeping in these, remember to put some socks on them, too.

- *One to three hats,* for warmth and/or sun protection.

- *Seven to ten pairs of baby socks.* Most books will tell you fewer, but I pretty much lost a sock a week. Darn dryer!

- *One snowsuit with attached mittens,* if you live in a cold climate—or if you just want to torture them and see what they look like all bundled up.

> **MM TIP:**
> Keep seasons in mind. Don't buy an adorable nine-month-size swimsuit if it will be cold where you live by then. Do the math ahead of time. Also, remember that babies grow at different rates. Jack was in a size two before he turned one. A lot of the sweaters I had bought for a calendar year after he was born were too small by the time the next winter arrived. Unless it's a fabulous sale, I say skip it.

> **MM FAVE:** Some of my favorite baby and toddler clothes stores are:
> - Target (www.target.com)
> - Baby Gap (www.babygap.com)
> - Boden (www.bodenusa.com)
> - Polo (www.polo.com) (remarkably reasonable for a fancy brand)
> - Hanna Andersson (www.hannaandersson.com)
> - Janie and Jack (www.janieandjack.com)

MM FAVE:
Carter's onesies from Target. I don't know what made them different, but I tried many brands (in a desperate hope that it was his onesie causing Jack to cry) and these were consistently the softest and easiest to button.

MM TIP:
Forget the cute socks and stick with basic white. That way when you're down a sock, you won't have to chuck the other. I promise, you'll have plenty of time to get them cute footwear in the future.

MM TIP:
While you may be happy with buttons and snaps, as your child gets older, you may want to help him with potty training and dressing himself by having clothes with elastic waists that he can easily put on and take off. Also, make sure clothes aren't too snug, as it's harder to get tight underwear and pants up and down.

Washing Your Baby's Clothes

A lot has been said in the last few years about harsh chemicals and dyes and trying to steer clear of washing your baby's clothes in normal detergents. And while you may think, *"Our moms washed our clothes in normal detergents and I'm just fine,"* consider this: the detergents that our parents used were far simpler, with a lot less fancy ingredients (meaning chemicals). Case in point—when Jen had Sam, her mom

MM TIP:
Although they tell you to wash all of your baby clothes before your baby wears them, *don't* wash everything immediately. Your baby might outgrow them before she's even had a chance to wear them. Just leave the tags on everything until you know she is going to wear it. And, in general, best to buy a size six months bigger than your child's age. If she doesn't fit it you may be able to exchange or regift it!

pulled out an old box of her baby clothes, seeing if there was anything that could be passed down. Some of the items looked to be stained beyond repair—and Jen's mom had no doubt scrubbed and scrubbed thirty-odd years ago to get them clean. But one load with today's detergents and the stains were all gone. On the one hand, it's cool that the clothes could be salvaged. On the other hand, it's scary to think what is in our detergents today.

With that in mind, Dreft is a really popular option for mothers who are worried about chemicals in their baby's wash. And while most babies won't break out or get a rash from normal detergent, if you can afford to go with a baby-friendly "light" detergent like Dreft, then why not? If you're on a budget, or simply can't be bothered, try doing a double rinse cycle to make sure that as many of the harsh chemicals and dyes as possible get rinsed out. Also, skip fabric softeners and fabric sheets until your kids are around two years old; they have been shown to give kids rashes.

If you are interested in more environmentally safe ways to reduce the exposure of your baby to harsh chemicals and toxins in and around the house, one of the best sources is *Household Detective: Protecting Your Children from Toxins at Home* put out by Children's Health Environmental Coalition (CHEC) and available at their website: www.checnet.org.

Still looking for foolproof ways to get out kid-size messes? Try the modern mom methods listed on the following pages.

MM TIP: If you are looking for an even more eco-sound route, try these options:

Laundry booster: To cut down on the amount of commercial detergent you need, add a half cup of baking soda at the beginning of the wash cycle if you're using liquid detergent, and if you're using powdered detergent, add a half cup of baking soda during the rinse cycle.

Fabric softener: To soften up the load without chemicals, add two cups of white vinegar (plus a few drops of essential oil to get rid of that nasty vinegar smell) to the rinse cycle. But beware—it can fade your colors a bit.

THE MODERN MOM'S GUIDE TO STAIN REMOVAL

The Problem	The Solution
Berries (all varieties)	Immediately place the garment stain side down on top of a clean, absorbent surface (such as white paper towels) and sponge thoroughly with cool water. If stain persists after sponging, apply a liquid detergent to the area and let sit for five minutes before rinsing with hot water over a sink. Next, use a stain-removing solution and wash regularly. Quick tip: for *very* fresh berry stains only, hold the garment over a sink or tub and pour boiling hot water through the stained area.
Blood	Saltwater is key here. Either submerge the garment in heavily salted water or rub a saltwater mixture directly on the stain until it goes away. Be sure that the water is cool; warm to hot water will set the stain. For a smaller stain, you can forgo the salt and simply try rinsing with cold water or club soda. For a more stubborn stain, add a bit of water to some meat tenderizer and let the paste seep into the stain for about fifteen minutes, then sponge off with cool water and wash garment as advised.
Butter or margarine	First, eliminate chunks of butter or margarine from the area, and then sop up excess grease by covering with cornmeal or flour and rubbing or shaking off it. Next, apply a prewash stain remover and rinse. If the stain is old, use WD-40 to reactivate it before following the directions above.
Chocolate	Blot or scrape to remove excess chocolate before soaking the garment in an enzyme-based prewash solution (Biz detergent and Axion are good options). After about thirty minutes, apply a liquid detergent to the area and thoroughly rinse with cold water.
Crayon and colored pencil	Coat both sides of the stained area with WD-40 (using several layers of paper towels as a blotter). Let stand for about ten minutes. Work dish detergent into the stain and then wash in hot water with regular laundry detergent (and bleach if necessary).

Crayon, melted	Set iron on high setting and put aside. Lay the garment (stain side up) between several layers of paper towels so that there is adequate padding on both sides (like a sandwich.) Pass iron over the stained area so that the paper towels absorb the crayon. Replace soiled paper towels with clean ones as you go until the stain is gone.
Dirt	Remove excess dirt. Immerse garment in water with a presoak solution and let sit (thirty minutes for a new stain, several hours for an older stain). Launder as usual. If the stain persists, repeat process as needed.
Food dye (from various liquid food/drinks)	Sponge the stain immediately with cool water (which may be enough to remove it). If not, mix one tablespoon of ammonia with one cup of cold water and apply to the affected area. Next, work some table salt into the stain. Repeat process as needed and launder. If the stain is red, orange, or purple in color, try treating with a red wine stain remover.
Formula (infant)	Mix water with meat tenderizer to get a paste-like consistency. Apply the mixture to the stain. For white clothing, lemon juice also works. Just treat the affected area with juice and allow garment to sit in the sun.
Fruit (fresh)	Immediately remove excess fruit and rinse the stained area with cold water. Work liquid detergent into the stain and let sit for at least five minutes. Hold the garment over a sink and rinse hot water through the back of stain. Apply a stain-remover solution and launder with detergent. For white garments, try treating with hydrogen peroxide, lemon juice, or white vinegar if stain persists.
Fruit juice	Treat immediately for best results. If the stain has dried, try reactivating with glycerin. Attempt to loosen the stain with cold water or club soda. Next, treat with white vinegar, using a sponge to clean the area. Apply a stain pretreater and wash as usual. If stain persists, soak the garment in an enzyme solution for fifteen minutes and launder again.

Glue	Remove with a wet (hot water) cloth if the stain is fresh. If the glue has dried, scrape off the excess with a knife or spoon. Soak the garment in hot water if substance persists and launder as usual.
Grass stains	Immediately sponge with warm water and rubbing alcohol. If the stain persists, try sponging with white vinegar. Work laundry detergent into the soiled area and wash as usual.
Ice cream	Soak the garment in cold water for five to ten minutes. If stain persists, treat with detergent and soak in lukewarm water for about thirty minutes. Apply a prewash stain remover and launder as usual. If the stain has dried, scrape off the excess ice cream before following these steps.
Ink	Place the garment on a pad of paper towels. Saturate the soiled area with rubbing alcohol (or alcohol-based hairspray) and blot up the stain with a sponge or paper towel. Repeat as necessary. If the stain persists, rub it out with traditional, nongel toothpaste.
Markers (washable)	Despite the name, not all washable markers are completely washable. The trick is to treat the stain immediately by rinsing the soiled area with cold water. Next, place the garment stain side down on a bed of paper towels and sponge from the back with rubbing alcohol. After blotting the stain away, treat with liquid detergent and launder as usual. Before drying check to make sure the stain has disappeared. If not repeat this process as necessary.
Milk	Soak the garment in cold water for five to ten minutes. If the stain persists, treat with detergent and soak in lukewarm water for about thirty minutes. Apply a prewash stain remover and launder as usual.
Mustard	Remove excess mustard. For colors, treat with glycerin and let sit for about one hour. Launder as usual. For whites, douse the affected area with hydrogen peroxide and let it sit for approximately thirty minutes. Launder as usual.

Paint (acrylic)	Some acrylic paints are permanent, but your best bet is getting to the stain before it dries. To do this, rinse vigorously with cold water and soap until the stain is removed. If this doesn't work, treat with a commercial stain remover. Launder as usual.
Pencil	Try "erasing" the mark with a clean eraser. If the stain persists, treat with a commercial stain remover and launder as usual.
Rust	Sprinkle salt onto the affected area, saturate with lemon juice, and place the garment in the sun. Keep the area moist by periodically applying more lemon juice. If stain persists, add more of the salt/lemon juice mixture and rinse with boiling water. You can also try soaking the garment in white vinegar, followed by a soak in a hot water/white vinegar solution (half and half). Once the stain is gone, wash as usual.
Stickers	Apply an ice cube to the stain and then use a spoon to scrape away the frozen residue. Repeat the process. If the stain persists, dab baby or cooking oil onto the area to loosen remaining residue. Apply commercial stain remover and launder as usual. You can also try using undiluted heated white vinegar. Saturate affected area with the solution and eventually the adhesive should peel off easily.
Tomato/tomato-based products (ketchup, tomato sauce, barbecue sauce, etc.)	Immediately remove the excess tomato or tomato product and flush the soiled area with cold water. Apply white vinegar and repeat a cold water rinse. If stain persists, treat with a red wine stain remover.
Zinc oxide (commonly used in diaper creams)	If the stain has dried, reactivate it with WD-40. Apply undiluted dish detergent to the stain and work it through the affected area. Launder as usual.

Okay, so you have the gear. Now what do you do with the actual baby?

CHAPTER 2

Experts, Epidurals, and Everything Else
Before Baby

By this point you've probably mastered pregnancy. You no doubt have found cures for everything from heartburn to swollen ankles to midnight cravings. And while the actual birth is still looming, you are pretty much a pro at all things pregnancy.

Yeah, that's how I was, too. And I hate to burst your bubble, but guess what? In a few short weeks, it's no longer going to be about you and the various kicks you feel, sugar cravings you have, and shortness of breath you're experiencing. There's actually a baby coming and—gasp!—you need to know how to care for him.

While you've probably thought about many of the things covered in this chapter, here are some tips that will save you time, money, and a lot of headaches. Given the pain you'll be feeling in other parts of your body, a headache is the *last* thing you need.

Now, I know you're organized. Heck, you wouldn't have time to be reading this book if you weren't. But if you haven't done the following, there are still a few last details you will want to take care of before the baby comes. Some are optional (like shopping for fun baby gear; see chapter 1) and others, not so much.

Choosing a Pediatrician

Choosing a pediatrician is a very personal decision. This is someone you and your child will need to feel at ease with, and you need to be comfortable asking questions without feeling intimidated. The best place to start is to get a list of recommended pediatricians from your OB/GYN. Also ask friends, colleagues, and family members who have children and cross-reference that with your doctor's list. Do your homework on the pediatricians, and narrow the list down to two or three. Then, it is very important to meet with the doctor, so set up a new-patient consultation. Some doctors may charge for this, but it's worth it, as this will be a lasting relationship. It also helps you get a feel for the office and the doctor without having to fully commit. Here are the most pertinent questions to ask:

- Where is the doctor's office located? It needs to be convenient.

- Is the doctor accepting new patients?

- Does the doctor have convenient office hours, including weekends and evenings?

- Does the doctor have partners, and is someone always on call?

- Who takes the calls, the doctor or nurses? How quickly does a doctor call you back?

- In emergencies, will she make house calls? (If you find this person, please send me the name and I will happily fly him or her to visit me in a pinch.)

- Do they offer a sick-child waiting room or entrance?

MM TIP:
For a fee of about $10 you can do a search on a doctor to find out whether there are any outstanding cases filed against him or her at www.docinfo.org.

MM TIP:
Don't ask me how, but babies *know* when it's a weekend or holiday and always choose *that* day to get a fever, turn a color not known in nature, or spit up something resembling a bad scene from *The Exorcist*. Trust me; you want someone available on the weekends.

> **MM TIP:** This won't matter when *your* precious angel has the sniffles, but when your healthy bumpkin is waiting for a well visit and a hive-ridden, phlegmy, fever-spiked child wipes his nose on a toy *your* child then sticks in his own mouth, I promise you'll wish there were a separate area for those with what suddenly seems to you like the plague.

- Do they accept your insurance, and if not, what are their fees?

- Is the doctor certified by the American Board of Pediatrics?

- What is the doctor's educational background?

- What are the pediatrician's hospital affiliations, and are those hospitals near you?

- Will the doctor come to the hospital to see the baby after he is born and examine him there?

- Did the doctor answer your questions respectfully and take time with you, or did you feel rushed?

- Are the doctor's child-rearing philosophies in sync with yours?

In the end, follow your instincts when choosing a doctor. Before Jack was born I went to visit "the" pediatrician. I had to have a friend call to get me in. (Heck, it was a longer wait than for my Balenciaga bag.) When I finally got a meeting I found him not warm, not funny, and not the kind of guy I could ask my embarrassing questions to. Instead, I went to a doctor with a newer practice who had a child a little older than mine. Not only was she smart and kind, but she related well to me as a mother. I didn't run into anyone famous in her waiting room, but I never felt rushed or unimportant, and both of my children loved her. But alas, we moved . . .

Bracing for Delivery Day

Finally, the big day is upon you. I've always said the pregnancy is strangely set up perfectly. You spend the first three months sick as a dog, just trying to get used to the idea that you're pregnant. You spend the second three months glowing and very excited about being pregnant, and finally have energy again. By the last three months, you feel so big and tired all the time, and so sick of being pregnant that the fear of actually giving birth subsides to the fear that *this thing may NEVER come out!* Thus, you welcome the birth in a way that you never thought you would.

MM TIP:
When scheduling appointments with a pediatrician, try to go for the first appointment in the morning or the first appointment after lunch. This is when doctors are most likely running on schedule. After-school hours are usually the busiest.

MM TIP:
If you think a visit will require getting shots for your baby or child, schedule it for earlier in the week. If your baby has an adverse reaction, you may want to be able to bring him to the doctor's office rather than making an emergency room visit or calling your doctor at home on the weekend.

MM TIP:
According to many pediatricians, the thing that most drives them crazy is when a parent leaves a rude message on the machine. Yes, your baby is important and it's scary when she's sick, but there's no need to be rude.

And while I will certainly be there for you any way a modern mom could, I'm not a doctor and don't claim to be one. So when it comes to birthing methods, here are some insights, and some great sources to check out.

Some Great Books on Labor and Delivery

What to Expect When You're Expecting, by Heidi Murkoff

At this point, this book has probably been your month-by-month encyclopedia to your pregnancy (if not, there's always next time!). Well, it won't let you down on delivery either. It gives straightforward information without taking too much of a stand on one method over another.

The Birth Book: Everything You Need to Know to Have a Safe and Satisfying Birth, by Martha and William Sears, MD

This book is divided into three parts: Preparing for Birth, Easing Pain in Labor, and Experiencing Birth. It covers everything about vaginal births, cesareans, VBAC (vaginal birth after cesarean), water births, home births, best birthing positions, drugs, pain, and how to design your own birth plan. Bonus: pages of birth stories.

The Thinking Woman's Guide to a Better Birth, by Henci Goer and Rhonda Wheeler

This book provides scientific references, summaries of the articles, and logical recommendations, all in a highly readable, user-friendly format.

Ina May's Guide to Childbirth, by Ina May Gaskin

If you are going for natural childbirth, this is a great source. Ina May is the founding member and former president of the Midwives Alliance of North America, and she gives encouragement and practical advice on natural childbirth in an upbeat and informative way.

Natural Childbirth. The Bradley Way, by Susan McCutcheon

This is another great source for natural childbirth, laid out according to the popular Bradley method. While sometimes books covering this method employ fear tactics, many readers have found this book informative because it provided them with the ability to recognize when medical personnel were undertaking a procedure for your best interest. She provides you with information and proven tools to make informed decisions and take responsibility for yourself.

Birthing Methods and Ways to Ease the Pain

You have many choices when it comes to birth. Some women (like me) choose drugs to ease the pain. Other women opt for more natural birth methods such as Bradley or Lamaze, while others prefer the assistance of a doula or a water birth. Here are some short descriptions on what is what. If one sounds more interesting than another, I encourage you to seek out more information on your own about these methods.

Epidurals

I gave birth to my second child in Los Angeles, at one of the more prestigious hospitals where many celebrities tend to go. And in true Hollywood form, the nurse said to me, "Our idea of a natural childbirth means no makeup." And while this is not the route for everyone, for me, I was all about pain management.

Epidural anesthesia is the most popular form of medicinal pain management for labor and delivery. It can be used for a normal vaginal birth, and even sometimes for a cesarean. In a conventional epidural, you are given a shot of local anesthetic in your lower back, which numbs the epidural space around your spinal cord. This numbs the nerves that bring sensation from the uterus and birth canal. The initial prick (that's an understatement) is probably the most painful part of the procedure, but truly, not that bad. It is important that you are still for this, so it is necessary to time this between contractions if possible (this is why some women are told they can't have an epidural if they are too far along in labor). The epidural does wear off, and since it is a constant flow via a tube into your spine, you can receive more as you go. The trick is to rotate your body from side to side so that it distributes evenly.

As with any medication or procedure, there are also risks. The major complication from epidural anesthesia is a drop in the mother's blood pressure. Most hospitals will try to prevent this by giving the mother intravenous fluids prior to the administration of the epidural. An epidural can also lead to fetal distress, slowing of labor, and increased risk of forceps or vacuum extraction. Make sure you talk to your doctor about your potential risk factors and what you'd like to do.

> **MM TIP:** An epidural can fall out. Yes, I know, it's your worst nightmare. I wouldn't have believed it if I hadn't seen it. One of my best friends, Clare, was in unbelievable pain during her delivery. Both her husband and I couldn't understand why, as they said they were giving her more medicine. Well, when she finally moved forward, the needle was on the bed, not in her back. She made it through, but boy was she pissed!

Natural Birth Techniques

Many people are attracted to the idea of giving birth to a baby who isn't exposed to drugs, and also to the idea of feeling the sensation of birth. For these women, the two predominant birthing methods are the Bradley method and Lamaze. Bradley was developed by Dr. Robert Bradley in the late 1940s and emphasizes an extremely natural approach, with few or no drugs and little medical help during labor and delivery. This method stresses good diet and exercise during pregnancy, teaches deep relaxation techniques to manage pain, and educates a woman's husband or partner so he can be an effective coach.

Lamaze was developed by Dr. Ferdinand Lamaze and is based on the idea that the best way to control pain is through knowledge and relaxation. The method emphasizes breathing techniques. If you are interested in either of these methods, you should definitely take a class to learn the proper techniques. www.babycenter.com has some great information about Lamaze and a guide to centers by zip code.

Doulas

Consider a doula to be your own personal trainer for labor. This is an option many women find incredibly reassuring, as it means that someone is there coaching and encouraging you through labor, and acting as your personal spokesperson to make sure your labor plan is attended to. This is an especially great option if you're a single parent or if you're worried your husband may not be able to hold it together in the delivery room (think of Hugh Grant fainting in *Nine Months*). As a bonus, researchers have found that women attended to by labor assistants have shorter labors—by up to two hours!—fewer labor complications, and fewer problems with newborns.

Most doulas are certified childbirth assistants and have coached hundreds of women through labor and delivery. Their fees typically include the delivery, as well as preparatory and follow-up visits. Doulas of North America (DONA), an association of doulas, has a referral line (801-756-7331) that can help you locate a doula in your area.

Water Birth

Many birthing centers and more and more hospitals are offering women the chance to use a birthing pool to ease the pain of labor, and even to give birth in. Many women have found that wallowing in deep warm water during labor allows them to relax, and gives much relief from the discomfort of contractions. Some choose to get out of the water in the second stage to deliver their baby. Others actually give birth in the water, so that the baby's first moments of life outside of the uterus are underwater—which is similar to their environment in the womb.

> MM TIP: Many centers that offer water birth are located close to a hospital in the unlikely event that something goes wrong. Now while I knew I was an epidural girl, this idea intrigued me, and the proximity to the hospital made it pretty appealing. Pretty, not very.

MM TIP:
Even if you've spent your whole pregnancy planning on delivering naturally and begin to do so during labor, don't feel like a failure if you change your mind halfway through and ask for drugs. Childbirth is painful. It hurts. I don't know how else to say it. Some women can handle this pain; I know I could not. You are not a better or worse mother because you didn't succeed at natural childbirth. And your child will be just fine either way.

MM TIP:
Some doulas will massage your feet or shoulders during labor. While it probably won't make all the pain go away, it's more fun than watching your husband pace the room.

While You Still Have Some Time on Your Hands

At this point, you are basically ready to deliver the baby, and probably don't have energy to do anything beyond lie on the couch and kick your feet up. Well, before you lose that free time—and trust me, you are about to lose your free time—here are a few things to consider doing. Don't worry; you won't have to exert too much energy.

Ordering Announcements

One of the best things I did before the baby arrived was to preorder my announcements. Whether you are ordering printed ones or making your own, you need to decide on the style, create your list of recipients, and buy your envelopes ahead of time. This way, when you are lying on the couch with your feet up, you can address and stamp all of your announcements. Most stationery stores are used to this request and will gladly send off your envelopes separate from the announcements. Then, once your baby arrives, you can simply call in the name and stats (you'll want to see a proof, of course) and have them printed.

> **MM TIP:** Consider ordering matching thank-you notes for your baby. You'll be getting a lot of gifts, and the sooner you write the notes, the better. Go for small four-by-six cards so that you don't have to write too much. And begin writing as soon as you receive gifts—even if the baby hasn't arrived yet.

MM TIP:
If you don't know the gender and want the announcement to be gender specific, simply pick out two styles and call them with the right one once you know what you've got.

MM TIP:
To that end, *do not* get overly Type A and order the announcements themselves in advance. Heck, you may change your mind on a name or have a surprise when it comes to the sex. Call me superstitious, just wait.

Preserving Memories

Whether you plan to put together a baby book, a photo album or scrapbook, or simply write a journal, it's great to have it ready before the baby comes. It's nice to be able to include your very first thoughts and memories in the books, and the longer you wait, the more you forget. During your time in the hospital you'll actually experience quite a bit of downtime, as the baby sleeps a lot. This can be a fun time to make some notes in a baby book.

I have always been a horrible journal-keeper. But I decided with my son that I would write a little something a few times a week for the first year. I gave myself an end date, as it made it seem more attainable (and I didn't feel as guilty when I stopped at eight months). I also made sure to include feelings and milestones rather than activities, which means so much more as I look back.

> **MM TIP:** Get a big box in which to store memories. From his first clip of hair to the sonogram tape (yup, I've got that), just toss everything in. As long as you have a designated place, it's okay if you don't organize it into a scrapbook or whatever. The first outfit, photo, and so on will make the beginnings of a treasure chest for your child to dig through in a few years.

Writing a Will

With a new life about to enter your house, pondering your own death is downright unpleasant. But while it might be okay to defer thinking about who gets your stuff when you pass on, you must think about who would look after your child and how his needs will be met.

The thing that scared me into finally writing a will was being reminded by a fellow mother that in the event of my husband's and my death, without a will, the court (basically the laws of the state in which we lived) would appoint a legal guardian for our children and determine how our assets would be distributed. And while a judge will try to select the best possible guardian for your child and direct your assets to take care of your children and/or spouse, these choices might not reflect your specific wishes.

One of the strangest things for me about having a child was that I suddenly became frightened for my own safety. I was terrified that if something happened to me and my husband, there wouldn't be anyone to provide for and take care of our children. Writing a will *will* at the very least put some of your fears and worst-case scenarios to rest. It is one of the most important things you can do for your child and for yourself. It is your safety net. It is there to ensure that in the event of

MM TIP:
Many people will ask you if they can lend a hand after you have had the baby. Take them up on it. Stuffing your announcements into envelopes is an easy task to hand off to your mother-in-law or girlfriend, especially if you've preaddressed them all. That way, you can take a short snooze!

MM TIP:
If you're not into writing, get a small personal tape recorder. Sometimes just talking can be a lot easier.

your death, your assets and property will be distributed in the way you would want them to be. Even more important, it is the means for you to designate a legal guardian for your child in the event that something happens to you.

Don't assume that you don't have enough assets to make a will necessary. One of the biggest misconceptions about a wills is that they are for the wealthy, but this couldn't be further from the truth. The purpose of a will is not limited to passing down money and property; it can also be a means of passing down your wishes, values, and sentiments to your children. You can leave your great grandmother's fiftieth wedding anniversary ring to your daughter; you can donate a certain amount of your money to charity, and you can even write up guidelines for how you want your children to be raised in your will. Don't cheat yourself out of preparing what is an important message from you to your children. As you hand down your assets to the next generation, you may feel more in touch with your own heritage and history, and you might become more aware of how much you really *do* have (monetarily or not). It can also serve as a jumping-off point for financial planning; analyzing and really looking at your assets, debt, and property may start you thinking about and consequently planning for your child's financial future. So don't put it off. I promise you will feel a big sense of relief and peace of mind when you finish. You can then put your will away in a safe place and get back to enjoying the more pleasant parts of being a mom.

Consulting a Lawyer

Consulting a lawyer is one option when drafting a will, but it isn't the only one. For some, the perceived cost of going this route can be a primary reason for putting it off. In fact, the majority of Americans today don't have a will, and it's often because they think hiring a lawyer will be too expensive. But it's not as costly as one might expect, and for those with more complicated and/or valuable estates, I definitely recommend this route. One upside of hiring a lawyer is that it may help protect you from making unnecessary mistakes that could cost your beneficiaries money down the line. Depending on where you live, the lawyer you choose, and the level of complication, drafting a will can run anywhere from a few hundred to a few thousand dollars.

Chances are that you'll have friends or family (especially if they have children) who have been through this process. Ask them what lawyer they used, what their experience was like, and how much it cost them. If they had a good experience, ask them to refer you. Most people will be happy to help guide you through this process. The American Bar Association's website (www.abanet.org) is also a great place to get started. It will provide you with a list of certified lawyer referral services in your area that will help guide you to someone who specializes in probate and estate planning.

Get Prepared Before You Go

Now that you've found a lawyer, save money by starting to prepare *before* your appointment:

- Calculate how much you have in assets by adding up the value of all of your property, including your real estate, 401K's, IRAs, bank accounts, stocks, bonds, life insurance, and so on. Then subtract your debt from this amount (which includes how much you owe on your house).

- Make a list of the people you'll want to provide for in the event of your death. For many of us, this list is short, but it's an important consideration, particularly if you have a larger estate.

- If you are married, draft a separate will from your spouse and leave your assets to your spouse, as he will most likely be the one to take care of your child/children in the event of your death.

- Think about who you may want to be the executor of your will. This is extremely important, because if you don't designate an executor, the courts will do it for you. Technically, you can choose anyone for this job (a friend, a relative, or even your lawyer), but make sure it is someone you trust implicitly; they will have the responsibility of

MM TIP:
The upside of hiring a professional is that they will have emotional distance and will most likely be more skilled at some of the responsibilities involved with being an executor, such as paying off debt and taxes. The downside is that some of your estate will need to go toward paying your will's executor (which may mean a bit less money for your children).

MM TIP:
Should you choose a family member to be the executor, you may want to write a provision in your will to pay them, but it's not required.

MM TIP:
If you don't have a complicated estate, work with your lawyer on drafting a will that is somewhat general, so that you won't have to update it as often. This will save you money down the line.

MM TIP:
Remember to revise your will if you have another child or if your property and assets significantly change. In any case, it's a good idea to look at your will every three to six years to make any necessary revisions.

MM TIP:
Create a separate list in your will that designates where nonmonetary assets should go. This will save you from having to meet with your lawyer every time you want to add one of these assets to your will. You can simply amend the list.

executing the wishes outlined in your will. If you have a family member who may disagree with your wishes, it's better to not make him or her the executor. Choose someone who can be impartial. Whomever you decide to use, I recommend choosing someone who is responsible, organized, and has some knowledge or skill in dealing with financial affairs. A good friend's father passed away when he was sixteen and his mother was appointed executor of a fairly complicated estate, which was more than she could really handle. As a result, she made several honest mistakes that cost them a great deal of money and could have been avoided by someone more familiar with this kind of responsibility. Remember to talk to the person you have in mind for this job before you meet with your lawyer to make sure he or she is comfortable taking on this responsibility.

MM TIP: You and your spouse should create different wills, even if it seems more efficient to create just one document. A joint will binds the survivor to the provisions of the joint will (which is usually written with the children in mind, not the spouse), which doesn't leave a lot of room for the surviving parent to change his or her mind on financial and other matters if circumstances change radically.

Writing a Will on Your Own

Don't let the mental or financial intimidation of meeting with a lawyer be an excuse for putting off your will writing. There are many ways to create a will on your own.

There are numerous sites online to get you started; www.nolo.com is my personal favorite. You will find valuable information there on anything from writing a will to drawing up a trust (see page 58), along with several downloadable software programs, such as Quicken, to guide you through the process and provide the necessary forms. Quicken Willmaker kits cost from $40 to $80 and can also be purchased at www.amazon.com. You can also find free legal will writing forms at the Self Help Law Center (www.selfhelplaw.com). Here's what to do next to make sure your will is legal:

- It should be typed, not handwritten. Handwritten wills aren't legal in all states, so best to be on the safe side.

- You'll need to state somewhere in the will that it is your will; for example, "This is the last will and testament of _____." All your decisions about what should happen to your property and assets (to whom they should be directed) should be contained in your will. Your will should also appoint a legal guardian for your children.

- Date and sign your will in front of two or more witnesses. In Vermont, three witnesses are required.

- When you have finished writing your will, put it in a safe place, and let a few people that you trust know where it is (your spouse/partner, parents, legal guardian, trustee, or executor). Make sure it's a place that these people have access to. You may want to avoid safe deposit boxes; in the event that both you and your spouse pass away, it might be difficult for others to gain access, which could hold up the transference of your estate and the appointment of a legal guardian.

MM TIP:
Even if you plan to sit down with a lawyer in the future, your will can act as your family's safety net in tho moantimo.

MM TIP:
Contrary to popular belief, a will does not have to be notarized to be legal, but I do suggest going to a notary and signing a "self proving affidavit" in front of witnesses. This may save time later having to call witnesses and gather affidavits.

Appointing a Legal Guardian

This is one of the most important and emotional decisions you will make and probably the biggest reason not to put off drafting your will. But if you think contemplating your own death was hard, try thinking about someone else raising your child. While actually *designating* a guardian in a will is as simple as filling in a blank, *choosing* whose name to put in that blank can be extremely difficult. While the chances that you (and perhaps your spouse) won't be around to raise your child may be slim, it can happen. And if you still need more motivation to start this process, just think about a judge deciding who should raise your child. It's a scary thought, but that's exactly what will happen if you die without having appointed a legal guardian for your child.

Now be warned. Even if you've somehow survived the first few months of motherhood without hurting anyone's feelings (friends, mother-in-law, coworkers), you're sure to hurt someone's feelings while choosing a legal guardian. I recently spoke to a friend whose sister is giving her the silent treatment over this very issue. Evidently, she confided in her sister that she was considering naming one of her close friends as the legal guardian of her children. When her sister asked why, she rattled off a laundry list of her friend's strengths, from having children of her own to the stability of her friend's marriage. (This was like salt in a wound for her sister, who had a struggling marriage and was trying desperately to get pregnant.) While her sister tried to make a case for herself as a legal guardian, she kept listing reasons why her friend was a better choice. Needless to say, they aren't speaking to this day. The lesson: don't even *speak* to the people that you *aren't* considering as legal guardians about the decision you are attempting to make. I promise, it will hurt someone's feelings, and believe me, you have more important things to worry about.

But the essential thing is that you pick the right person/people as legal guardians, and having gone through this process myself, here are some questions you may want to ask yourself while trying to make this difficult decision:

- Who are some candidates that you and your spouse might agree on? This may be more difficult than you think. Your husband may want his parents to be legal guardians, while you may consider them too old to raise young children. It may be hard to come to a consensus, but it's essential that you do. Otherwise, the judge will have to choose between your different appointed legal guardians if you have chosen separate people in your wills.

- Who will love your children *nearly* as much as you do? I know this isn't really possible, but it was important for me to pick someone who genuinely cared for my children. In my opinion, love can go a long way when it comes to good parenting.

- How old is the prospective guardian? You don't want to pick someone who is so old that caring for young children will put a great strain on them. They should be healthy enough to care for someone other than themselves, but mature enough to handle the responsibility. A legal guardian must be eighteen years of age or older.

- Are the guardians you're considering financially solvent? Would they be able to provide for your child in the case that your will cannot?

- Are their values and morals similar to your own?

- Do you have similar religious and political views?

- If they have children of their own, how are they raising them?

- Are their parenting methods compatible with yours?

- How well do they know you? Should you pass away, would they be able to tell your children about you, the type of person you were, how much you loved them, and stories that they remember? Having a guardian who intimately knew the deceased parents can help a child to process grief and feel more grounded.

- Do they have the time to devote to your children?

- Do they have other children? How old are they? Many parents like the idea of their child having playmates, but too many children close in age can be overwhelming.

- Where does your child's prospective guardian live? It may be difficult for your child to relocate—it's important to keep a few things stable in a time of turmoil—so weigh this with other factors. If they don't live near you, do they live in a neighborhood or city where you think your child might have a variety of opportunities?

- How do they feel about the idea of being your child's legal guardian? If you are still having a difficult time making a decision, speak to the people that you have in mind. Their enthusiasm about taking on this kind of responsibility may greatly impact your decision.

- Can this person care for all your children? Most parents prefer that their children stay together, but if there is a large age difference between your children, this may not be as important to you. Your children may also be close to different people and have preferences of their own, so keeping them together should be weighed against these factors.

MM TIP:

Keep in mind that you can change guardians in your will as often as you like. Perhaps you feel that your parents are the best choice to watch your child now, and your sibling isn't in the best financial place to take on this endeavor. Ten years down the road when your child is facing the teenage years, you may feel that your parents are past the point of dealing with these trying times, and your sister has come around. Just know that this decision can change as your child grows up.

MM TIP:
Be sure to name a
guardian and one alternate
guardian in the event that
your first choice cannot
accept the responsibility.

MM TIP:
If you are divorced but feel
strongly that if you should
you pass away, it wouldn't
be in your child's best
interest for the other parent
to have legal custody,
include a letter in your will
detailing why you believe
that person to be an unfit
guardian. Just know in
advance that in most
cases, despite your
wishes, unless the court
feels there is some kind of
proof to back up your
feelings, they will grant the
surviving parent custody.

MM TIP:
Include a letter in your will
stating how you ideally
want your child or children
to be raised.

- What does your heart tell you? If there is one thing that comes along with being a mother, it's a heightened sense of intuition. Trust yourself. You ultimately know in your heart what is right for your child, so listen.

A Living Trust

A revocable living trust is a good addition to a will, or shortcut to a will, as you can include in it a simple statement designating a legal guardian for your child. A trust involves transferring all of your assets to the trust and typically naming yourself and/or your spouse as trustees and beneficiaries until you pass away (at which time your children become the beneficiaries). Instead of an executor, you name a successor trustee to manage your assets for your children in the event of your death. One advantage of a trust is that your trustee's responsibilities don't necessarily expire when your child turns eighteen; they can continue watching over the assets of your estate for your child indefinitely. Another advantage is that you can revoke or change the provisions of your trust at any time. But perhaps the biggest advantage of trusts is that they don't have to go through probate, which can be a costly delay for family members. (Probate, by the way, is the act of proving that an instrument purporting to be a will was signed and executed in accord with legal requirements. This is a great option if you have blown off doing a will, and then you find you and your husband needing to travel without your child at the last minute and are a little freaked out about getting on a plane without a few loose ends tied up. This happened to Jen.) Despite the advantages of trusts, many people seem to stay away from them, because they assume they are far more complicated that wills, but this isn't really true. Ask your lawyer about a living trust option or go to www.nolo.com for advice and do-it-yourself trust-writing software.

Dollars and Sense: Planning for Your Child's Financial Future

At a time when there just seems to be no money to spare (whether it's things you bought or things you're planning to have), you're hearing other moms and dads talk about the college fund they just set up for their unborn child. Whatever you do, don't be intimidated into *not* doing anything. Even if you don't seem to have any extra money once you're done buying groceries and paying off your hospital bills, you should start planning and saving at least *something*—even just a piggy bank in which you put your extra change. Just think for a moment about the cost of a year's tuition at even a public in-state university, which today averages at least $10,000 a year; multiply that number by at least 5 percent inflation a year, and you'll have some idea how much four years of college will cost you eighteen years from now. It might be overwhelming, especially if you have more than one child, but don't let that stop you; every little bit makes a difference. The piggy bank earns no interest and thus works more as a mental incentive.

I recommend opening a savings account for your child as soon as you discover you are pregnant (okay, sorry, probably too late). But the point is, open an account now, and make a goal to contribute a set amount of money to your child's savings account each month. You'll be amazed at how quickly it grows. There are many alternatives when it comes to saving for your child's financial future, and this is one area where I strongly recommend paying to meet with a professional. Don't put off making the most important investment you will ever make. Here's what you should ask your financial planner about at your first meeting:

- Roth IRAs

- Education IRAs

- Hope Scholarship credit

- State college savings (529) plans

- Prepaid tuition plans

- Life insurance policies

- Uniform Gifts or Transfers to Minors Act (UGMA/UTMA)

- Stocks

- Mutual funds

- Trust funds

MM TIP:
Fan of the BlackBerry or
not, e-mailing is certainly a
faster and less taxing way
to spread the word of your
newest arrival. Consider
creating a mailing list
ahead of time so that the
e-mail is all ready to go.

Compiling a Call List

Okay, now on to the birth. Look, we all have friends who would freak
if they weren't contacted the minute you gave birth. Typically
(strangely), they are not your closest friends but the ones who need
you to *prove* to them how close you are by the very fact that you called
them to tell them the news of the birth. But the last thing you need is
to be reminding your husband who to call and then frantically looking
up their numbers yourself. And after a day (or two) of no sleep (on
both your parts) and the joy of a baby, truth is you might have forgot-
ten to call each other had you not been there. So I recommend making
a list of the most important people you need to contact, along with
their phone numbers. Pack the list in your bag for the hospital.

Packing for the Hospital

My husband laughs to this day about how much stuff we took to the
hospital. I was settled in and comfortable in the delivery room (God
bless a good epidural!), and my husband went back to the car to get my
suitcase. As he was wheeling in our rolling suitcase, along with a nice
big boat-n-tote, a third-time father passed my husband in the hall,
chuckled, and said, "First time, eh?" Well, clearly this is one of those
things you learn only from experience.

If you took any prebirth classes, you probably received a lengthy
list of about 100 things you *must* have with you for your stay in the
hospital—both in the delivery room and afterward. Since we had no

idea what we were doing, we spent the last two weeks of my pregnancy going all over town buying things like a mini-battery-operated fan, sour sticks to suck on, a six pack of apple juice boxes, ginger ale, magazines, books, massage oil, back massage doo-dad, and the list goes on. Well, trust me, you will never use half the stuff on those other lists. I left 90 percent of it with the nurses, who probably packed it away in a locker full of similar stuff. Most hospitals have most of the things you will actually want (ice chips, clean gown, etc.). You may want to pack two small bags, simply to keep things separated for labor and then later. Hospital essentials include:

For Labor

- Cosmetic bag with a hair band, lip gloss or balm, toothbrush and paste, moist facial wipes, contact solution and holder if applicable.

- Socks or slippers (depending on whether you are planning to walk or simply lie in bed with an epidural).

- Anything to distract you: trashy magazines, a mini-DVD player, iPod, funny friend, whatever. I spent most of my labor with Lilia on my Blackberry. While it truly drove my husband crazy—and convinced all my friends that I was redefining the Type A personality— I found it a great distraction (although I don't recommend contacting lost friends with the starting line, "Hi, how are you? I'm in labor and thought I'd reconnect . . ." Sounds like you're fishing for a baby gift. I wasn't! Just the first time in a while I didn't have much to do!).

- Camera and/or video camera with all battery rechargers and extra film.

Optional

- Your own nightgown if you are okay with throwing it away afterward. I personally preferred the hospital's gown, as it was easier.

- A watch with a secondhand or stopwatch for timing contractions (*if* you feel like it—I didn't even bother. Pre-epidural I was in too much pain; post, I couldn't have cared less).

MM TIP:
Please, for the love of the horror film *Carrie*, use black-and-white film. Babies covered in blood in black-and-white photos are artistic; in color, they're quite freaky.

MM TIP:
I preferred PJs because of the open front for breast-feeding. Personally, I just wore the PJ top and kept a blanket over my lower half.

MM TIP:
It sounds strange, but the hospital gives you these bizarre mesh panties that aren't so comfortable. Use them, but don't spend a lot of time on these; they will definitely get ruined, so simply throw them away.

MM TIP:
Lansinoh is good not only for sore nipples, it's great for sore chapped lips and as a cuticle softener—a great use when you find you've got too much on your finger.

MM TIP:
Consider just a tinted moisturizer. You won't want to be putting on your full face, but this will add a little glow and keep your skin from drying out!

For Afterward

- Clean nightgown or PJs.

- Your own pillow. Now this is something that I wouldn't have traded, as silly as I looked walking in with it. It really did provide me my only rest in my first nights of sleeplessness.

> **MM TIP:** Consider buying an inexpensive but comfy pillow to bring with you but not bring home. You'll leave with twice as much as you came with—and not just a new baby. With gifts, flowers, supplies, and more, you may not feel like lugging a big pillow home.

- A special treat or snacks or a good friend to get you carryout. I was completely famished after my labor, and the rubber chicken the hospital served didn't quite do the trick.

- Cell phone, battery recharger, and address book.

- Five pairs of maternity granny-panties (in case you're in that long with a c-section).

- Nursing bra, Lansinoh cream, and Soothies to help soothe sore nipples.

- A few more cosmetics: your facial soap, lotion, shampoo, hairbrush, and perhaps even makeup if you are planning on having visitors.

- A going-home outfit. Just bring your most comfy maternity outfit, as you will still look about five to six months pregnant when you go home (don't worry, I'll get to that later). Also, bring flat, slip-on shoes.

- A going-home outfit for your little one, including a hat, socks, and receiving blanket.

Eight Unpleasant Things You Need to Know About

Okay, so you're pretty much ready to go. There are just a few last things you need to know. Look, it's my duty to let you in on not only the good, but also the bad and the ugly of childbirth. Just when you thought it was safe to go into the delivery room . . .

But seriously, these are the things I wish *someone—anyone—*would have told me.

Pooing on the Table

First up, pooing on the delivery table. It is only natural, with all that pushing, that *other* things beyond the baby are going to get pushed out. I was one of the first of my friends to have a baby and had no idea this was a possibility and was horrified by the thought of it. How embarrassing! How gross! But rest assured that your doctor has seen it all and is not fazed by a little feces. The nurse will literally push it away and get back to business. Given that my husband wasn't allowed to look below the thin paper separating my hips and the great unknown, I was pretty sure he wouldn't see, but I just couldn't get it out of my head.

So if you don't want to be trying to push and thinking about poo, pick up an enema to have on hand. While some hospitals will provide you with one, others won't. You can give yourself one either before you leave for the hospital or once you get there, depending on how your labor is progressing. Or ask your doctor when you're discussing your birthing plan and she may be able to order one for you. (FYI, in retrospect, getting an enema may well have been more embarrassing.)

Tears and Episiotomies

If you've been pushing a cantaloupe-size head out of your vagina, you've likely experienced one of two not-so-pleasant things: a cut in your perineum called an episiotomy that makes a little more room for the baby to come out by cutting the skin between your vagina and your anus, or a tear that may or may not be the most symmetrical of openings on your body. And if the baby's head didn't rip you wide open, then the shoulders were right there to finish the job. So chances are pretty good that you've got a couple of stitches down there (totally normal) or at the very least, a great deal of swelling. Here are a few tips to dealing with *this* lovely new obstacle:

MM TIP:
You may have done this in case of your water breaking (which actually happens in only about 10 percent of women)—buy a nice, waterproof mattress cover to put under your sheets. This will not only come in handy in those first few days of oozy-ness, but also when your breasts leak from engorgement (more things to look forward to!).

- You will be bleeding. Lots. And likely gushing a lot of other stuff that, well, I guess I should just say it's better if you don't know what all of that stuff is (another good reason to wear their gowns instead of your own PJs. Who wants to be reminded of all that ooze later on when washing!?!). The hospital will provide you with an endless supply of sanitary pads, but it's not a bad idea to bring a nice big box of your own, especially if you're partial to a certain kind. And have some on hand at home, too. Who the hell has maxi-pads around the house anymore?

- Don't look or touch down there for at least three weeks. Trust me. You will be horrified, and will likely never want to have sex again if you look too soon. Do use the spritz bottle you get at the hospital to wash.

- Know that time is your friend, and before long you will feel a lot more normal!

Peeing and Pooing Post Pushing

I know what is running through your mind right now. Open wound. Swelling. And the *same* opening with which you also have to go to the bathroom. Don't panic. After what you have just gone through, this will seem like a walk in the park, and I promise, it is scarier in your mind than in reality. Here's what to do:

- While the first time you pee may burn a little, get a spray bottle of water and spray yourself over the area while you go the first time. This will cut the acidity in your pee and make it burn less.

- Start taking stool softeners and laxatives the second you give birth. You will be constipated, and it eventually has to come out that supersore area. Don't psych yourself out, and know that this too shall pass—literally.

Pain Pain Pain!#@%#$*^%!!!!!

I don't know if it's some unspoken mother's code, or if mommy veterans are simply trying to protect us delivery virgins from the inevitable, but for some reason, no one—and none of the books for that matter—told me how downright painful recovery is. Let me just put this out here: it's excruciating. You will hurt. It sucks. I don't know how else to say it, but someone ought to let you know. Everyone tells you about labor. Somehow they forget about recovery. Unless your baby has a head in the twenty-fifth percentile like Lilia's (I *knew* I liked that girl), you will just plain hurt. And guess what? Even with a head in the twenty-fifth percentile, I still hurt! You assume that the labor is the worst part. Look, it may be. But if you've had an epidural like I did, the shock may very well be the next day when the drugs wear off.

The day after I delivered, it was as if my body had been used in some bizarre tug-of-war ritual where my legs had been pulled apart. I certainly wasn't expecting all that blood, and who knew that I wouldn't be able to sit for about two weeks? When I compared notes with my friends who had c-sections, the prognosis wasn't much better. They may have been sitting prettier, but cutting through a layer of skin and muscle in the abdomen is no walk in the park, and lifting their baby, or sneezing for that matter, was something else entirely. Either way you go, you're going to be in a huge amount of pain.

And to make matters worse, it's almost as if once they get the baby out, the doctors are on to smaller and more precious matters. Although sweet and lovely, short of the one visit the next day—in which he simply talked to me about how I was feeling, but didn't even look down there (perhaps it was too scary even for him)—I was on my own. I was shocked to learn that my doctor didn't even want to see me for a month (and we were so close).

MM TIP:
You may also find that you can't control your bladder the way you used to and may pee when you laugh, cry, or just stand up. In most cases, this problem will correct itself, but it's another good reason to do your Kegel exercises (which I'll describe in a bit).

MM TIP:
Prune juice mixed with pear juice makes a great and palatable laxative. It cleans your whole system right out.

Now, I'm not writing about this to scare you, but rather to tell you what I wish someone had told me. Just don't plan to do much walking, moving, or much more than cooing at your baby. And if you're thinking the pain will never end, I promise that it will. After all, many women do it all over again—by choice. I just want you to be prepared and have a few tips on ways to make it better:

MM TIP:
Go to a hospital supply store before you give birth and buy one of those donut pillows used by people who break their tail bone. It will be one of the few things you will be able to sit on after you deliver.

- *Pain medicine.* In my opinion, this is not the time to be all noble about trying to experience birth. The baby is out. This is finally about you. And even if you're nursing, it's okay to take some pain medicine. If it's being offered, take it. If it's not, ask for it.

- *Ice is your friend.* Keep the nurse (or your husband) on speed-buzzer for those rubber-glove-filled ice packs and stick 'em down there. Nothing works quite as well.

- *Pass the peas, please.* When you get home, you may find that frozen maxi-pads or small plastic packs of frozen peas work well. They don't leak and are refreezable. These are also great for children's boo-boos. Just mark this bag with a permanent marker so that you don't accidentally serve it for dinner. Gross!

MM TIP:
Stock up on some hemorrhoid cream *before* you go into the hospital. You'll want to have it when you need it, not when your husband finally gets around to picking some up. I'm also a big fan of Tucks wipes. Sitz baths also help. Ewww, I know.

Hemorrhoids

If you think pooing on the table was bad, wait till you see your special little delivery present. All that pushing has likely made a few other things flare up. If you're used to Tivo'ing through those Preparation H commercials, guess what, you're currently their latest target demo. Even if you didn't get hemorrhoids during pregnancy, the pressure of the labor may cause them after. Chances are they will go away, in time, but for a while they'll be a literal pain in the ass.

Bizarre Side Effects

If it weren't enough that you can barely sit or lift—depending on which area your baby popped out of—you will likely experience several other side effects from delivery. Some of the most normal ones include:

- *Headaches from epidural or other medicines.* This is incredibly common, and the headaches can vary from slight to intense. Food and drink are just what the doctor ordered because chances are good that most of what you are feeling is due to a drug-induced hangover. Usually, it's nothing a good greasy plate of fries from the cafeteria won't fix.

- *Facial swelling.* Although you feel as though you are supposed to start losing weight the second you give birth, your face may stay swollen for several days. Time will make it go away.

- *Broken blood vessels.* This can happen from hours of bearing down, and they can occur in your eyes (makes you look a bit like a vampire, but they go away after about a month) and in the little capillaries on your face. Most facial capillaries will go away, but if they don't, they're easily zapped by a dermatologist's laser.

- *Dehydration and chapping.* Chances are you haven't had a thing to drink for hours, not to mention all the fluid you've lost giving birth (I had to remind you of the ooze again, didn't I?). Anyway, make sure you have a good lip balm and start drinking as much as possible. Water is the best, although juice is a fine alternative.

- *Itchiness.* This is a typical side effect of an epidural or a general anesthetic that includes morphine. While you may want to rip your skin off, the itching will go away as the medicine wears off.

- *Hair falling out in clumps.* Okay, so you probably noticed how wonderfully thick your hair got during pregnancy. Well, just like you got the baby out of you, now it's time—cruel as it is—for your newly lush locks to go away. It may fall out little by little, or do it in clumps, but don't worry. You're not going bald. You're simply giving back what really wasn't yours to begin with. You will soon simply have your pre-pregnancy amount of a mane. If you're breast-feeding, you may keep that gorgeous hair until you wean your baby. But don't think you've come out with a baby and locks that look like extensions. As your hormones change, it's likely to fall out.

- *Back pain.* If you had "back labor"—and if you have to ask what that is, you didn't have it—then you are probably trying to decide what

MM TIP:

If you had a c-section, all that loose skin around your waist coupled with your incision can make the act of standing up very painful, especially as your belly drops to your ankles. Grab a pillow and press it against your incision every time you get up. This will help ease you into position.

MM TIP:

To help heal your c-section scar, rub vitamin E oil and Maderma on the scar. Most drugstores sell these products. They really work, but you have to apply them religiously—like fifteen times a day!

hurts more, your privates or your spine. Chances are that your tailbone has been bruised from the inside. While it can unfortunately take months to heal, it will go away completely. This is one of those "only time helps" annoyances.

* *You still look pregnant!* Okay, so this is one of the more depressing things. You will look at your stomach and, well, still look fat. But instead of your skin being stretched tight across a big ball, it will be all mushy and lumpy. And gravity—never kind to women in my opinion—doesn't do us any favors on this front. Every time you roll to the side of the bed or stand up, there hangs your belly. It will get better each and every day, and your muscle tone will come back. Unfortunately, you really can't do any exercises until your doctor gives you the go-ahead, which is usually about six weeks after birth.

Sex

I know. It's the furthest thing from your mind, right? I know it was for me. But let me let you in on a little secret: The thought has crossed your husband's mind . . . five times a day . . . since the last time you had sex. Oh, and that medicinal "bend over the bed in a strange position to try to have sex to make you go into labor" sex didn't quite cut it. To make matters worse, your hormones are readjusting, which can zap your sexual desire, while his libido is likely at an all-time high. And then let's not even talk about the fear of sticking anything in there, certainly not after what came out!

Now don't get me wrong. Many women jump right back in the saddle after the "recommended waiting period" of six weeks, feel little to no pain, and enjoy a completely fulfilling sex life right away (surprisingly, these people do exist outside of the Playboy channel). For the rest of us, try out these tips to get you going again:

* *Loosen up.* Most husbands can flick on their sexual desires like a light switch. Women are bit more complicated, and after the stress of a day with a screaming baby, getting in the mood can be the

biggest challenge. Take a bath or warm shower, have a glass of wine, ask for a shoulder rub. Get yourself in the mood.

* *Warm up.* Unless your baby is screaming, indulge in lots of foreplay to make sure that the juices are flowing.

* *Lube up.* Altered hormone levels—especially for those who are breast-feeding—can make the vagina uncomfortably dry. This is normal. Don't skimp, and use plenty on you and your husband. If necessary, ask your doctor to prescribe topical estrogen to lessen the pain.

If you experience a great deal of discomfort the first time you have sex, don't worry. Your vaginal walls are a bit like a rubberband. I know it sounds funny, but they have to stretch out a little bit. The other thing you may feel is the sensation that, when your husband is completely inside of you, he is hitting something. This actually might be the case. With your switch in hormones, your vaginal cavity can temporarily shorten. Know that it will get back to normal over time.

If you're still feeling a great deal of pain after several attempts at sex, talk to your doctor. A friend of mine had pushed her baby out so fast and torn so much, that when her doctor stitched her up, a few things fused too tightly. After several failed rounds of topical estrogen cream and estrogen inserts to try and loosen up the area, she ended up

MM TIP:
You may notice slight spotting after intercourse. This could be a result of skin flaps at the site of incisions or tears. If it doesn't go away on its own, don't worry. They can easily be repaired by your doctor.

MM TIP: Some women come out of delivery feeling "stretched out," leaving sex to not feel quite as good. Time helps tighten you up, along with Kegel exercises. In case you don't know about Kegels, these are exercises to tighten the muscles in your pelvis that (I'll be blunt here) make it easier for you to squeeze to control your bladder or heighten your man's pleasure. The great thing is you can do them anywhere, anytime, and you'll never break a sweat. You want to make sure you empty your bladder and then squeeze what feels like your vaginal muscles together. If you can't figure out what it is, next time you're peeing, try to stop midstream. THAT's the muscle that you are trying to exercise. It's different from clenching your butt muscles. Hold for three seconds and release. Try doing three sets of five once or twice a day for a week, and then try increasing this to three sets of eight strong squeezes.

going in for a local anesthetic and a minor snipping of the area to create more room. While this sounds excruciating, it didn't hurt all that much, and in the end, made for much better lovemaking.

Postpartum Depression

I don't know a single woman who felt so overjoyed and ecstatic at the birth of their child that they never even had a moment's doubt or regret. But strangely, I know very few women who ever talk about it. Perhaps it's all of those movies in which someone has a baby and the couple is so happy and constantly cooing over their new little one. Or maybe it is simply too taboo to think about anyone not being instantly in love with a brand-new baby. But the reality is that 60 to 80 percent of women experience the "baby blues," which usually occurs within the first week of giving birth.

And until recently, even the medical community swept the baby blues, and worse, postpartum depression, under the proverbial rug, leaving women to suffer through it alone, ashamed, and unrecognized. Well, thank you, Brooke Shields—and doctors around the country—who have made it a better-known ailment. Recently, many hospitals have even required that women take home literature that discusses the signs of the baby blues and postpartum depression and provides a checklist for women and their husbands to go through and evaluate how they are doing.

So what are the signs? The baby blues typically include crying and irritability, sleep problems ranging from insomnia to sleeping the day away, appetite swings from all to nothing, and the inability or lack of desire to take care of your baby. This is very common the first week, and usually subsides by week two. But if it continues or become more intense, then you may be among the 10 to 20 percent of new mothers who suffer from postpartum depression. PPD can develop out of the baby blues, or may not come on until after your first menstrual cycle or when you wean your baby. And exercise and fresh air are typically not the cure. There is real treatment for PPD, but you need to get help immediately. Here's what to do:

- Call your physician and get your thyroid levels checked out. This may be a simple explanation for your mood swings. However, if they appear to be normal, seek out help from a therapist who specializes in PPD.

- Make an appointment with a therapist promptly. Counseling coupled with antidepressants such as Zoloft or Prozac (which appear to be safe during lactation) can make things better fast.

- If the idea of antidepressants makes you nervous, try light therapy, which is very effective for some women.

MM TIP:
For more help, contact one of these great sources:

• Postpartum Support International. 805-967-7636, www.postpartum.net

• Postpartum Assistance for Mothers: 925-552-5127, www.postpartum depressionhelp.com

• Depression After Delivery: 206-283-9278, www.ppmdsupport.com

Whichever route you choose, know that you are not alone, but you need to take care of yourself quickly. PPD can prevent the very necessary bonding that you and your baby need. It can also have devastating effects on other relationships in your life—with your husband, other children, and parents. But don't stress out about it if you need a little time to work through your issues. Babies are blissfully unaware of your emotional state—unless, of course, you are completely neglecting them or putting them in physical danger—and in the end, won't notice a thing about your depression.

Okay, at this point, you are pretty much good to go—I'm sure I don't need to tell you that. Rest up; you'll need your energy for the birth (and the next eighteen or so years). My other suggestion is to spend as many evenings as possible going to the movies. Not only is it a cool, comfortable place to hang out (especially for those of you having summer babies), but also, it will be one of your last opportunities to see a movie for a while. Once you're ready to leave the house, the idea of spending $50 for a baby-sitter to go see a movie that could be a hit or miss quickly makes you switch to a Netflix account.

Deciding About Cord Blood Banking

Cord blood banking is a relatively new medical advancement in which the blood from your baby's umbilical cord is collected, frozen, and stored for future medical use. It's all completely painless and safe for you and your baby, and takes about ten minutes to gather. Once the blood is collected, it's shipped to a cord blood bank, where it's processed and frozen for long-term storage.

Cord blood is valuable because it is rich in stem cells, the building blocks of blood and your immune system, which can then be used to treat a host of diseases. For example, leukemia patients undergo chemotherapy to kill off the diseased cells and then restore new, healthy blood cells. If normal cell production resumes, then the disease goes into remission and the patient recovers. But if the treatment doesn't work or the disease recurs, that is where the cord blood can be handy. By using a transfusion of this blood from a healthy donor, a new blood and immune system can generate, thus making recovery more likely. Further, since cord blood cells are immature and haven't learned how to attack foreign substances, rejection by the patient occurs a lot less frequently than in other types of traditional treatments like bone marrow transplants.

That said, the American Academy of Pediatrics says it's tough to recommend that parents store their children's cord blood for future use if there is no history of disease. It can be a relatively costly insurance plan that most families never cash in on. However, if you have another child or family member that already has a condition that can be treated with a stem cell transplant, such as sickle cell anemia, thalassemia, aplastic anemia, leukemia, metabolic storage disorders, and certain genetic immunodeficiencies, it could prove to be a life-saving choice. In this case, you should definitely try to bank your child's umbilical cord blood.

Currently, there are many companies that specialize in storing cord blood. This is something that you *must* arrange prior to giving birth, as they send you a special kit that allows your doctor to properly store the blood. Most companies then use medical messenger services to pick up the cord blood from you directly at the hospital. Also, be sure and discuss your choice with your OB/GYN so that she knows to collect the blood (in all the excitement, you may forget). Below are a few companies to look into and various prices.

Family Cord Blood Services: A California Cryobank Company
800-400-3430, www.familycordbloodservices.com
Apply online or over the phone. There is a one-time, nonrefundable enrollment fee of $75. Then, for the collection kit, processing, and licensing and storage (excluding shipping), you pay based on the number of years they store the blood. The rates range from $1330 for one year up to $2715 for twenty years of storage. Shipping cost is an additional $150 nationally; local shipping of less than 100 miles is $45. The fee includes $125 for reimbursing your physician for the cord blood collection. Shipping with a specialized medical courier are included in the fee. After collection, you just call the courier for a pickup. A payment plan is also an option.

Cord Blood Registry
888-CORD BLOOD (888-932-6568), www.cordblood.com
A processing and banking fee, which includes all costs associated with your collection kit, processing your baby's sample, administrative costs, follow-up materials, the cell separation process, and testing costs $1700. Additional costs include one-step shipping for $150 and then an annual storage fee of $125 for the first year and every year thereafter until contract expires. There is a $150 discount for online enrollment and an option that allows clients to save up to $400 by prepaying for eighteen years of storage up front. They also offer several payment plans.

ViaCord
866-668-4895, www.viacord.com
The price at ViaCord begins at $1800 for collection, delivery, and processing of the cord blood and then $125 a year for storage. Since the blood is saved for up to twenty-one years, the total cost would be about $4425, unless you prepay for storage, which can save you big bucks. They also have a variety of monthly payment plans.

Sibling Donor Cord Blood Program
www.chori.org/siblingcordblood/home.html
This program is at Children's Hospital of Oakland. You can bank your child's umbilical cord blood there for free if you meet their eligibility

MM TIP:
Look, the thing is I didn't do it because, well, too many people thought it was unnecessary (as it really was very new) and (I'm embarrassed to admit) I had overpaid on curtains and just had reached a breaking point in my budget. I am incredibly lucky that to this point my children are healthy, but should something happen and cord blood banking might have helped, I'd burn the curtains and never forgive myself. If you're interested and price is an issue, consider asking for it as a shower, birth, or baby present from close family or friends.

> **MM TIP:** You may decide that instead of banking your newborn's cord blood, you'd like to donate it to a nonprofit cord-blood bank for research or to save the life of another child. If you'd like to donate your child's umbilical cord blood, contact your local chapter of the American Red Cross or a local university hospital, or check the National Marrow Donor Program's list of registered cord blood facilities that accept donations.

requirements, which include having a child with a transplantable condition or a prenatal diagnosis of a transplantable condition, or having an unborn child at high risk for having a transplantable condition.

Help Is on the Way!

Now that you've gotten the medical experts and considerations taken care of, it's time to think about expert help for you—oh yeah, and the baby—once your little one arrives. Some moms are lucky (and brave) enough to be able to stay at home and go it alone. But for many people who work out of the home or need an extra hand, hiring a nanny or finding a terrific day care situation is a great option.

Choosing a Nanny

If you choose to go the nanny route, it's great because it allows your child to stay at home in a controlled environment with one-on-one attention. If your child is sick, someone is there to take care of him and you can go to work (day care has strict rules against bringing ill children). Some nannies also clean and cook, which frees up time for you to be with your child when you come home. Of course, it also costs a lot more than day care, and you become responsible for reporting taxes, Social Security, and worker's compensation insurance. Your child may have less socialization with other children, and if your nanny is sick, you have no built-in alternative for care.

However, if you decide to hire a nanny, it can prove to be a rewarding choice. You can choose to go through an agency, in which you will pay a hefty fee. Otherwise, you can search out recommendations of friends or try newspaper ads. Another great source is www.craigslist.com for your city.

Of course, anytime someone comes into your home to care for your child, you'll be anxious. Here are a few tips to help maneuver through the nanny process:

- Do the initial screenings over the phone. This will save you a lot of time in the end. Once you find one or two great candidates, then meet in person.

- Find out about past caregiving experience, the ages of the children they cared for, and why they left that family. Then ask for the number of that family and follow up with them for a reference.

- Decide if you want a nanny who speaks your language, or if you want to introduce a different language and culture to your child.

- Determine if it is important that the nanny have a valid driver's license.

- Be up front about expectations in terms of hours and responsibilities.

- Decide whether you want a nanny who has her own children. If so, set up clear guidelines up front as to when she can or can't bring her children around.

- Discuss price. Remember, you can always go up; it's much harder to go down. Don't suggest a price you know you can't afford or will resent.

- Find out if the nanny can work legally in this country.

> **MM TIP:** Look, of course you should hire only people who are in this country legally, for legal reasons. But there are practical ones, too. I've had friends whose nannies "snuck" home, never to return as they were denied entrance, and everyone was miserable. Also, if you ever plan on traveling to another country with your nanny, you can't do that if she isn't legal.

MM TIP:
It may sound anal, but write up as specific a nanny list as possible. A friend of mine even wrote different responsibilities for different days of the week. This is a great way to help keep you both from getting frustrated. She knows what is expected, and you won't worry that the laundry isn't ever going to get washed, but know that it is due to be washed tomorrow.

MM TIP:
Similarly, if your nanny will be doing any chores or shopping, write a specific list of brands and even sizes you prefer. After no sleep, baby spit-up, and an early meeting you're late for, the wrong brand of butter may push you over the edge. But it's unfair to expect your nanny to be a mind reader and remember everything you like. I even did my list as a "shopping list" divided into sections and printed out about fifty copies to have on hand. We keep it in the kitchen and that way when we are out of something I check it off on the list and our nanny knows to buy it.

MM TIP:
Whether your child is going to be cared for by a nanny, a relative, or even at a day care center, it is important that whoever is watching your child has a letter of medical consent in their possession. Emergency rooms have become incredibly strict about caring for children when they are not with a parent, due to fear of lawsuit. It can be a simple letter stating the name of the child, your name and number, and the name and number of the caregiver, and that you give them permission to treat your child. Make sure you sign it. Further, you can add your insurance company information to the letter, which will make the emergency room react that much quicker (sadly) because they know they will be paid.

MM TIP:
It's not foolproof, but if the caregiver seems uninterested in holding or really looking at your child, she may not be the right person. If you sense that she's just shy, suggest that she hold the baby and see how she responds. Also, see whether she washes her hands first.

- Make sure she doesn't smoke.

- Ask if she is CPR trained and, if not, if she would be willing to become certified (look for more information on this in chapter 4).

> **MM TIP:** Be very clear on what holidays and days off your caregiver will be getting throughout the year. Those pesky holidays like President's Day and Columbus Day always seem up for grabs, and you should decide in advance what you want to do. Also, if you are providing two weeks' vacation, consider having one week be at her discretion, and one that overlaps with your vacation.

> **MM TIP:** If you're a working mom, think about having your nanny start a few days a week before you go back to work. Not only will it be nice to have a couple of hours to yourself a few times a week, but it will help make the transition of handing your child off that much easier.

Choosing Day Care

For many moms, day care is a more economical option that provides many advantages over nannies. It is a much more social environment that lets your child interact with other children, which can be a bonus developmentally (and you benefit from a built-in support system of other moms with children the same age). There are also multiple caregivers at once, so you are not relying on just one person for your baby's well-being, which is a comfort to many mothers. Most day care centers also allow for early dropoffs and late pickups.

Some children in day care get sick more often, as they are exposed to more runny noses and other illnesses (this can also prove to be a benefit later on when your child goes off to preschool—his tolerance may be higher). The provider-to-child ratio is also a bit higher, and the schedule may not be as flexible.

But since day care is licensed by the state, which controls the standards set in the day care centers, many are a very safe and wonderful option for families. Here are some things to look for:

- Is the location convenient?

- What is the child-to-adult ratio?

- How many children are enrolled?

- Can parents visit anytime? Never consider a program that's off limits to parents for even part of the day!

- What is a typical day like for a child (meals, naps, time outdoors, etc.)?

- What are the hours of operation? Are early dropoffs or late pickups available? What about holidays?

- Is part-time care available?

- Is the day care center clean and childproofed?

- How many cribs and beds are there? How is nap time handled?

- What do the meals consist of, and do they follow any special diets?

- Do they allow sick children to come and, if so, where do they stay?

- Will they dispense medicine to sick children?

- How do they handle potty training?

- What is the cost, and are there options for payment?

In the end, you may find that you try a nanny at first, and then move to day care, or vice versa. When it comes to having someone else raise your child, know that you will pretty much torture yourself either way, one hundred times a day. I know I did. But rest assured that millions of women have had to make these decisions and their kids have been happy, healthy, and well cared for.

MM TIP:
While you are doing a day care tour, take a very close look at the air vents. Even if the day care looks spotless, the air vents tell the real story. If there is dust and dirt on the vent cover, it's not as clean as it should be.

MM TIP:
A big part of day care is the ratio of caregiver to child. According to the National Association for the Education of Children, ratios should be as follows:

• One caregiver for every three babies (birth–15 months) if there are six infants in a group and one for every four if there are eight babies in a group. Eight babies should be the maximum number in any group.

• One caregiver for three toddlers (12–36 months) in a group of six, a one-to-four ratio for eight children, one-to-five for ten, and one-to-four for twelve. Groups should have no more than twelve kids.

MM TIP: I would advocate visiting the facility on several different days so that you can observe many interactions between the children and the day care providers; first impressions count, but you'll want to look for repeated signs of warmth and affection.

CHAPTER 3

The Babymoon: The First Few Weeks Home from the Hospital

I'll never forget the day I came home from the hospital with my son. The night before, my husband and I decided it would be best if he went home and got a good night's sleep so that at least one of us was well rested for the homecoming (last decent night's sleep *either* of us has had in years!). Lucky for him, but for me, well, that night was one of the worst I can remember. My baby finally woke from his two-day zombie-like state, and was up all night with an open mouth like a baby bird wanting a worm dropped in. If you've ever taken up working out after being lazy for a few months, you're well aware that you feel great after that first workout, sore the next day, and basically can't move the third day. Well, giving birth is really similar. The day after, you basically feel like hell, and the third day you typically feel like you have been hit head-on by a Mack truck (more on that later). I could barely sit up, let alone skooch down the bed to hold him and feed him.

So there I was, painfully skooching, trying to satisfy his hunger, and of course, dealing with second-day soreness of the nipples, too. And while all of the nurses up until that point had been more attentive than a husband first seeing his wife's pregnancy boobs, my nurse on *that* night must have been down to her panties in a game of strip poker with some hot doctor, because she was pretty much MIA.

The next morning, I called my husband for sympathy and, well, a life vest. Meanwhile, he was in the best mood ever and bragging about his Ambien-induced night of great sleep. If I could have slapped him over the phone, I would have, but instead, I just started bawling. I think this was clearly my first sign that I had the baby blues. And while I was thrilled to be coming home with my new bundle of joy, that morning was just the beginning of a *long* and trying couple of weeks.

Not only are you adjusting to a major change to your immediate family—whether it be going from two to three, introducing a sibling or even a family pet—but you are also likely having to deal with parents, in-laws, and other visitors and their excitement (and sometimes invasion) about getting to know the little one. Couple that with the fact that you're damn sore and are simply a hormonal wreck who is best compared to twelve sorority girls all getting their period on the same cycle—needless to say, this can be a trying time. Don't be fooled, the babymoon won't be just like your honeymoon but with a baby.

Introducing Your Bundle of Joy (and Screams)

New Siblings

So, it's time to bring your new baby home and interact with the rest of your family. Remember them? And while a baby's homecoming can be an exciting event, it can be a bit overwhelming for a small child. You may have heard this great analogy: to a child, bringing home a new sibling is the same to the child as your husband coming home one day and saying to you, "Hi. I love you, but meet my new girlfriend. She is going to live with us from now on." If you keep this in mind, your patience and understanding for your older kids will be firmly in place. And depending on your child's age, these feelings can be amplified. How you handle the homecoming will no doubt accentuate your child's greatest expectations or worst fears (no pressure here). I had heard that you shouldn't walk in holding the baby. My husband didn't want to either. We thought about having the FedEx man bring Lilia in, but feared Jack would subconsciously hate packages for the rest of his life. Instead, we brought the baby onto the doorstep, and I went in, got Jack, and had him help me carry her inside in her car seat.

Here are a few tips to help your older child adjust:

- If a sibling is coming to the hospital to meet the baby, make sure the baby is in the bassinet when they arrive so that your arms are open to greet your oldest.

- Have him be a part of the homecoming team as opposed to the team waiting at home for the arrival. This may help him feel more a part of the process and give him a bit of ownership over the baby. If he can't come to the hospital, then have him be a big part of the action by letting him set out decorations or lay out diapers. Also, try to come in first, without the baby, to have a few minutes of time alone with your older child, and then have your husband follow with the baby.

- Have your child help "present" the baby to other members of the family who might be waiting at home (grandparents, neighbors) rather than having a baby be presented to him.

- If you're particularly worried about germs around your new baby and you have a toddler who is in day care or preschool, consider having your child wear a mask when they meet their new sibling. You can make a game out of it by letting them pretend they are a doctor or nurse. Personally, I wouldn't worry about it.

- Have your older child sit on the floor next to you and "hold" the baby in his lap. Being on the floor makes it a lot safer, but still lets him feel as though he is helping out.

- Try to spend as much time as possible with your older child in the first few weeks when the baby is no doubt sleeping a lot. Have your husband or the grandparents take your oldest out for a special outing—to the zoo or even to a favorite restaurant—as a fun treat.

- It's important not to send the message to the sibling that the baby will be the only priority. Unless you're feeding the baby, try to put her down in the swing or the bassinet and actively play with your

MM TIP:
Toddlers and preschool-age kids are walking petri dishes of diseases and germs. While you want your child to feel a part of the process, you don't want your baby to be exposed to all those germs. Always have your toddler wash his hands before touching the baby, and a great rule for siblings and small children is that they can only touch the new baby's feet when he or she comes home from the hospital. The feet are safe since babies don't put them in their mouths as often as they do their hands.

oldest. At night, once your oldest is asleep, then feel free to spend hours holding and cuddling the baby. The baby won't know the difference the way a two-year-old will.

- Use feeding sessions as a time to read stories to your older child, as it will make him feel a part of the process. If he's old enough, start a big chapter book that you can read bit by bit. Then, your child will look forward to feedings and so will you.

- Avoid idolizing your baby when possible (cooing over your new little one in front of the older child). Instead, point out things your eldest can relate to: "Her fingers are so little. Did you know that your fingers were once that little?" Or, "Wow, her poopy really smells. Can you believe you were that stinky?"

- If your older child wants to stay home from nursery school when the baby first arrives, let him. You don't want him to feel as though you are pushing him out of the house or trying to get rid of him—even though you may want to. Just make sure you set up parameters in advance, so he knows how long his little holiday will be.

- Expect a bit of regression from your toddler when you welcome a new child to the family. That's a nice way to say that they can basically turn into the temper-tantrum-throwing baby you never knew you had. If you've made great progress in toilet training, bedwetting, thumbsucking, or pacifier and bottle use, don't be surprised if old habits resurface when you bring home the baby. Try to be patient and sympathetic (don't punish), and know your child will likely work through these Chucky-like issues when things calm down a bit.

MM TIP: Have about a dozen small, wrapped gifts ready to go for your older sibling (great thing to put your mother-in-law in charge of!). They don't need to be large gifts. More important is that they are activity related, such as crayons, a paint set, or something to build so that it occupies him for some time. While savvy guests will bring a gift for both children, many guests will not. Dispense the little gifts when necessary, and keep this tip in mind when *you* bring baby gifts to friends who have older children.

MM TIP:
Okay, so you may find yourself in the enviable position of receiving gifts from afar. I know all of those gifts coming to your door can be the highlight of any girl's day. I got so bad that I used to simply open the door when I heard the UPS truck come barreling down the street and wave to Martin, the UPS guy, just knowing he was coming to me. It felt as if I had been dumped by a boyfriend when he slowed down with the gifts and started bringing stuff to *other* neighbors (the two-timer!). Resist the urge to unwrap gifts that arrive by mail or UPS. Stash them in a closet or leave them on the front stoop if you can. Once your older child has gone to bed, then have a little new-baby opening session

Furry Friends

If this is your first baby, and you've had your dog or cat for some time, there's a good chance that prior to the birth of your baby you've counted the *pet* as your first child. I'm sure my cats remember their prebaby life fondly: Long cuddles every day. A prime spot on the bed. Belly rubs for no reason at all. Leftovers and treats at their bidding. And, of course, they got the first feeding in the morning. Now, the poor guys are lucky if they are picked up (other than to be removed from the kids' rooms) or even fed at all. (Oh, stop, you don't need to call the ASPCA, it's an exaggeration.) If this prebaby pet scenario seems at all familiar, there's a good chance it will be a little difficult for your furry friend to roll over when your baby arrives. So, just as there are things that you need to do to acclimate a sibling, your four-legged loved one deserves the same consideration. Cats and dogs react in a similar way to a new baby, so the tips below work for both. If you've got a canary or an iguana, you're on your own. If you collect snakes or insects, time for a new hobby.

For the safety of your baby, it's a good idea to take your pet to the vet for a checkup to make sure he is free of worms and up to date on all of his vaccinations. Here are a few other things you should do:

Before the Baby Arrives

- If you have friends with babies, invite them over so that your pet is used to seeing you interact with babies. If your friends don't mind, under careful observation, let your pet explore near the baby to become familiar with the smells. (I remember the first time we did this, our dog went into the nursery, which we were already in the process of setting up, and peed all over the floor. Sounds a lot like a two-year-old's reaction, no?)

- As you buy things for the baby, let your pet sniff and explore them a bit. This will help them become at ease with the various scents that will eventually be surrounding your baby. Don't punish them for snooping in the nursery (unless, of course, they chew up the new bedding; in that case, try not to give your pet up for adoption).

- Invest in a baby-size doll, and begin a routine in which you change the baby with real diapers and something baby-scented like baby powder or baby lotion. Make sure your pet is in the room and sees/smells you doing this. If your pet gives you a weird look, well, it's probably deserved. You are changing a doll, after all. I don't know anyone who has done this, but it is recommended by many experts so you may want to try it.

- Download baby crying sounds from the Internet (www.acoustica .com/sounds.htm) and burn them onto a disc. Then, occasionally play it and comfort your baby size doll. Let your pet get used to the cries. (Don't let your neighbors hear you doing this, or they may commit you.)

- Make any adjustments to your pet's routine before the baby arrives. If the family pet is used to sleeping in then bed with you and won't be postpartum, or has a feeding station that will eventually move when there is a crawler in the house, move it before the baby arrives so that your pet doesn't resent the baby for the change.

Once the Baby Arrives

- After delivery, but while you're still in the hospital, have your husband bring home an unwashed piece of clothing, blanket, or burp cloth for your pet to sniff so that it gets used to the smell.

- Just like with siblings, when you arrive home, let your husband carry the baby, and you greet the pet first (second if there are other siblings in the mix, duh!). Similarly, let the pet be involved in the new flurry of activity over the baby. Pushing the pet away can cause resentment and retaliation.

- Let your pet sniff a well-swaddled baby while protecting the baby's head and face with your arms. However, never let a dog or a cat lick your infant.

MM TIP:
When you bring home an item from the hospital that smells like the baby for your pet to sniff and get used to, place the item somewhere that is associated with a good feeling for your pet such as their food bowl or near their bed. This way, they associate the smell with positive experiences.

MM TIP:
Although actual cases of babies being suffocated by cats are quite rare, better to keep the cat out of where your baby is sleeping.

Dealing with Wanted (and Unwanted) Visitors

When your baby arrives, it is a time of joy, excitement, and happiness—okay, so that's really only the first fifteen minutes. Then, you quickly learn it's a tough job and *you've* got to do it. Add on top of it some immediate pain and recovery and many sleepless nights, and it can be the longest few weeks of your life. And while some people see this as a time in which they really want help from friends and family and the more houseguests the merrier, others simply want to lock themselves up and not see anyone for several weeks. Whichever plan sounds more appealing to you, inevitably your friends and family will want the opposite.

Keep in mind, this may be the first of many times when you have to stand up for your own new family and be strong. The most important thing is to set the rules early so no one is expecting you to be hospitable. Visitors and houseguests can be taxing enough, without postpartum recovery thrown in the mix.

Drop-By Visitors: At the Hospital and at Home

My good friend gave birth to her son on New Year's Day, so her husband called all his friends to spread the news. By one o'clock in the afternoon there were twelve hungover oglers in her recovery room—many of whom she didn't even know. When they finally went home, the open house continued since everyone was in town for the holiday and wanted to get their chance to see the baby. My friend had a constant migraine because of the epidural and was absolutely miserable. But she was so worried about what everyone else wanted that she put up with it for four days. Finally, she just told everyone to go home. When her second child was born, *no one* was allowed in the hospital, and she asked people to stay away for weeks once they got home.

While this is not the norm, it's what can happen if you don't have a plan going in. Be very clear and up front with people about what your wishes are. Okay, now that I've said that, I have to tell you, for most of my mom friends, and for me, this was the hardest thing next to the actual delivery. I don't know what it is about women, but we are typically too worried about what everyone else wants—to the detriment of ourselves. Well, it's time to prepare for mommyhood, and you, your wishes, and your baby must come first. Here are a few tips to make your postdelivery visits what you are hoping for:

- Have every guest who walks through the door wash their hands. Whether or not they want to hold the baby, it's a good blanket rule to have. While you may feel a little weird asking people to do this, they should know better and wash on their own.

- Put your husband in charge of traffic control. If you want guests at the hospital, have him spread the word. If you don't, have him keep everyone away. If you're going to be breast-feeding at all hours for the next few months, this is the least he can do. If your husband's not up for the challenge, better to pick a trusted friend or relative who is. You'll have enough reasons to resent him without adding this to the list.

- Establish a secret code with your husband ahead of time, like, "It's time to feed the baby," or even something more awkward and obvious like, "It's time to change my ice pack." This will likely elicit a quick exit by your guests, or, if they are incredibly dense, will at least let your husband know you need help getting them out.

- Don't feel as if you have to sit and talk with people for hours on end just because they've made the trip to the hospital. Ten minutes is plenty if that's all you want.

- When you have visitors at home, never plan it around a meal unless *they* are bringing the food. No one should expect you to entertain, and if they do, don't have them over.

- If your close friends want to stay for a while, put them to work. I had one friend who passed her baby off to friends and excused herself to take a nap. If you have friends like this, by all means, have them come over. Often!

MM TIP:
Keep several bottles of antibacterial gel, such as Purell, around the house. It's an easy way for a lazy guest to get clean.

MM TIP:
Although you may be tired, if you know a lot of people want to see you immediately, consider encouraging them to come to the hospital. In the hospital, there is nowhere to sit and no drinks or snacks to serve, and it's a quick in-and-out visit. No one expected me to get out of bed and entertain.

MM TIP:
If you feel like taking the first couple of weeks to adjust and don't want to have *any* guests, blame your pediatrician. Tell guests that your *doctor* is very worried about germs and doesn't want any visitors for the first two weeks. People may think your doctor is a bit extreme, but it's better than their being angry with you—or invading on your space.

- Don't be afraid to tell people it's time to go. Assert yourself and make no apologies. Breast-feeding or needing a nap is a great excuse.

- Turn off the ringer and turn on the answering machine. If you feel like hibernating with your husband and baby, do it. The visitors can visit in week three or four when you're feeling more like yourself.

> **VERY IMPORTANT MM TIP:** It is very important in parenting that you and your partner are allies on the various issues that will come up. You'll feel this way over and over and over again. It will likely first occur to you when it comes to guests once you've brought your baby home. Two things to keep in mind: Discuss your feelings on the issue ahead of time (if possible) and alone. Even if this means making an awkward departure out of a room, do it. Second, whatever you decide, stick with the plan. In the beginning, it will feel as if he is making a lot of compromises for your feelings (which, frankly, is how it should be—you just pushed that baby out). But in the long run, it will even out.

Friends with Toddlers

MM TIP:
I had one friend who came over with her husband and her toddler, but quickly whisked her toddler off to our guest room with a new video. He was happy as could be watching his new show—it's not like *he* wanted to see the baby—and my friends got to meet our son. It's also a great way to make sure the visit is short and sweet. When the toddler's video is over, they will be quick to exit.

I had a good friend tell me to not allow any friends with toddlers to come over to visit with their kids in tow. Since I was a new mom, this seemed like a reasonable thing to request, as I didn't want my child to end up with some weird illness a toddler had picked up at preschool. But then, as my son got older and I had friends who had babies, I realized how difficult it was for my husband and I to go pay our visits. We didn't want to get a baby-sitter for what amounted to a thirty-minute visit, yet we didn't want to impose our toddler on them. In the end, I missed out on meeting a lot of friends' kids when they were little.

Overnight Houseguests

This is typically a trickier obstacle to maneuver, as people who expect to stay at your house are automatically closer friends or family, who inevitably come with a unique set of baggage—and I'm not talking the fall Louis Vuitton line. This is a special time for you and your family, and one in which you will likely want to bond privately with your baby and adjust to your new life and routine. I know I feel as if I missed out on this a bit because I was so concerned with what my relatives wanted to do—come stay with us. Don't let someone spoil this for you simply because *they* want to see the baby. On the other hand, if there is someone you want to stay with you to ease the burden, then the most important thing will be to set up boundaries ahead of time.

- Adopt an all-or-nothing policy. If you say yes to your mother, you will likely have to say yes to your mother-in-law. A good excuse is to simply explain to everyone, "If I let you stay, then I will have to let my mother-in-law/best friend from Chicago/stepdad come and stay."

- If you don't want people in your house, have guests come to town, but see if one of your friends has a spare room and could host your guest. If it is really important, offer to put your guest up in a hotel or split the cost. (Most guests won't let you pay.)

- Ask guests to wait for two weeks. This is typically the amount of time it takes you to start feeling better and to begin to want people around. If you've had the first two weeks to yourself, you may actually welcome guests by then.

- Keep overnight visits to three nights or under. Any more and you will inevitably be entertaining.

- If you do choose to have a guest stay in the house, be very clear that they can only come if they will work—and put them to work. Whether they do your laundry, run to the grocery, cook a meal, or simply watch the baby so you can take a nap—this is the price of their room for the time they are there.

Babyproofing

Okay, so you will be tempted at this point to go out and buy basically anything and everything on the market to keep your child safe from any sort of danger or harm that may come her way. After all, she's so little and helpless. Well, that's kind of the point. She is helpless and will likely be that way for the next six months until she learns to sit up on her own, and eventually crawl sometime around seven to eleven months. There is very little trouble she can get into on her own and, well, putting your child in a bubble is pretty much looked down upon these days. So the way I look at it, why should you torture yourself every time you need to open the cabinet beneath the sink, go down the stairs, or plug something in by having to deal with those annoying childproof devices?

Well, you shouldn't. Milk those last few months of cabinet-opening, stair-climbing, direct-stereo-accessing freedom the way you would a night out with your husband with no baby in tow. But do keep in mind that you will need to babyproof at least a month or two *before* your child starts crawling. If you put up gates before crawling is an issue, then the baby has always seen it as part of her environment. If you put it up once she starts to crawl, it may feel more like a re-straining device that's there to keep her from doing what she wants.

Here are a few problem areas you will want to look out for:

- *Outlets.* You can stick those little outlet covers into every socket, but I always found that I broke a nail pulling them out (hey, who wants to ruin a good manicure when you have alternatives?). I also find that eventually, a crafty two-year-old can pull them out. So I chose the ones that had you replace the entire face plate and screw on a new one that had safety latches over the plugs that spring into place to cover the outlet.

- *Cords.* This is a great excuse to finally bundle all of those cords under your stereo, by your computer, and from lamps near walls. Buy covers that secure your cords to baseboards, roll up long cords and secure with a twist tie, or buy those long cord hiders.

- *Phone cords.* Nothing's more fun to grab than those curly cords. One pull and bonk! Right on the head. Replace with shorter cords, or buy a retractable one.

- *Heavy objects.* Anything that is light enough that your child could pull it over but heavy enough that it could do harm should be secured or strapped to a wall: fireplace screens, small book shelves, standing floor lamps, TVs, and so on.

- *Electronics.* Move your video or DVD equipment out of reach or shield it. There's nothing like a PB&J sandwich shoved in a VCR to make you wish you had.

- *Doors.* Make sure all doors can be locked or unlocked from either side, or that you have a key. Children love to slam doors, and it's awful when they—or you—are stuck on the wrong side.

- *Screens and windows.* Know that screens won't support your child if she leans on them. For high-floored windows, install safety bars (it's the law in many cities) or make sure windows are opened from the top.

- *Drapery cords.* Wrap up all long cords for curtains and drapes, as they are a huge strangulation risk.

- *Stairs.* Install safety gates at the top and bottom of the stairs, and avoid a tension bar at the top of the stairs, as a child could lean on it and dislodge it.

- *Sharp edges.* Use table bumpers for sharp edges and glass tables. There also are adhesive ones for fireplace edges.

- *Swimming pools.* Don't ever skimp on babyproofing your pool. It needs to have a gate all the way around it—no exceptions—with latches up high, out of little ones' reach. It protects your own kids *and* kids in the neighborhood.

- *Cabinets.* Put baby latches on dangerous cabinets where chemicals, sharp objects, or things that are breakable are stored.

MM TIP:
Put a bell on any door that leads to an area you would want to be alerted if your child entered: the back door, the garage door, and so on. This way you will be alerted the second they leave. You can get this device at many baby stores or Target.

MM TIP:
I'll talk more in chapter 7 about creating "yes" alternatives to the word "no." On that same theory, keep one cabinet in the kitchen accessible to your child so that she can explore, like the bread drawer or the Tupperware cabinet. This way, she won't get frustrated with everything being off limits. As an added bonus, hide one of her toys in there for her to find.

MM TIP:
Switch from tablecloths to place mats. Kids love to pull on things, and it's not only a mess, but dangerous if your child pulls the contents of an entire table down onto himself.

Reality Check: Everything Has Changed, but Your Life Will Come Back

I had a good friend tell me, about a week after giving birth, that I would be surprised at the fact that one day, in the not-so-distant future, I would experience little moments when I would realize I had a bit of my life back. In the midst of midnight feedings, sleep deprivation, and utter soreness, I found this a little hard—okay, downright impossible—to believe. But she was right. Granted, it wasn't some major monumental reminder of my old life—like sipping a chilled dirty martini on a hot date out with my husband (still waiting for that one a few years later)—but there were little signs. About six weeks in, my husband and I actually sat down and ate dinner together while catching one of our favorite TV shows, a former ritual. Then there was the first time we made it back to a movie again. Then there was sex. The point is: it does come back. Here are a few ways to get it back faster:

MM TIP:
Get a regular baby-sitter on a weeknight. You have more of a chance of actually using the freedom to reconnect with your husband and do something just for the two of you. If you get a sitter only on weekends, you will likely use the opportunity to see friends or hit social functions.

- *Regular baby-sitting.* At first you may not feel as if you can do this, but by month three, it is a must. Ideally, once a week—whether you want to or not. Whether you have time or not. Whether you are fighting or not. Just get out of the house together and reconnect. It's easy to forget about your relationship when you are so taxed being parents.

- *Take your baby out*—once your pediatrician okays it—as much as possible to do the things that you like to do. They are still at an age in which they are easy to cart around (read: they sleep all the time), and you will feel like more of a person if you go out to lunch or shopping once in a while. Added bonus: the baby will start to assimilate to your lifestyle.

- *Take a shower every day.* I know it is tempting to blow this off in the first few weeks—I think I went four days at one point. But you will feel like so much more of a human if you do this. And your husband will thank you, too!

- *Lip gloss!* Doing a full face of makeup is not only out of the question on most days, but a criminal waste of good product! But there's nothing like a little sheen on your lips to make you feel a bit pulled together.

- *Take walks.* It will energize you, help get you back in shape, and give you a nice bonding session with your baby (and your new fancy stroller!).

- *Buy transition clothes!* There's nothing more depressing than wearing maternity clothes six weeks after you've given birth. And unless you're regularly being photographed for *US* magazine, you're likely not back into your pre-pregnancy clothes. Hit Target or some other store, and stock up on a few cute, basic transition outfits. You'll look and feel better instantly.

CHAPTER 4

Food for Thought (and Little Tummies)

A true Modern Girl can fake it when she needs to, right? I mean, after all, I've learned how to cheat my way through a dinner party without really cooking (all hail a sprig of fresh rosemary on a store-bought chicken), change a tire in stilettos and look damn good doing it, and even master the medical miracle of curing a hangover. So I can handle anything, right?

Well, flash to 2 A.M., eyes blurred, feeling like I'm in the middle of some strange nightmare in which my nipples are being pierced during what can only be described as a torture-induced state of insomnia. Once I've pinched myself twice and realized that not only does it hurt, but I'm awake, it comes to me: this is just my nightly breast-feeding ritual with my newborn son. And guess what? There's no way to fake this! He's hungry, and I've made the decision to breast-feed him. And contrary to what Ben Stiller said in *Meet the Parents*, you *can't* milk anything that has nipples—so my husband and cats are out of the question as copilots on this journey. Even if I decide to switch to formula on the spot, clock my husband over the head (partially to wake him and partially because, well, he's asleep and I'm not) and beg him to make a bottle, my darling little bundle of joy doesn't even know how to drink from a bottle. Short of calling 1-800-wet-nurse (and believe me, I've thought about *that* as my next business idea), this is my new Modern Girl life. Not exactly the picture-perfect idea of motherhood I had in mind.

Well, guess what? It will get better. Then worse, and then better again. And while I had one baby who cried his way until age two and another who never cried until two but then didn't stop for a year, I can say that breast-feeding typically gets easier. It's also important to realize when you're reading this chapter that in the first several months, sleeping and feeding are (usually) explicitly linked. It's kind of like taking a road trip. You can't be expected to drive for several hours on an empty tank. Babies are the same way. Typically, the fuller their tank, the longer they sleep. Now, of course, every child isn't as easy to decipher as the gas gauge on your car, but hopefully, with these feeding tips, it will make the road a little less bumpy.

Your New Bosom Buddy

For years I had heard friends gush about the incredible bonding experience of breast-feeding their child. Just the two of you, cuddling, cooing, feeding in the middle of the night. Well, my first few weeks of breast feeding couldn't have been further from that. First of all, I've been cursed with what my husband affectionately refers to as a "no fly zone." In other words: sensitive breasts. So having an infant with a mouth like a Hoover vacuum sucking away for dear life on my nipples was, let's just say, a gift that only a mother could give a child (my husband is still a little jealous).

The best piece of advice I got was this: If you commit to breast-feeding, then make a pact that you will stick with it for at least three weeks. That is how long it takes most women to get over the initial hurdle of the sore nipples, the rigid schedule, and the general discomfort. If it doesn't get better, skip it. You tried. But more likely, you'll find it does and it will be well worth it.

Chances are your first three days of breast-feeding will be the hardest. Breast-feeding is a learned skill and a really frustrating and difficult one at that. Maternal milk flow depends on nipple stimulation to begin with, but after an initial period of wakefulness immediately after delivery, babies are too tired to go to the breast on their own and often too tired to stay awake at the breast for any extended length! They're generally zonked out for their first day of life and need to be woken up for feeding attempts. When they do get some energy on their second day of life and are all ready to go, most new mothers' milk hasn't quite let down. So if you can make it to day three, the combination of an awake, crying baby and a full breast will finally start working together.

Now listen, I'm about to make a bunch of enemies. I breast-fed both of my children—Jack for six months, Lilia for four (clearly, I loved him more). And I felt guilty that I didn't feed him longer, that I didn't feed her as long as him, that I ever supplemented formula, that I didn't want to have sex with my husband because I felt like a milk truck, and so on and so forth. While I was glad to be breast-feeding, I found it impossible to have any sort of life (Jack ate every two hours for the first two months). I was tired, cranky, sore, and miserable. But I did feel virtuous. There is tremendous pressure to breast-feed. And I know that it is healthy for your baby and studies show that. I KNOW. So if you do it, great. If you don't, give yourself a break. Don't let anyone sway you. Make the decision for yourself. If your baby gets a cold, it is not because you didn't breast-feed. If the idea of it all freaks you out, don't worry. Truly. A happier you will make for a happier baby, breast- or bottle-fed.

Advantages of Breast-feeding

- Breast milk is said to be perfect food for your baby. It has all the nutrients babies need, so you don't have to worry about what to feed them.

- It's easy for your baby to digest and cuts down on the chances of allergic reactions to various formulas.

- Breast milk has been shown to boost a baby's immune system.

- Your baby will be protected from gastrointestinal trouble, respiratory problems, and ear infections, thanks to breast milk.

- It can guard against your baby's getting allergies.

- It may boost your child's intelligence.

- Breast milk can protect against obesity later in life.

- Breast-feeding may protect your baby from childhood leukemia and developing Type 1 diabetes.

- With preemies, it may protect against infections and high blood pressure.

- You will save hundreds of dollars on formula.

- The bonding—once you get past those sore nipples—is something truly special.

MM BONUS:
Okay, so the reason you breast-feed *should* be about the baby, but there are two added bonuses for mom. First, It's been shown to reduce the risk of breast, uterine, and ovarian cancer—the longer you breast-feed, the greater the reduction. And it's a great way to get back into those coveted pre-pregnancy jeans: breast-feeding moms burn 800 more calories a day than moms who don't, and in the first few weeks, it triggers contractions in your uterus that help return it to its original size.

How Long Should You Breast-feed?

Any doctor will tell you that some breast-feeding is better than nothing. But women will get mighty competitive about how long they went. When I told one woman that I had stopped breast-feeding Lilia at four months, you would have thought I said I'd locked her in a closet for four months. Mothering is hard. We're all looking for ways to "prove" we're doing a good job. But there are no rights and wrongs (well, there are some, but I'm not going there). And being a judgmental power breast-feeder doesn't qualify as right in my book. And anyone who is breast-feeding until kindergarten may be providing great nutrients, but I've got to imagine there are some other issues going on, no?

Although the American Academy of Pediatrics recommends breast-feeding exclusively for the first six months, I'm guessing not many of them were working mothers with toddlers at home.

Latching and Learning the Ropes

Of all the predelivery classes I suffered through, the one on breast-feeding actually proved to be the most helpful—not to mention the most entertaining. Nothing quite like watching a room full of men trying to act supportive and comforting of their wives as another woman demonstrates latching techniques on her own breast. The key to successful breast-feeding—and reducing the pain for Mom—is a good latch. Here's what to do:

- Brush your baby's lower lip or tickle her chin to make her open up her mouth wide. Wait until her mouth appears to be almost in a yawn, and then quickly insert your nipple into your baby's mouth (it sometimes helps to pinch your breast flat to get more of it in her mouth).

- Your baby's mouth should cover your entire nipple, and her lips should be puckered so that you see the inside, pink portion of her lips. If she is just sucking on the nipple and not the entire areola, pull her off and try again.

- Once you've achieved a good latch, try to go for fifteen minutes before you switch sides. Many of the best nutrients are in the hind-milk that comes at the end of each feeding on that one breast, so you want to make sure you try to "empty" one breast before you move to another. You'll typically get your baby to go longest on the first side.

- Always alternate which side you start on the next time.

> **MM TIP:** To remember which side to start on, each time you finish, leave yourself a reminder by putting a hair rubber band or a bracelet on the wrist of the side you should start on next. I know you think you'll remember, but I promise by the third day, it will all become a blur.

MM TIP: If you are having trouble breast-feeding and it is important to you to continue, there is a lot of great support out there. Your hospital should provide you with a lactation consultant while you're still there, but if they don't, request one. This is also a good place to start once you've left the hospital. Breast-feeding groups are also becoming very popular and give moms a chance to compare stories and helpful tips.

MM TIP:
Rule of thumb: Your baby should have at least six wet diapers a day. More is fine, but less likely means she's not getting enough milk. Keep track and you'll quickly see how she's doing.

- When it's time to switch sides, don't just pull the baby off (ouch!). Insert your finger between your breast and his mouth to relieve the suction, and then ease him off.

Once you've mastered the latch, it's time to set up a system. First, to give your baby the best chance of latching on, make sure—if you are physically able—that you have the nurse bring you your baby as soon as possible in the hospital so that you can try to start feeding. Even a trial of breast-feeding in the delivery room is appropriate and helpful: suckling will stimulate the release of a hormone called oxytocin, which helps stop uterine bleeding. It's important he gets used to the breast and not the bottle if that's the route you've chosen. In the beginning, you'll be giving colostrum, the thick, nutrient-rich "pre-milk" that can sustain a newborn for several days. Also, the more stimulation to the breast, the quicker your milk comes in. (It's also nice for the baby to practice on a relatively empty breast.) Here's the general routine:

- For the first several weeks, during the day you should feed your baby every two to three hours. Measure the two to three hours from the time you started the previous feeding, not when it ended. In

MM TIP: Worried about your milk production? Pick up some Mother's Milk tea or Mother's Milk homeopathic pills to help increase your flow. Added bonus for you beer lovers: it makes your milk come in really strong, so pick up a six pack of a nonalcoholic variety like O'Doul's or Kaliber.

MM TIP:
Okay, I'll admit it. Contrary to my advice above, Lilia could sleep a good four-hour stretch during the day from the moment she was born. She was a big eater and would drain both sides in twenty minutes flat. So I didn't wake her, and she gained weight by her two-week checkup. So I fessed up and the doctor said that was fine. I'm not saying you shouldn't wake your baby, but I am saying that some babies sleep more from the beginning and you might have lucked out. Maybe see how the first few days go before you do the waking every three hours.

MM TIP:
You will find that you are parched the minute you start breast-feeding. So having a glass of water handy (or a husband handy who is willing to get it for you) will be a blessing.

other words, if you feed your baby at noon, even if it takes forty-five minutes before he's done, you should start your next feeding sometime between 2 and 3 P.M. (two to three hours from noon, not two to three hours from 12:45). Right now you're probably realizing that this doesn't leave you a lot of time for a shower, a nap, or well, anything. Welcome to motherhood! You will quickly learn a whole new meaning to the words *time management*.

During the day, wake your baby to make sure he's fed on schedule. Your mother/mother-in-law/grandmother has probably told you a thousand times to *never* wake a sleeping baby, but trust me. This is a fairly new theory, but during the day, it is important from the beginning to set a schedule, and make daytime an active, happening time (we'll get into this more in chapter 5). Daytime should be marked by lots of feedings and lots of activities. This means never letting your child sleep more than three-and-a-half hours during the day, and feeding every two to three hours. The more regularly you feed your baby during the day, the better your chances of getting him to sleep for long intervals at night.

> **MM TIP:** Ideally, breast-feeding should be a time of quiet bonding between you and your new bundle of joy. And the first few weeks will likely be that way. However, if you are at all like me, sitting still for forty-five-minute jaunts five times a day can start to drive you a little crazy. I rented a bunch of movies (albeit quiet, not violent ones) and Tivo'ed a bunch of shows I had wanted to catch up on. It made the time pass much quicker, and my son didn't seem to mind. Then, I always made sure the first and last feedings of the day were quiet and involved just the two of us with no distractions.

> **MM TIP:** If your baby has a cold and is having a hard time breathing and breast-feeding, try turning on the shower and feeding in the bathroom. The steam should help clear his nasal passages enough to feed comfortably.

- From birth to four months of age, babies should have five to ten feedings of breast milk a day.

- Set yourself up with everything you'll need *before* you get started. Have a large glass of water, nice background music, reading materials, the remote control—whatever—plus a burp cloth for the baby within arm's reach.

Feeding on Demand

There is quite a bit of controversy as to whether or not to feed an infant on demand. Some say yes, as infants need to have unrestricted access to their mother's breast (and more stimulation will help the mother's milk come in faster and more plentiful), while others say no, this will just lead to a habit of a baby's only being able to soothe himself with the breast. I rest somewhere in between. The first few months with an infant can be tricky as he finds his way into the world and you begin to understand his needs and habits. I certainly believe you need to feed your baby more during the day and less at night. You also need to closely monitor your child to make sure he is gaining weight and producing the recommended amounts of wet diapers. If all things are in check and you are feeding your baby every two hours during the day—from start to start—and the baby takes forty five minutes to drain both breasts, then in reality, you are really only holding out on your child for one hour and fifteen minutes between feedings. This is quite a bit of feeding, although it's on a schedule, not on demand. This teaches your baby to delay gratification early on, but not in a harsh way. This also teaches him to be able to soothe himself in other ways in between—which he needs to be able to do in order to get through the night.

The other thing that can tend to happen with feeding on demand is that every time a baby cries, a mother assumes her baby is hungry and therefore gives the child the breast. He could simply be tired, or wet, or need a change of venue, or not like your shirt. The point is, you need to look for signs in your child to see what is the matter. If you

MM TIP:
I'm not a big fan of the breast-feeding pillows. I received a beautiful one at my baby shower and, while I loved having it, I rarely used it. It was never where I needed it and I was always getting the baby, water, a burp cloth, and so on and didn't have that free hand. I also found that a regular pillow was just as effective. And pillows can help when learning how to position babies comfortably in the early stages of breast-feeding by getting your baby at the right height (which can alleviate some breast-feeding soreness). So while some people love them, I could have skipped it. They do, however, make a great place for your infant to sit up in safely as he gets older.

MM TIP:
Many children by nature have a very strong sucking urge. The pacifier can work incredibly well to satisfy this urge without constantly giving the breast. And if you're worried about breaking that habit, I have some tips in chapter 8 on how and when to get off the pacifier!

search out all of these questions and your child is still crying, put your finger in his mouth. If the finger sates your baby, then you know he's not hungry because there is no milk coming out of your finger (I hope!). It's important to try foodless soothing. By nature babies are automatically dependent, so we want to slowly teach them to self-soothe.

Problem Eaters

All right, so this is all well and good *if* your child will eat for fifteen minutes on each side every two to three hours during the day. But what if he won't? It seemed as though Jack had much better things to do than be pinned down for forty-five minutes to breast-feed. He preferred a nice ten-minute snack and then was done with it.

Like all things in motherhood, it depends on your baby. Some latch on and hang out for what seems like an eternity. Others gulp, go for it, and get on with it. And others, like Jack, seem less than interested. It's your job to check and see if your baby is sated. Go through all the checks to see if the signs are right (wet diapers, isn't cranky, happy after feedings). If it checks out, chances are your baby simply doesn't need as much, or perhaps eats less during the day, and more in the morning or evening. If things don't check out, then pull him off a little sooner on the first breast and put him on the second breast before he's lost interest. Perhaps your baby is getting frustrated with the draining process and likes more of a steady stream. The other thing to try is to let him fall off the breast, burp him, play with him a little bit, and then put him back on. It's all about increasing his ability. He has to learn to do this thing called breast-feeding. Gaining an extra minute here or there is a major accomplishment for a little one.

Your Baby Is What You Eat

Your breast-feeding diet is a lot like your pregnancy diet, but with a few catches. Now, flavors are actually getting passed to your baby. Some babies react badly to onions, others to garlic. I couldn't eat green beans, broccoli, peppers, or tomatoes—they made my baby gassy. Unfortunately, this is one of those trial-and-error things, as sometimes it takes twenty-four hours for the food to get into your breast milk. Just monitor closely what you are eating, and then watch how your baby reacts. If you have a piece of garlic toast and then your baby is crying and pulling his legs up to his stomach (this is a sign of gas pain) after the next feeding, it's a pretty good sign you should skip the garlic for a while. And trust me, if you have a screamer like I did, you'll be willing to subsist on water and bread (not necessary) if you think it will decrease your baby's crying.

Here are some of the foods that commonly cause issues:

- *Anything with caffeine.* Chocolate, coffee, tea, sodas, even some medicine (although a cup or two of coffee is probably fine, you will want to limit your intake).

- *Some vegetables.* Broccoli, Brussels sprouts, cauliflower, cabbage, cucumber, onions, peppers, turnips.

- *Spices.* Chili powder, cinnamon, curry powder, garlic.

- *Citrus fruits (and juices).* Grapefruit, orange, kiwi, lemon, lime, pineapple, strawberry.

- *Laxative-inducing fruits.* Cherries, prunes.

- *Dairy products.* They can cause an allergic reaction in your baby, so be careful.

- *Allergens like corn, eggs, fish, nuts, peanuts, soy, and wheat.* "Stray" proteins from these foods can be absorbed into your bloodstream and thus into your milk.

- *Alcohol.* It's okay to have an occasional drink. Just wait at least three hours before feeding again. If you have to feed before then, consider giving a bottle and pumping and (sadly) dumping your breast milk.

- *Nicotine.* Sorry, smokers. I'm trusting you quit while you were pregnant. Stay clear while breast-feeding, as tobacco can get into breast milk and heavy smoking can decrease milk production, as well as cause vomiting and restlessness in babies.

MM TIP:
I imagine you're looking at this list wondering what the heck you *can eat!* Well, remember that not every food causes problems in every baby. So just be aware of these foods and watch your baby's reactions. If they seem gassy, try to cut the food out. I must admit I subsisted on pasta, plain chicken breast, and a heck of a lot of bread. Man, was I glad to move on to formula!

MM TIP:
Okay, so I know it's tempting after nine months of packing on the pounds to think about those 800 calories you're burning every day by breast-feeding as a nice little diet. But you're still eating for two. It's important that you take in about 500 extra calories a day (above your pre-pregnancy diet) of healthy fruits, vegetables, grains, and proteins. You also need to drink a ton of water—twelve eight-ounce glasses a day!

MM TIP:
Exercising typically increases the lactic acid in your milk, which, while safe, can make your milk a little sour. So exercise *after* you nurse.

Ouch! Sore Nipples

One of the things that made me want to scream was the lactation coach at the hospital who said, "If your nipples are sore, then your baby isn't latching on properly." Okay, first of all, I've never done this before, and second, *he* definitely hasn't done this before. So what do you expect? The reality is, I've met very few women who didn't have some sort of discomfort in the first few weeks. It's sort of like going out and running a few miles if you haven't run in a while (or ever, for that matter!). It's only natural that you're going to have a general level of soreness until your body acclimates. Well, here's the "Advil" for breast-feeding:

- Lansinoh is great for soothing sore nipples. Dab some on after each feeding, and don't worry, it's not harmful to the baby if there's still a little on your nipple when he starts feeding again. Plus, it makes a great lip gloss!

- Putting some breast milk on your nipples can also help heal the soreness.

MM TIP:
If you want a home remedy, try refrigerated cabbage leaves in your bra. They work and are considerably cheaper (but considerably smellier). Just don't make the mistake I did in grabbing purple cabbage—it stains clothes.

MM TIP: There's really nothing more embarrassing than a wet T-shirt contest. And no, I'm not talking about that one your best friend dared you to participate in (but thank God you never did) during college spring break in Ft. Lauderdale. I'm talking about going about your day and discovering your nice little breast pad has had its fill and has decided to leak through your bra and onto your shirt. Major embarrassment. This is one of those times when you will have wished you stuffed your bra twice as full.

Breast pads do the trick on most days with most shirts. They're fairly absorbent and come in different thicknesses, just like maxi-pads. However, I also found a great trick for those slightly trickier outfits. They are called Lily Padz and are made out of a rubbery plastic that feels vaguely like a thin piece of calamari. While it sounds gross, they adhere perfectly to your breast (like pasties without glue) and hold the milk in. They are fairly comfortable, effective, thin, very hard to see through your bra, and completely reusable; you simply rinse and reuse. Do beware, however, that they are holding your milk in and not letting any trickle out. This can cause you to feel a bit engorged, so limit your use of these or they can hurt a bit. They're available at http://www.evalillian.com.

- There are all sorts of great nipple soreness relief pads out there. I really liked Soothies, which you keep in the fridge and place over your nipple (skip the Lansinoh when you're using these) to cool the burning sensation (www.soothies.com).

- Never leave a wet pad in your bra or stay in a wet bra. It can cause an infection and allow bacteria to grow. In fact, go braless and wear loose-fitting shirts when possible. This will allow your nipples to dry and heal from any scabbing. I was pretty much topless at home for the first two weeks—my husband couldn't have been happier.

- Avoid underwire bras. They can reduce milk production and cause mastitis, a breast infection.

Pumping

I'm a big believer in pumping. First of all, for any woman who is planning to go back to work while breast-feeding, it's an absolute necessity. Second, once your baby has mastered latching on, if you can get him to *also* take a bottle, it gives you the flexibility of letting other people get in on the feeding fun, especially at 2 AM. (Husbands, look out!) It is also helpful to feed them a bottle before bed, something we'll touch on a little later on when we get the all-important topic of sleep.

There are plenty of hand pumps, but these take forever and are a pain in the arm. I strongly encourage you to spring for an electric one. You can rent an electric pump from most hospitals (you will need to buy your own breast shields, tubes, and bottles) or, if this is your first child and you're planning on having a few, you may want to invest in your own.

The other advantage of an electric pump is that you can pump both breasts at once. They even make special bras that you insert the pump shields into so that you can have your hands free the entire time (www.easyexpressionproducts.com). I talked on the phone, wrote e-mails, even put on makeup, all while pumping.

While most lactation consultants will encourage you to not introduce a bottle to your baby too soon, as it may give your baby nipple

MM FAVE:
Pump in Style Advanced Breast Pump by Medela. Okay, I didn't really feel in style with suctions on my nipples, but it's a great machine.

MM TIP:
Pumped milk lasts three hours at room temperature, three days in the refrigerator, and three months in the freezer. Get some oil pencils and mark directly on the bottles the date the milk was pumped. Always throw away any milk your baby doesn't finish from a bottle, as bacteria will enter the bottle while your baby is sucking.

confusion, I found it wasn't a problem. My little Hoover guys had no problem switching between breast and bottle as early as two weeks. Other friends said they had a hard time getting their baby to take the bottle when they introduced it. This is something you will likely have to gauge yourself, based on how strong of a sucker he is, and if he is having any latching problems. The safest timing is believed to be three to four weeks. One thing is for sure, though: the sooner he can do both, the sooner you can have help with the feedings.

> **MM TIP:** I was a fan of pumping and feeding the breast milk from a bottle, especially for the last feeding. I never knew whether Jack had gotten enough milk with the breast, and with a bottle I could see exactly how many ounces he had consumed.

Hitting the Bottle

Breast-feeding doesn't work for everybody. Don't feel guilty if it doesn't work for you. Rest assured that formulas these days are very good, and your baby will be just as happy and healthy in the long run. Here are some great reasons to go straight to the bottle:

- Anyone and everyone can help out with feeding the baby. This means that you can actually get some rest and let your husband handle a middle-of-the-night feeding.

- You know exactly how much your baby is getting, taking the guess-work out of sleeping patterns, crying fits, and mood swings.

- Formula is denser that breast milk and takes longer to digest, which means your baby has a better chance of sleeping through the night sooner.

- You will likely get your period sooner—good news if you are looking to have another baby quickly (although if you're even thinking of having sex, I'm impressed).

- You can go back to whatever diet you want after nine months of worrying about what you're feeding your baby. And that means finally having a cocktail—cheers!

Not every formula works for every baby. Start with what your pediatrician recommends and try it out for a few days. Let your pediatrician know if anyone in the family is lactose intolerant, as she may choose to put your baby on a soy formula. If you notice that your baby is spitting up a great deal, is colicky, or hasn't gone poo for several days, it may be time to switch formula. Give your doctor a call and see what she says.

Choosing a Formula

- Cow's milk–based formula is best for most babies.

- Look for an iron-fortified formula, as this is one thing breast-fed babies are getting naturally that you need to be supplementing in the formula.

- Don't automatically choose soy-based formula unless a doctor recommends it. If your baby is allergic to milk, there's a good chance he'll be allergic to soy, too.

- Babies don't absorb as much calcium and other nutrients from soy formula, so you have to choose one that's fortified to meet your baby's nutrient needs.

- If all things are equal in terms of your baby's nutritional needs, then consider convenience and cost—not brands—when shopping.

- Never make your own formula or add anything to prepared formula unless a doctor suggests it.

MM TIP:
The iron in the formula does *not* cause constipation. This is a big concern for a lot of mothers, but don't worry about it!

How Much?

From birth to four months, your baby should drink sixteen to thirty-two ounces of formula a day. The range accounts for different size babies and different appetites.

Bottle Do's and Don'ts

- Sterilize new bottles, nipples, and rings, by submerging them in a pot of boiling water for five minutes. Then allow them to dry on a clean towel. But after that, you don't really need to sterilize them. Stick them in the dishwasher or clean them in hot soapy water.

- Try starting with bottles served at room temperature. If your baby never gets used to heated formula, he'll probably never miss it. While I spent crying minutes waiting for hot water with Jack, Lilia had room temp from the start and never seemed to mind. But if your baby is not taking the formula, try heating it.

- Don't go back to a bottle a baby hasn't finished if it's been sitting there for more than an hour. Bacteria can build up, which can be harmful to your baby.

- Buy age-appropriate nipples. The openings are bigger or smaller depending on how much they should take in at what speed for their age. I was feeding my six-month-old son for several weeks before I noticed that the nipples on his bottle were for a three-month-old. Once I switched, he was able to drink the bottle without getting discouraged.

- Use tilted bottles or bottles that help filter out the air. Another great trick is using bottles with disposable liners in which you can push the air out ahead of time.

MM TIP: Okay, so every book you will read says to never microwave a bottle of *formula,* as microwaves tend to heat unevenly. And I'd recommend that you don't, but in a pinch, it doesn't diminish the quality of the formula (although it *can* break down some of the immunologic components of breast milk). It is just a bit risky due to hot spots in the heating. Nuke it for twenty seconds, shake it well, and test it against the inside of your wrist. (Microwaves vary greatly. My microwave makes it scalding after 20 seconds, while Jen's needs a full minute to get it lukewarm. Make sure you experiment and test the milk before giving it to your baby.)

Burping, Colic, and Crying

Now that we've gotten through *how* to feed your baby, we now need to cover the inevitable side effects of feeding your baby. While many lucky moms will never have to deal with spit-ups, gas, colic, or acid reflux, I didn't happen to be one of them.

Spit Happens

My daughter spit up all the time. I swear sometimes I thought there was as much coming back up as there was going in. But as most doctors will tell you, typically spit-up is more of a laundry problem than a health concern. Spit up often happens because when drinking, babies get not only milk or formula but also air. The air gets trapped and when it comes up, the liquid does, too. Also, typically, newborns' stomach muscles aren't fully developed and may bring the food back up. It can also be the result of excess mucus that needs to be cleared or simply from overeating.

While there are few foolproof cures to spit-up, there are several things you can do to help:

- Burp your baby as you feed him; don't wait for one burping session at the end (see tips below).

- Avoid feeding your baby when he is taking in a lot of air—like when he is crying.

- Keep your baby upright while feeding, and for a while afterward as well.

> **MM TIP:** The best way to get spit-up out of anything is baby wipes. Keep some on hand and dab up spit-up as soon as it happens.

> **MM TIP:** If your baby tends to spit up the second you put him in the crib after a feeding, place a few books under one side of the crib mattress to keep the head-end elevated. Oh, and don't put him right back in the crib. Keep him upright for a bit.

MM TIP:
The good news is that most babies stop spitting up around six months or once they learn to sit up.

- Don't put a lot of pressure on his stomach. Avoid too-tight diapers or pants, and don't put his stomach on your shoulder when burping him.

- If your baby spits up a great deal when you try a new formula, it could be a reaction to that brand. Check with your doctor and try a new formula to see if that helps. If your baby's spit-up is more of the projectile vomit type or has blood in it, consult your doctor immediately, as this could be a sign of a much more serious condition.

Burping Your Baby

Never will a simple bodily function cause you as much grief as burping. You'll sit there at 3 A.M. hoping, praying, and waiting for one darn little belch. It is important to burp your baby throughout the feeding, and not just wait until one big burp session at the end. Otherwise, he may be less likely to eat as much as he really needs (feeling full from gas, not burps) or be more likely to spit up afterward. For bottle-fed babies, this means burping every two ounces, and for breast-fed babies, between breasts. There are three easy ways to burp your little one:

- *On your shoulder.* Hold your baby against your shoulder (but without pressure on his stomach) while supporting his butt with your hand. Gently pat and rub his back with your other hand. Oh, and don't forget a burp cloth for your shoulder.

MM TIP:
Our grandmothers used to think that whacking a baby on the back helped burp him, but it doesn't really help. Instead rub your hand gently in upward strokes on his back. This may help bring up any air.

MM TIP: If your baby is incredibly hard to burp, try these two techniques, but beware. If you have a child that spits up, try and avoid these positions, as they are likely to bring quite a bit up.

- With your baby's head on your shoulder and his body vertical, bounce him up and down a few times to loosen the bubbles.

- Place your baby over your shoulder, supporting his head and back, and lean forward to rock him down to your lap and then up again until you get a burp.

- *On your lap.* For this position, your baby should be face down on your lap with his stomach over one leg and his head on your other leg. Hold him in place with one hand and pat with the other. This position is especially good for colicky babies.

- *Sitting up.* With your baby sitting on your lap, support his chest with your arm—letting him lean slightly forward—and pat his back. Be careful his head doesn't flop back. This is the best position for a baby who spits up a lot.

Colic

If you have a colicky baby, you lost the baby lottery (like I did). I remember calling my friend Sarah, who had a baby girl two days before I had Jack. I would call her and find that she was blissful, showered, and well rested, and I barely heard a peep from baby Lola. I hadn't showered for days, Jack hadn't stopped crying in as many, and I was wondering what the return policy was on an infant.

Many people think that colic is some sort of a stomach disease in babies in which they have gas or acid reflux. In reality, colic is better described as a state in which babies cry uncontrollably and regularly for several hours a day, causing their parents to pull out their hair, and can be caused by many different things—some related to their tummies, and other times related to their environment (such as over-stimulation). And some are downright inexplicable. (I blamed one night on Jack not liking his outfit and never put him in it again.)

One in five babies suffers from colic. And while doctors typically diagnose colic based on the "rule of three" (three hours in length, at least three times a week, and beginning at three weeks of age), normal signs of colic include a baby who pulls his knees up to his chest, clenches his fists, and cries uncontrollably for several hours on end. Side effects include a disruption in eating and sleeping patterns, and it can cause a baby to increase bowel and gas activity, search frantically for a nipple only to then push it away after several sips, and adopt a cry most resembling that of a tortured hyena.

The good news is that, while it seems like it will never end as it's happening, it really gets as bad as it's going to get by six weeks of age

MM TIP:
Sometimes your baby needs a change of venue when he is crying. Take him outside onto the front porch. Sometimes the change from warm to cold or dark to light can do a lot to calm your baby.

and is typically gone by three months. Below we've outlined a few reasons why it may be happening in your baby and a few tips to ease the pain:

MM FAVES:
Two lifesavers for colic, especially when it involves stomach issues, are Mylicon and Gripe Water. Mylicon is sold at most drugstores and helps relieve stomachaches and gas. It is safe to give your child several times a day, and I had friends who put a few drops in every bottle. Gripe Water, made by Baby Bliss, works well for not only stomach issues, but also teething, hiccups, and general colic issues. It's a more natural remedy with ginger and fennel and can be purchased in baby boutiques or online.

MM TIP:
Often in the first three months, your child is simply suffering from overstimulation—adjusting to the world outside the womb. I know it sounds slightly bizarre and institutional, but place your baby in front of a blank wall. Sometimes this lack of stimulation will calm him down. This is the same idea behind using white noise to help block out the rest of the world. Turning on fans or the monotonous drone of a clothes dryer are all worth a try.

- *Immature digestion.* This is typically more common in boy babies or preemies than in fully developed girl babies, as boys typically develop slightly more slowly. As their immature digestive tracts pass gas, their intestines contract violently, causing pain.

  - *Solution:* This is what Jen likes to call the "grandma hold." Her mother discovered this with her son, and it worked like a charm. Lay your baby stomach down on your forearm, with your palm cradling his head and his legs straddling your arm. The pressure on his belly will force the air out. Also try laying him on his back on a bed and bringing his knees up to his chest. This forces the air out of his belly.

- *Acid reflux.* Reflux is much like heartburn in adults, in which acid in the stomach backs up to the esophagus, thus irritating it and causing spit-up and sometimes vomiting. While this is typically a separate issue, it is often diagnosed as colic. Keep a watchful eye out for excessive or forceful vomiting coupled with the colicky symptoms, as your baby may need medication.

  - *Solution:* While there isn't a cure, the key is to make your baby feel better until he outgrows it. Your doctor may prescribe medicine that neutralizes stomach acid. Otherwise, avoid overfeeding. Feed smaller amounts more frequently. When your child is old enough to eat solids, opt for thicker rather than thinner or runnier dishes. Try to keep your child propped up after feeding.

- *Overstimulation.* For many babies, experiencing the stimuli of a normal environment—new sights, sounds, smells—can cause their systems to simply overload by the early evening hours, having taken in literally all they can handle for that day. The result is a child that can't take in any more stimuli. This is particularly helpful to recognize, as most parents—like me—will try to calm a colicky baby by bouncing, walking, and singing to the child to make him feel better. In reality, this is the exact opposite of what he needs. Learned that the hard way!

- *Solution:* Sooth your child in a dark, quiet room. Lay him on his belly and rub his back. Don't bounce him, walk him, or make loud noises.

- *Insufficient milk supply.* You tend to have the least amount of breast milk toward the end of the day, right around the time your child starts to get colicky. Coincidence? Perhaps not.

  - *Solution:* Consider pumping a bottle for this time of day or supplementing with formula.

- *Smoke.* Tobacco smoke in the home has been shown, for whatever reason, to contribute to colic. The more smokers in the house, the higher the likelihood.

  - *Solution:* Don't do it or be near it.

MM TIP:
Dealing with a colicky baby can be extremely trying on a new parent's nerves. Try switching off every hour or so with your partner. If you are stuck alone with a colicky baby, don't feel bad for putting him down in his crib for fifteen minutes to cry it out a bit. Sometimes this brief break does you a world of good to be able to continue caring for your child, and it won't harm your baby at all.

Everybody Stay Calm! Making the Most of Pacifiers

I tortured myself over giving Jack a pacifier. I had heard it ruins their teeth, that they'll never give it up, that they don't *need* it and should be soothed otherwise. I didn't give him a pacifier and endured many hours of crying. Having said that, I did give Lilia one, and breaking her of the habit was as hard as breaking me of shopping trips to Saks (I didn't say we'd accomplished either yet). So while I personally think they're fine, here are some things to keep in mind:

- Some kids have a definite oral need. They are born with this reflex. Other kids are not. A pacifier can be a great way to soothe an intense sucker and helps your child learn to self-soothe.

- A pacifier can be a great way to comfort a child between feedings when trying to keep to a schedule.

- For children with an intense sucking need, a pacifier is a safe alternative. Some children who aren't allowed to use one find other, more dangerous objects to suck on and satisfy their oral fixation.

- A pacifier habit is easier to limit and break than a thumb-sucking habit. You can be in complete control of when they do and don't have the pacifier. A child's thumb will always (hopefully) be with him.

- By five or six months, a pacifier should be limited to bedtime only: not in cars, not in shopping malls, nowhere out of the house. This will make your transition off of it much easier.

- Most parents are done with having their child suck a pacifier by two years. Most kids will be done with it somewhere between three and five. If you can limit it to bedtime only, don't torture yourself if they are still using it to fall asleep at this age.

Of course, there are natural pitfalls to pacifiers. You will have to decide where you draw the line when they hurl it out of their crib in the middle of the night and scream for you to come and get it. (It's not exactly "self-soothing" when you have to come and grab it for them.) Some parents just can't stand how it looks. And then there's also the issue of eventually having to break the habit. While I can't exactly help you with the first two issues, I do have some great tips in chapter 8 on how to break the habit.

Still want to use a pacifier? Here's what to look for when choosing one:

- Make sure the pacifier base has ventilation holes the right size so that it won't block his nasal airway.

- Make sure the sucking piece is the right density for the age of your child. You will need to move on to a stronger pacifier once the first tooth is cut. Pacifier packages typically will tell you the age it is appropriate for.

- Use only one-piece pacifiers that can't break or separate.

- Check your pacifiers regularly to make sure that they don't have any tears or holes in them.

- Regularly run your pacifiers through the dishwasher or immerse them in boiling water to disinfect them.

- Do not tie the pacifier around your child's neck, as he could be strangled.

- Always have an extra two or three pacifiers on hand to avoid the "missing binky" nightmare.

Introducing Solid Foods

Just when you thought you'd gotten the hang of breast- and bottle-feeding, it's time to add another element into the mix—solid food. I remember my husband and me looking at each other totally dumb founded, trying to figure out what to feed this little baby of ours. What? You mean a delivery of spicy beef and broccoli won't work? What about Domino's? We were in trouble. And not only are you expected to *serve* your baby a well-rounded meal, but some mothers go so far as to prepare it on their own. You can process, blend, and grind your own food or simply grab the stuff that's pre-pureed and call it a day, but one thing is a must: grab your camera. Those first few sweet-potato–faced baby shots are ones you won't want to miss.

Six to Ten Months

Okay, so your little one is probably still toothless, so you gotta start slow. You'll know your baby is ready by his age and his interest in food. If he is gazing longingly at every french fry and piece of pizza you eat, chances are he's getting ready. You also may find that he just doesn't seem sated by milk or formula. Most doctors suggest starting with cereal only. While you will get to introduce a wide variety of fruits, vegetables, meats, and grains, all these foods will need to have a smooth consistency—solid food is a bit of a misnomer, as it all basically looks like runny tomato sauce at this point. If you're going for jarred food, rest assured that there are many great options to go with.

Either way, the following principles apply:

MM FAVE:
I was a fan of the Gerber cereals. Once we moved on to baby food, I liked Earth's Best, which is organic, but a bit pricier than other brands. Also try www.homemadebaby.com for homemade baby food direct to your door.

- Introduce foods one at a time, and isolate each new item for three days to make sure your baby tolerates it. Start out with rice cereal. Mix it up with a little breast milk or formula and give that to your baby for three days to make sure there are no allergies before you add a fruit into the mix. Repeat the process for each new food. Allergic reactions can include diarrhea, rash, or vomiting. If your baby reacts in this way, call your pediatrician immediately.

- Begin with about one teaspoon of dry rice cereal mixed with four to five teaspoons of breast milk or formula (it'll be very runny).

- Gradually thicken the consistency and increase to have one tablespoon of dry cereal and mix it with breast milk or formula, twice a day.

- Once you've mastered rice cereal, move to oatmeal mixed with formula, milk, or water and then mixed with fruits—again, one by one. Your baby will likely prefer his rice cereal with fruits once he's given that option.

MM TIP:
Introduce new foods in the morning, so that you are with your child awake most of the day to be able to check for allergic reactions.

- Food order is a funny thing. My doctor always said to start with the icky stuff (veggies) as once they tried the sweetness of fruit, they would never go back to the bland vegetables. Jen's doctor had her do just the opposite, and sure enough, her baby Sam prefers the bland vegetables. Go figure. I think in the end, the order matters less than the isolation of each food to be able to test for allergic reaction. In the end, your kid is likely going to love or detest broccoli for his own reasons.

- Once your baby has tolerated fruits and vegetables, move on to a few meats.

- You need to wait until they are twelve months old to introduce cow's milk, but you can offer yogurt at around eight months, because the active bacterial cultures make it easier to digest than cow's milk.

- Go for a spoon with a rubber-coated mouthpiece. It's much easier for your baby and won't hurt as much on their teeth and gums when they bite down hard (which they will).

Like everything else with a child, be patient. If they aren't into solid food in the beginning, wait a few days and try it again. If they don't like a food one day, don't give up on it completely. Try it a few more times. Sometimes a baby can be full or teething, which affects his appetite and taste preference in the end, he may really like that food.

Great Foods

You should experiment with many different foods; however, these pureed foods are tried-and-true hits with babies because they are fairly bland and easy to digest. Remember, the only thing they've had up to this point has been breast milk and formula.

- *Fruits.* Bananas, apples and applesauce, pears, peaches, apricots

- *Orange vegetables.* Carrots, squash, yams, sweet potatoes

- *Green vegetables.* Peas, spinach, zucchini, beans

- *Meats.* Lean ground beef, lamb, veal, chicken or turkey

How Much?

From six to ten months, your baby should eat approximately:

- Three or four feedings of breast milk or sixteen to thirty-two ounces of formula (depending on how much of the solid food they are eating)

- Infant cereal, cream of wheat, oatmeal (two or three servings daily)

- Mashed vegetables (one or two servings)

- Cooked or raw fruit (one or two servings)

- Meat, chicken, fish, egg yolk, yogurt or cottage cheese (one to two tablespoons a day from eight months on)

MM FAVE:

I tried every bib available and felt like Goldilocks. The plastic ones were too hard, the cotton ones too messy. Finally, I found ones that are lightweight, easy to clean, and have sleeves with elastic wristbands. Bumpkin bibs are washable and it saves you many dirty-outfit changes. You can find them at www.rightstart.com.

MM TIP:

Most sensible moms put a bib on their baby, but go into feedings, well, unprotected themselves. Babies love to spit, throw, and raspberry their food all over the place. So always dress for work *after* feeding the baby, and grab an apron for you when you bib up your little one.

MM TIP:

You may notice that with the introduction of formula after breast milk, rice cereal, and more solid foods that the consistency of your child's poo will change quite a bit. This is normal. Typically, there will be a period of a few days of diarrhea or quite solid poo. Keep an eye on it, and if it doesn't normalize within a week, call your doctor.

Foods to Avoid

Allergies are very common in babies, and can be very serious. For this reason, avoid the following foods with babies under age one:

- Beans

- Berries (not only can they be allergic, but it may be easier for them to digest after a year)

- Cabbage

- Chocolate

- Cinnamon

- Citrus fruits and juices (less about allergies, but usually too acidic for babies)

- Coconut

- Corn

- Cow's milk (yogurts tend to be okay, as it is typically less allergenic)

- Egg whites (although egg yolks are okay at about eight months)

- Honey (it can cause botulism)

- Mango

- Melons

- Mustard

- Nuts and peanut butter: peanut allergies can be deadly, and it has become a more common allergy these days. Avoid giving any peanuts, peanut butter, or peanut oil to your child until preschool age.

- Onions

- Papaya

- Whole peas (pureed are fine)

- Pork

- Shellfish and fish (although fish allergies are less common, there is a risk)

- Soy products

- Tomatoes (they're too acidic)

- Wheat

- Products that contain yeast

MM TIP:
If your baby is being breast-fed and refuses to be fed solid foods by you, try having your partner feed the baby.

Gas in Children

Nothing is more hysterical to little kids than farts and burps. But the laughs can quickly turn to tears if your little one is suffering from intense gas pain. Here are some foods that are known to cause gas in children, so you may want to avoid them:

- Beans

- Carbonated beverages

- Cucumbers

- Dairy products

- Mushrooms

- Cabbage-family vegetables:

  - Broccoli

  - Brussels sprouts

  - Cabbage

  - Cauliflower

- Onions

MM TIP:
Some vegetables (such as spinach, beets, turnips, and carrots) can be high in nitrates (even organic ones). And lots of nitrates can lead to a certain kind of anemia. So you may want to avoid these foods when making your own. Baby food companies have to test for nitrates, so the store-bought ones shouldn't have any.

Making Your Own Food

For some moms, making their own baby food is the best way to ensure that they know exactly what their baby is eating. While this is definitely a more time-consuming option, if you and your blender are a good team, go for it. Here are a few tips to keep in mind:

- Make a large quantity at once, then pour it into an ice-cube tray and freeze the food. When it's frozen, pop out the cubes and store them in like groups in labeled plastic bags (with the type of food and date of freezing) for easy access and to cut down on the space of the trays.

- Always use the earliest-dated food first.

- Don't defrost baby food for long periods of time on the counter, instead, pull out what you need at least three hours in advance and defrost it in the fridge. Remember, the baby food you make doesn't contain preservatives.

- Never refreeze previously frozen food.

- Avoid adding spices, sugar, salt, honey, or pepper.

Drinks and Things

There are lots of theories on when your baby should use a bottle, a sippy cup, and a regular cup, and even more on what you should be putting in them. I don't think any solution offers foolproof drinking. Some suggest going from breast to sippy cup or cup and skipping the bottle. Others suggest going from bottle to cup and skipping the sippy. (Whatever you decide, I have some great tips in chapter 8 about transitioning and weaning.) To some degree, this will all depend on what you and your baby desire. Since I've covered the breast and the bottle, here's a little bit about sippy cups, and what to serve your child to drink.

Sippy Cup

The sippy cup can offer a good transition from the breast or bottle when your baby has the motor skills to handle a cup, but would still spill it. Some babies can use them as early as five to six months, others at seven to nine. It gives him independence, but you don't spend the day running around with a roll of paper towels. They're great for long trips, bringing to restaurants, or on airplanes. They're also great if you have a thirsty baby who wants to drink something at night.

If you're transitioning from a bottle, try giving him half of his formula in the bottle then switch to the sippy cup for the second half. However, some babies will not drink breast milk or formula from a sippy cup but will drink water or juice. That's why some wait to introduce the sippy cup until about age one when their baby is ready to start drinking whole milk.

Although I'm a fan of sippy cups and still use them (well, my kids do, that is), I sort of feel the sippy cup is more for the parent than the child. If you allow them to practice with a cup, they will get the hang of it. But, frankly, I liked the portability of sippy cups and got tired of cleaning up spills. If you do want to use sippy cups, make sure your child also develops the skills to use a regular cup, so only use sippy cups when spilling is an issue or if you're on the road.

One risk of sippy cups is the same as that of bottles used after age one: frequent sips during the day keep children's teeth essentially bathed in a sugary fluid and increase the occurrence of tooth decay. Use them specifically at meal times or else fill them only with water.

> **MM TIP:** Never let your child take a sippy cup of juice or milk to bed. The liquid can pool in their mouth and then the sugar can cause terrible tooth decay. My mother let me have a sippy cup with apple juice from two to three and all my teeth fell out—oops.

MM TIP:
Be careful of cups with "no spill" valves: these require children to suck and won't help them learn to sip, which is really the whole point!

MM FAVE:
I loved the Magic Toddler Spout with handles from Avent. I found these were easy for my toddlers to hold, and didn't spill. However, washing the tops was a bit of a pain.

MM TIP:
As they get older, children love pouring, and pouring their drink is a great sign of independence. But it can be messy. Try having them practice pouring with cups and a pitcher in the bath. Then have them pour over the extended dishwasher door to avoid having to clean up spills.

MM TIP:
If you want to skip the sippy cup and go straight for the cup, try Gerber's Lil Trainer Cup. It's sort of like a travel coffee mug in that there is a lid so not too much liquid can come out at once. Your child still has to learn to sip like a real cup (there's no spout), but it just cuts down on a few messes.

Juice

Fruit juice has become a very controversial drink for kids these days. Many juices are so packed full of sugar it's like giving your child a liquid upper. Some moms avoid juice altogether. If you can get your child to enjoy water (typically, they will if they've never had the sweet sensation of juice), then you're probably better off, as your child won't immediately crave sweet things. However, if you choose to go the juice route, here are a few things to keep in mind.

- Look for pasteurized juice.

- Try to go with the all-natural kinds that don't add a lot of sugar.

- Avoid juices that contain high-fructose corn syrup, an additive.

- Dilute the juice with water.

> **MM TIP:** I'm not a huge fan of juice boxes, as you can't dilute them. Also, your child grabs it, and the liquid gushes out of the straw. But when you use them (which you will, especially at birthday parties), try this. Unfold the corners on the top and "pop" the top up, sort of making a triangle. This makes the box less dense and slightly less likely to spill liquid out of the straw.

Ten to Twelve Months

At ten to twelve months, your baby probably has several teeth that have broken through, and lumpier food is now on the menu. You will also want your child to begin to experiment with finger foods so that he can take a crack at feeding himself.

- For finger food, start out with dry food, which will be easier for your child to pick up. Gerber makes these great fruit and veggie "puffs" that are better than Cheerios because they dissolve in your baby's mouth, so there is no danger of choking.

- Give your child only a few pieces at a time, as he will likely grab at it all and try to shove it all in his mouth at once.

- Rather than using a plate, try a bowl with high sides. That way, it's easier to scoop, as the food won't slide right out.

- Pastas are a great thing to add at this point. Opt for ones that you can cut up a bit, like penne or rigatoni.

> **MM TIP:** Many moms make the mistake when their child starts to eat more solid, lumpy food of switching immediately to traditional "kids' foods" such as chicken nuggets, macaroni and cheese, and tater tots. If your child has liked vegetables and other healthy foods up to this point, continue on this path. You have a far greater chance of getting your child to keep eating his vegetables if he has never been spoiled with the fried alternative. I mean, come on, if you had to choose between plain sweet potatoes and a tater tot, what would you pick?

> **MM TIP:** When your baby starts crawling and picking up food on his own, it is very important to wash his hands before every meal—a near-impossible feat to accomplish. I kept a tub of baby wipes in the kitchen and wiped my son's hands once he was strapped down in the high chair. At least then I knew his hands had been slightly disinfected.

How Much?

From ten to twelve months, your baby should eat:

- Three or four feedings of breast milk or sixteen to twenty-four ounces of infant formula a day

- Cereal, bread, rice, noodles, pasta, crackers (two to four servings a day)

- Cooked or raw vegetables (one or two servings a day)

- Cooked or raw fruit (one or two servings a day)

- Protein-packed food such as lamb, beef, pork, fish, poultry, egg yolks, cheese, yogurt, beans, tofu (one or two tablespoons a day)

> **MM TIP:** By ten to twelve months, you should give your child the chance to test out his dexterity by using his hands to pick up food.

Food Safety

As adults, we take food safety for granted, but with kids who are learning a new skill with each bite of every new food, it can be a challenge. Follow these guidelines to avoid burns, choking, and other potential hazards:

- Always test the temperature of your baby's food before serving it.

- Never let your child eat while walking around. Make sure he is seated—and preferably strapped in!

- Don't shove food in your child's mouth when he is crying or laughing. He is likely to inhale it.

- Cut your child's food into small bites, as he likely will be gumming it to break it down. Also, go for softer foods rather than hard ones that don't dissolve easily.

- Don't cut hot dogs into coin-shaped slices. They can cause choking. Instead, cut them into chunks.

- Avoid food with small bones, such as fish.

- Always watch your child when he is eating—even if he is feeding himself.

- For choking reasons, avoid the following foods for kids under two:
  - Gum
  - Hard candy
  - M&Ms
  - Whole grapes
  - Olives
  - Breads and bagels with seeds
  - Popcorn, pretzels, chips, or any nuts
  - Raw carrots, celery, whole peas, or whole corn
  - Raisins

MM TIP: Although you may think raisins are a great snack for your child, many doctors recommend against them. They are very sugary and sticky, so they are likely to get stuck in your child's teeth and can be worse for his teeth than, say, a piece of chocolate.

It's also a good idea for you, your husband, and anyone who regularly cares for your child to get certified in CPR and the Heimlich maneuver. Even if you have been certified, a refresher course is a must. Typically, it's not a skill you use all the time, and on a baby, it's a whole different method. Some groups will offer in-home courses, which can be a great excuse to have a bunch of new parents over, and you can all chip in to split the cost. A great source for more information is www.redcross.org; you can put in your zip code and find the phone number for a location near you. The class for infant CPR is three and a half hours and applies for infants up to twelve months, but they also offer a five-and-a-half-hour course that applies for infants and children up to eight years old. The classes are available in English and Spanish.

One Year and Beyond

Healthy Eating Habits

At this point, with the exception of peanut butter and shellfish (which you should hold off on giving your child until preschool age), your child can pretty much eat anything. The bigger issue is, what *will* he eat?

Just like all things with children, as soon as you get used to a routine, the child grows, changes, or otherwise throws you for a loop. Well, this couldn't be truer than when you are trying to feed a twelve- to thirty-six-month-old. One day they love and devour broccoli, and the next day they want nothing to do with it. And on those days, it's tempting, and quite frankly easier, to give them a plate of tried-and-true mac and cheese or chicken nuggets. The thing you have to keep in mind is, while we all feel like we are born with a predisposition toward junk food (which is great rationalization for my lack of willpower), the truth is that a child's palate is actually a clean slate. The tastes he'll develop depend on what he is presented with. That means that how your child will ultimately eat—picking whole-wheat bread over white, an apple over a cookie—will be influenced by what you put in front of him. And while kids can vary from day to day about what they like—often as a reaction to teething, fatigue, or quite simply not being hungry—pickiness is no reason to give up on healthful food altogether. Honestly, this is one of my biggest regrets in raising Jack and Lilia. I pegged Jack as a picky eater from the start, and I was so worried about my plump cherub starving that I resorted to the same four foods over and over again. It's no surprise that now he truly has become more of a picky eater, as I didn't expose him to as many different foods as I could have. Lilia, on the other hand, is a bit more adventurous. I've offered her a variety of foods from the beginning and she is much more interested in at least some of them. So keep on trying, and even if something is rejected one day, try it again another.

Some theories suggest that you may have to expose your child to a food ten times for it to become a part of their repertoire. (The point is to keep trying.)

- Hold off on the sweets as long as you can, which will allow more opportunity for them to develop a taste for tangy and tart. There is some evidence that suggests that if you avoid sugar in the first year, they are less likely to crave it later.

- Don't assume that they won't like plain yogurt or plain crackers and spread jam all over them or mash in a banana. If they grow to love tart foods, you'll probably have a better time with vegetables.

- *Do not* make food an issue. Refusing to eat is partly their way of showing some independence. If your child won't eat something, don't make a big deal out of it. Don't turn "eating another bite" into a battle. Don't cajole, bribe, or barter. Respect their judgment and let them be finished. But don't give him something else in exchange—especially a treat—until the next meal.

- Don't fill your child's plate unrealistically. Give him small portions so that he can feel control and finish his meal. If he wants more he'll ask (or you can offer).

- Toddlers have smaller stomachs and they're more active, so they do need to eat more often then we do. You should offer regular snacks; just make sure they are healthy.

- If you're introducing new foods, make sure there is something on his plate he likes. It's a bit unfair to offer only liver, rutabaga, and beans and then be upset if he doesn't want to eat anything. If all he eats is what he likes plus a taste of the other food, fine.

- Don't make things "forbidden fruit"; simply don't let their presence be known. It's only natural to want what we can't have. If you have cookies around the house and tell your child he can't have them, he will only want them more. Rather, keep them away until he is old enough to understand the concept of a treat.

- Eat all meals—including snacks—at the table. Not only is a child wandering around with food dangerous, but it also is an easy way to lose track of what they have eaten.

- Children love to play with their food, so why not introduce them to food that is socially acceptable to play with? For example, serve chicken and vegetables that involve a dipping sauce. Even baby spinach leaves with stems can be successful dippers! The act of dipping will be so much fun they'll forget that they are dipping something that is healthy.

- Kids like to prove they can do things on their own. Let them "sprinkle" their meal with fresh-cut herbs or dish out their own Parmesan cheese on their spaghetti. Tell them the number of spoonfuls they are allowed in advance, and count with them. Then it becomes a game.

- Let your child have part of the choice for dinner, but give him only two choices. Do you want spaghetti or chicken? This will give him a

> **MM TIP:** Watch out for foods with high-fructose corn syrup. It is used in so many of the kid-marketed foods because it makes the foods taste sweeter; but some experts feel it is a big contributor to the rising obesity in America.

MM TIP:
Kids should stay on whole milk until the age of two. Our culture is so worried about weight that many moms switch their children too young. In reality, babies need the fat whole milk contains for critical brain and body development. Consider springing for organic milk, as it may help avoid harmful hormones that are injected into cows in regular milk.

sense of control. If you leave the question open ended—what do you want for dinner?—it's too much for a little one to process and turns you into a short-order cook.

- Use the rule of age. If your child is four, then he needs to eat four green beans and so forth. While not a foolproof plan, it's a reasonable enough bribe for a kid and is a number they can understand.

- At some point, most children will hate having two different foods touch each other. Consider partitioned plates (Pottery Barn Kids has great ones) for a while, and this will most likely pass.

- I'm not saying that you should *never* let your child indulge—I have some friends who won't even budge off the no-sweets rule for birthday cake. But it is important to limit your kids' indulgences until they have come to accept a wide range of healthful alternatives.

Treats and Desserts

MM TIP:
If your kids are treat crazy, you should set a reasonable amount (one or two per day), but then allow your child to have them whenever he wants. If he wants them both before breakfast, so be it. But don't cave later in the day. In theory he'll learn to self-regulate.

As in everything, moderation is the key. Enjoying an occasional treat will do no harm, but there are some guidelines to keep in mind. Dessert *can* be seen as a reward for eating if it is presented that way (i.e., "no dessert unless you finish your vegetables"). So if your family enjoys occasional desserts after meals, they should be offered universally to all eaters, just as the pasta was during the regular meal. And because obesity is a worsening problem for all of us, children and adults alike, no one needs the temptation. Most pediatricians recommend buying treats in small amounts only for specific occasions so that there is no ice cream in the freezer or cookies on the counter for kids to see and want.

Dealing with a Fussy Eater

If you are well down the path of bad eating habits, don't worry—you can change and so can they! Here are a few things to try:

- Try simple things like switching from white to whole-wheat bread or sweetened to unsweetened yogurt.

- If your kids *really* won't touch their vegetables, disguise them. Puree the veggies and put them in omelets, meatballs, or pasta sauces. Your kids will never know they are there, and you will rest better knowing that your child *has* had his veggies.

- Change the names of food. My son would eat only penne pasta, and my mother-in-law had only rigatoni in her house. We renamed it "tricky pasta" because it was hard to get on your fork. Tricky pasta is now a favorite food.

- Try (harmless) games like "who can make the loudest crunching sound" with carrots, cucumbers, or broccoli.

- Try putting chunks of veggies or fruits on skewers. Just make sure the skewers aren't very sharp.

MM TIP:
If your child refuses to eat a meal, save it for later. Don't offer a new meal instead. If she's hungry before a meal, offer one of the courses like the vegetable as an appetizer.

Healthful Snack Alternatives to Sweets

- Smoothies made with yogurt and fruit (or milk)

- Yogurt mixed with all-fruit jam

- Dried fruits

- Apples with a light dusting of cinnamon sugar

- Buttered toast sprinkled with cinnamon and some sugar

- A banana frozen on a popsicle stick

- Whole-grain crackers

- Graham crackers

- Carrots and celery with ranch dressing

- Zucchini, apple, or carrot bread

- Pita bread

MM TIP:
Tofu hot dogs taste like the meat ones, plus they contain no nitrates. Nitrates interfere with the transport of oxygen by the red blood cells and, in high concentrations, can cause coma, seizures, and even death. At lower levels they cause blue skin discoloration, dizziness, and fatigue. Adults can handle small amounts, but infants are particularly sensitive to their ill effects. Nitrates and nitrites are added to meats like bacon, hot dogs, cured ham, and smoked fish to produce an appealing color (lovely thought) and inhibit the growth of germs and poisons. While they are not carcinogens, they can yield by-products that have been implicated in higher rates of cancer in animals. So why take the risk? You can find nitrate-free products in health food stores and some supermarkets. Just ask your local butcher or special-order nitrate-free products.

- Pretzels

- Shredded coconut

- Popcorn topped with Parmesan cheese or cinnamon

- Cottage cheese with cinnamon on top

- Drinkable yogurt with a straw

How Much?

Young children really only eat the equivalent of child-size one and a half to two meals a day. So if you're expecting a great meal at breakfast, lunch, and dinner, you're not going to get it. Also, don't stress too much over each meal. Many pediatricians suggest measuring your child's nutritional intake over a day or even a week—not just one meal. As long as they are getting a balanced diet overall, you're okay. And recognize that your child may not be as hungry as you think (or certainly as hungry as you are). Babies grow incredibly fast in the first year (nearly tripling their weight in twelve months), but then the growth will slow to about one tenth the rate, so don't expect leaps and bounds every month.

For a twelve- to thirty-six-month-old, your child typically needs:

- Cow's milk to replace some or all of formula and breast milk, sixteen to twenty-four ounces a day.

- Cereal, bread, rice, pasta (four or more servings a day of about one third of an adult portion)

- Vegetables (two or more servings a day)

- Fruit (two or more servings a day)

- Meat, fish, poultry, eggs, beans, tofu (two servings a day, about one ounce—about one eighth of a cup—each)

Vitamins

Your kid's a bad eater, so vitamins are the answer, right? Well, there is a bit of controversy over whether or not to give a toddler vitamins. The American Academy of Pediatrics (AAP) says you should really ask your pediatrician, but acknowledges that a supplement won't hurt (as long as it's taken in the right dose). Just don't see the vitamin as an excuse for bad eating habits, as it's still best to get the vitamins through food. In addition, smaller children sometimes think vitamins are candy (no surprise, given their colorful appearance). An overdose of iron could be fatal, so be sure to give your children only the recommended dosage and keep them out of reach.

> **MM TIP:** Other babies who may need vitamin supplementation are those at risk for iron deficiency. Most pediatricians will check a baby's blood levels around age nine months; this is when babies are rapidly growing and using up all their iron stores, which are essential for making more blood. Those babies with lower blood levels, or anemia, may be able to improve just by eating more iron-rich foods (green vegetables, beans, red meat), but some may need an iron-containing vitamin.

MM TIP: The AAP does recommend that exclusively breast-fed infants need supplemental vitamin D until they're getting at least 500 ml of a vitamin D–fortified formula or whole cow's milk. The reason is that vitamin D isn't readily available in human milk and the only other way to get it is for our own bodies to make it when our skin is exposed to sunlight. If you take supplements, it may not get through in a strong enough concentration. And since little babies shouldn't be out in the sun until they're six months old, they're at a total vitamin D disadvantage.

Family Dinners: You Mean Carryout Doesn't Count?

I hate to admit it, but my children eat carryout much more often than I cook. What can I say—I'm a working mom. In an ideal world, I'd have a June Cleaver meal on the table and ready to go for the whole family at 6 P.M. But the reality is, by the time both my husband and I get home, if I were to start a full meal, my kids would never get to bed before 10 P.M. That said, I've found a few shortcuts in menu planning that help us attempt to have a family meal at least a couple of times a week (after all, I have to support my local delivery guy!):

- Do the grocery shopping on the weekend, and plan out everything you'll need for the meals ahead.

- If you have a sitter at home who can do the shopping, create a "standard list" of your regular grocery items and photocopy it. Then, as you run out, you just have to check off what you need.

- Make several freezable meals on a Sunday afternoon that you can eat during the week: lasagna, a casserole, pasta sauces, or soup. Better yet, make a double batch, and freeze that for the following week.

- Always think about dinner before you walk out the door in the morning—especially when pulling something out of the freezer. It cuts down on the annoying "defrost" step when you get home that evening.

- Clean lettuce and make a "dry salad" as soon as you get home from the store. It will keep for several days, and you can simply serve out what you need and toss it with dressing the night of the meal.

- Cook up a bunch of ground beef or turkey, and freeze it in individual Ziploc bags. It's great for pasta sauces, tacos, or soups, and saves you an extra step at dinnertime. All you have to do is microwave it and you're good to go.

- Do try to eat dinner as a family. If this isn't possible every night, pick one or two nights a week that you can really stick to (Friday seems to work well) so that it becomes a regular tradition you all look forward to.

Table Manners

Most pediatricians agree that mealtime should be relatively relaxed (well, that is if you find noisy children half eating/half spitting their food relaxing). Basically, you want children to learn how to eat and at the same time reap the benefits of social time with their families. So don't offer games or other entertainments to keep kids at the table; TV and other stimulations will distract them from learning how to have a conversation between both children and adults. And kids need to learn how to figure out whether they're full or still hungry. They might eat longer if they're hypnotized by the Backyardigans, but they're less likely to tune in to their hunger cues.

Respond instead to their appropriate developmental levels. Kids two and under have about a fifteen-minute attention span (although be impressed if they make it five minutes); preschoolers can last a little longer, so keep your expectations realistic. Trust your children to know when they're full. Studies have shown that babies and children have an innate ability to self-regulate the necessary amounts of food—but, unfortunately, not an innate ability to determine healthy foods from unhealthy foods. That's where parents come in. And instead of demanding that plates must be cleaned or a certain food must be finished, allow your children to ask to be excused to a quiet activity in another room. The action at the dinner table will hopefully keep them interested in staying. And don't worry; we'll talk a bit more about manners in chapter 7.

MM TIP:
Children should be able to use a spoon at twelve months, a fork at eighteen months, and a knife between five and six years (although don't expect them to use the fork and spoon as well as you do). Encourage mastery just as you would for any other developmental milestone.

Dining Out with Kids in Tow

Okay, remember when you went to a restaurant with your husband to enjoy a calm meal, a quiet conversation, perhaps even a read through the Sunday paper? And remember that annoying family with the kid who wouldn't stop crying and the baby who kept throwing food into your new Marc Jacobs bag? Well, guess what? Now *you're* that annoying family. But, truth is, you can have meals at restaurants again; just don't bother bringing the paper. Here are some tips:

- Start young, and go often. Get your children used to dining out. When they are little, it's easy to go out, as they pretty much sleep in the car seat. Continue this as they grow so they get accustomed to being in restaurants.

- Go early and be reasonable in your choices. Don't go to a five-star restaurant and expect to be greeted with open arms by the maitre'd. Pick family-friendly restaurants, and get there on the early side. Not only will the other patrons not mind as much (chances are better it is a family crowd at 6 P.M.), but also you won't be quite so worried about ruining other people's night out if it's not so packed. As a bonus, the wait staff won't be as frazzled and the kitchen will be more able to accommodate special requests. A good rule of thumb is not to go anywhere where you would be bummed if a baby showed up.

- Ask for a large table in an out-of-the-way corner. You'll be less likely to impose on others, and will have more room to spread out with baby gear.

- Order your child's meal the second you sit down, and ask for it to be delivered first. The sooner his food arrives, the sooner he'll be occupied. If you are concerned about the restaurant's having something he will eat, bring your own food for your baby. It is not the restaurant's responsibility to satisfy your picky eater's whims.

- Pick one small toy—if your child is old enough, a time-consuming activity like a coloring book—to bring to the restaurant. Use this only in an emergency such as slow service. If you bring a whole assortment of toys, your child will believe that restaurants are a place to be entertained. It's better for them to learn that this is a place where the family sits together in a calm atmosphere.

- Never let your child out of the high chair to run around the restaurant. Once you start this habit, it's really hard to break, and it can be dangerous. Waiters carrying large trays may not see your little one, causing a big kaboom!

- For older children, treat a night out as something special. Practice table manners at home ahead of time, and let them choose a special outfit to wear. These rituals will likely make them take the experience more seriously. Afterward, praise and reward them for good behavior.

> **MM TIP:** Ask your waiter for a stack of clean spoons. Inevitably, your child is going to drop his silverware once or twice—or twelve times. This way, you won't have to bug your waiter every time this happens.

- Always tip your waiter 20 percent when you have children with you. Not only are you likely creating more work for them, but it will also make the waiter more eager to wait on other families if there is incentive for more money.

- Ask for the check as soon as your food arrives to ensure a quick exit when necessary.

No matter how well-behaved she is, going to a restaurant with an energetic one-and-a-half- to two-and-a-half-year-old is not going to be a lot of fun for you or your child. I'm not saying you shouldn't do it, but why subject yourselves to torture if you don't have to? From the moment Jack learned to walk until he was about three (okay, four) I rarely took him out in public to eat, but now (most of the time) he's a great companion, well behaved, and a pleasure to dine with. Lilia? Well, let's just say I'm looking forward to her third birthday.

MM TIP:
Many restaurants don't have high chairs with a tray attached, which means you need to feed your child off a plate. For little kids who are learning to finger-feed themselves, this can be dangerous, as my son loves to grab the plate and throw it. Pick up disposable table covers and keep them in your diaper bag. They are placemat size; they adhere to the table, creating a clean eating surface; and they can be tossed after the meal.

CHAPTER 5

Wake Up! We Need to Talk About Sleep

You grow up thinking you want diamonds, pearls, Manolos stacked so high you couldn't wear them in a month of black-tie benefits. Then you have a baby and you would trade all of that for three guilt-free nights of ten hours of sleep. Heck, for three nights of eight hours of sleep. Okay, even one night of six hours of sleep. Well, that's motherhood, and the goal once you have a newborn—beyond shimmying back into your favorite pre-pregnancy jeans—is to get that child to sleep through the night. There have been countless books and theories, controversial and sound, written on the subject. And while I'd be way out of line to dictate which method will be best for your baby, as many factors play into it—your child-rearing philosophy, your baby's development, weight, temperament, and so on—you might as well learn from my mistakes (and the things I actually did well). And while I wish I could say there is one golden rule or surefire answer to sleep, there isn't. But, hopefully, what follows will let you cut through the clutter without adding "reading all books on babies and sleep" to your ever growing (and never to be completed) to-do list.

The best thing to keep in mind is that all kids are different. And not just from family to family, but also within your own family. Sure, often baby boys' digestive systems aren't as fully formed as those of girls at birth, and thus baby boys have a harder time processing their food and may be gassier or have trouble sleeping, but girls are not necessarily better sleepers than boys. I know just as many girl babies who can't make it through the night.

Oh, and if you think trying to get the last pair of Ernest Sewn jeans at the Barneys Warehouse sale is stiff competition, wait until you start talking to mothers about their babies' sleep habits. One of the first questions you'll be asked when you meet a new mom is how your baby sleeps—what hours, with what accoutrements, and how often they wake up. If your child sleeps less than hers, she'll look at you smugly; if your child sleeps more, she'll look at you with jealousy. You'll find yourself dreading the question no matter what your baby's sleep habits. So here's a tip: realize that many women exaggerate. When a mother of a six-week-old tells you her newborn is sleeping through the night, dig a bit deeper. "Sleeping through the night" may mean midnight to 5 A.M. If you ask me, that's a red eye, not a full night's sleep. Some women are in denial. After talking to one woman who swore that her little boy never woke up at night after week four, I broke into a cold sweat (Jack was six months old and barely making it five hours at that point). Before I broke into a full-blown case of hyperventilation, her husband came up to me and told me that the truth was her child was up at least once a night. She typically slept through it and her husband didn't have the heart to break her idealistic view. Just as some people see the glass as half full, some moms see the best in their child's sleep habits no matter what. While it may drive you crazy to hear, it's actually a nice philosophy to subscribe to. Even after Jack turned into a marathon sleeper, I still characterized him as a "bad one." After my husband tallied how long it had been since he woke up in the middle of the night or early in the morning, I realized that my attitude—not Jack—was the problem.

So the lesson is: if you have a great sleeper you may be doing something right, or you may also just be darn lucky. Jack was a terrible sleeper—a real screamer from the moment he came out. Now at age four he sleeps eight till eight many nights, and wakes up happy as a clam most mornings. Lilia started out sleeping five hours at a stretch and slept through the night at about two months. Now at age two, she

MM TIP:
Honestly, the biggest fights my husband Marcus and I ever had were about what to do with Jack and sleeping. Usually, these occurred at 3 A.M. when Jack woke up screaming and we had conflicting ideas of what to do. Decide on your approach together, calmly and in the light of day—preferably before the baby comes and you're in the middle of the problem. Whatever method you choose, you will need to be consistent and united in it. A crying baby and sleepless nights are bad enough; fighting with your partner is a problem you don't need to have.

gets up twice a night. So before you count your blessings (er, sheep) or curse the sandman, know that whatever your lot, it will change.

So here's your month-by-month, year-by-year guide about why your baby is—or isn't—sleeping!

Birth to Three Months: From A to Zzz's

Sure, newborns sleep a lot—anywhere from fourteen to sixteen hours a day in those first few months. The trouble is, it never seems to be for more than four hours in a row. And while some infants can work up to an eight- to ten-hour stretch within six weeks, others don't accomplish that feat until six months (or even, nine months, like mine!). But you can help your baby—and you—reach this goal by establishing healthy sleeping habits early on:

MM TIP:
Ninety percent of babies over the age of three months are able to sleep six to eight hours without waking—that's the amount of time that's considered "through the night." Three months is just about when most babies will weigh twelve or thirteen pounds.

- *Weigh the issues.* The basic rule for infants is that babies who weigh in the seven- to nine-pound range are capable of holding enough milk to keep them asleep for three to four hours, while a baby ten pounds or over should be able to give a good eight hours. (You may be walking a little funny from delivering one this size, but this is one advantage to having a big baby!) So don't expect miracles from your preemie, and at the same time, if your baby is twelve pounds and sleeping only two-hour stretches at a time, it's time to get serious.

- *Pick up on signs he's tired.* Babies of this age don't really stay awake for more than two hours, and keeping them up longer can make them overtired, which, ironically, makes it tougher for them to then go to sleep (never understood that one, but it's true). Look for signs like your child's rubbing his eyes or having puffy, dark circles under his eyes. If that's the case, it's nap time. This will soon become second nature to you. When adults get overtired, we tend to sleep for days. But for whatever reason, when babies don't get enough rest, it gets twice as hard to put them down for a nap or for the night.

• *Discern between day and night*. If you talk to any expert about why your baby isn't sleeping at night, one of the first things they will likely ask is "What are your baby's days like?" Typically, the answer to your nighttime problem can be found in what you're doing during the days. Not only should you be feeding your child regularly during the day, as I mentioned in chapter 4; but it's important to let your baby know the difference between a daytime nap and a nighttime sleep, so his sleep cycle starts to get established and he can make it through the night sooner. This is something that babies have to be taught. Remember that babies had no day/night schedule while they were in utero, and in fact probably slept more during our daylight hours, when you were busy walking around and therefore rocking them to sleep without even knowing it. So it's up to us to help them learn that daytime is for playing and some naps, and nighttime is for "real" sleep. You have to encourage night as a time to sleep by making the daytime something different. From the beginning, avoid keeping a "quiet house" when your baby is sleeping. Not only will it drive you nuts to tiptoe around and avoid the phone ringing, but it is important for your baby to get used to ambient noise and learn how to sleep through it. Then, at night, when it is dark and quiet, if he wakes, don't talk to him, or if you do, speak in a soft, low voice. Don't turn on the lights when you come in to check on him. He will slowly learn tell the difference from when he should snooze for many hours instead of just a few. Here's how to do this:

- Let some natural light flood into your baby's room for daytime naps.

- Go about your business during the day, whether it is vacuuming, letting the phone ring and the dog bark, using the washer and dryer, and so on.

- Don't let your baby sleep more than three and a half hours at a time during the day.

- When the baby is awake, talk to him, sing to him, go outside, bounce him around. Make daytime a fun, happening time.

MM TIP:
If you have a really light sleeper, like Jack was, you have to teach him how to sleep through noise. Think of it as a sensitivity training. Start with a time in which you know your baby is really tired—perhaps the first morning nap after a very active morning. Create some white noise (like vacuuming) as a test. If he wakes up, this is a great time to try and teach him to go back to sleep on his own—because he is already really tired. If he's really screaming, go in to make sure he's okay, and then leave. It's a desensitization process, and slowly but surely he'll be able to sleep through ambient noise.

MM TIP:
Most people make the mistake of creating a totally dark room for their baby during the day. But think about the nursery in the hospital. Lights are on, noises are abundant. The second you bring your baby home, make sure his room has lots of light flooding in during the day. If you do this from day one, you'll probably be in much better shape.

- Feed him regularly during the day.

- At night, keep the lights dimmed even when coming in for a feeding.

- Don't stimulate or talk to your baby when checking in at night.

> **MM TIP:** Babies under the age of three months can't be spoiled, so don't worry if you go to him every time he cries. If he's awake and crying, chances are something is wrong (he's wet, he's hungry, something hurts). So respond quickly. After three months, start slowing your response time so that they don't learn to manipulate you by crying.

- *Put your baby down awake.* You would have thought I would have learned my lesson with Jack, but I remember that for the first several weeks, I would take Lilia into her room and rock her in my arms for thirty minutes or so until she fell completely asleep, and then put her down. While I loved this ritual, and wouldn't have traded it for the world at the time, it occurred to me one night that if I did this every night, she would come to *expect* it every night. The next night, as soon as she was done with her bottle, I put her down wide awake. Sure enough, she fell asleep on her own with no fuss. It turns out that *I* was the one who needed the ritual, not her. This is so important because the greatest gift you can give your child (and your marriage, for that matter) is to teach your baby to be an independent sleeper. And this is a habit you are establishing for later on. If you start it up front, she will never know the difference. Jodi Mindell, associate director of the Sleep Disorders Center at Children's Hospital of Philadelphia and author of *Sleeping Through the Night*, advises against rocking or nursing your baby to sleep, even at this young age. "Parents think that what they do this early doesn't have an effect," she says, "but it does. Babies are learning their sleep habits. If you rock your child to sleep every night for the first eight weeks, why would he expect anything different later on?" If your baby is constantly falling asleep by taking the breast or bottle before bed, wake him up (a little bit) again before you put him down. He must learn to go to sleep on his own. Now, don't misinterpret what I've said above. Obviously, your child is going to go to bed more easily *sleepy* than wide awake. It's just important that she is not sound asleep. Dr. Bill Sears and his pediatrician sons at AskDrSears.com have a nice explanation for those early months when babies are "lighter" sleepers and cry more frequently. They remind us that babies were designed that way so they would be protected; if they slept too long or too well, they wouldn't wake up frequently enough to fill their bellies or to alert their tired parents that they need to be checked on, to make sure they're in a safe position, and so on. Simply put, ignoring babies' cries in the first few months of life can be dangerous. As parents, we are still learning how to trust our instincts, and babies need to be checked on.

What If He Screams?

Your baby may scream at first when you try to put him down awake. And during the first month or two you will want to, and should, comfort him. The best thing to do is to soothe him with your voice and try not to pick him up once he's down. Otherwise, he will be mommy soothing instead of self-soothing. (This is, of course, assuming that all systems are go: he's been fed recently, had a nice burp afterward, doesn't seem to have a poopy diaper, isn't pulling his knees up in pain, and so on. Obviously, if any of these things are wrong, then pick up your baby and take care of him.) At a certain point, though, you are going to need to leave the room to give him a chance to fall asleep on his own. If after soothing with your voice, he screams, with a baby under three months, the rule of thumb is to leave him screaming for two minutes to test it out. If he doesn't settle down after two minutes, check on him and try again.

But by three months—again, assuming all other systems check out—grab the earplugs. Even if he screams, he needs to learn to fall asleep on his own when he first goes down or he will never be able to put himself back to sleep in the middle of the night when he wakes for

MM TIP:
Babies with colic are usually under three months of age, cry for more than three hours a day, and will cry the most during the afternoon and early evening. These are babies who really have a hard time self-soothing, and no number of two- or even five-minute checks will help during that time of the day. There are a variety of calming methods that can be tried on colicky babies, but the important things to remember are that babies outgrow colic (most by four months) and that studies have shown that colic causes no lasting problems for either babies or their exhausted parents.

MM TIP:
Don't be afraid of crying. I know this sounds silly, but I truly worried with Jack that his crying meant he was *mad* at me and that his crying was a sign that I was a failure as a mother. It's not. There are many reasons babies cry, and if it's not about being hungry, wet, or needing to burp, you can be sure it's *not* about *you*. He will not wake up resenting you for his crying the same way *you* may resent him!

whatever reason. Older babies can cry for about five minutes (that's actually looking at the clock or a watch for five minutes instead of just guessing under the stress of the screams). Longer than that and they should be checked and offered the simple reassurance of your presence.

- *Don't wake your baby in the middle of the night.* If she does wake up, feed her the breast or the bottle (for the first few months—see next item) and put her back to bed with very little stimulation. This means keeping the lights low or off and keeping noise and even soothing noises to a minimum.

- *Don't feed your baby every time he wakes up at night.* After the first month or two, when your child is of the right weight (as mentioned earlier) to get through the night, consider getting your child back to sleep using methods beyond feeding. Maybe you use the pacifier or perhaps your finger to sate him in some other way than with food. This will train your child—and his stomach—to be able to go for the longer stretches without food.

- *Let him side sleep.* Babies sleep the worst on their backs. But with sudden infant death syndrome (SIDS) being such a danger (more on that below), stomach sleeping is in no way an option. Try placing your child on his side, propped with side-wedge pillows. Chances are he will sleep a lot better.

MM TIP: For the first few weeks (or even months) it's perfectly fine—and quite helpful—to have your baby in the room with you in a bassinet, a cosleeper, or a Moses basket. It's convenient for middle-of-the-night feedings and establishes a closeness and sense of security for the baby (okay, and you too!). While some people choose to put their baby in bed with them, this is not the best idea. Not only is it dangerous with all of those flying elbows and pillows, but you need to establish a bit of separation between you and the baby so that he learns to sleep independently.

Getting on a Schedule

While there is no foolproof method short of tranquilizers (which I don't suggest—but can't say I haven't thought of it at 4 A.M.), here is a general schedule for the first few months that has worked nicely for many who have tried it.

In the beginning, a baby (at best) will go around three and a half hours between feedings. So, using simple math, if a baby is put down at 7 P.M., that means he will be up at roughly 10:30 P.M., 2 A.M. and again at 5:30 A.M. However, if you can manage to add in a last feeding of the day as late as possible (even if you wake your infant to do this), you can cut down your chances of having *two* feedings at ungodly hours (in other words, top off his tank for a last feeding at 11:30, and then you may make it to 3 A.M., and then 6:30 A.M., which you'll soon come to know as your wake-up call). This may not seem like a big deal, but psychologically, it can make a difference. And if you can get a little help on the journey, alternating shifts, then it makes a huge difference. (This is possible only if you are either bottle-feeding or have pumped breast milk.) Given that I had such a difficult time and Jen had a better one, I'm deferring to her experience on this:

Here's what she and her husband Ben did:

- Each night one went to bed early—anywhere between 8 and 10 P.M. The other person stayed up until 11 P.M. or midnight if possible for a final feeding to top off the tank (sometimes they would have to wake Sam for this feeding, but this is the only exception to breaking that rule). This feeding was *always* from a bottle, even if Jen was giving it (she would pump this bottle.) That way, they could monitor the amount they were giving him. This late night shift was called the bookend shift.

- The next feeding went to the person who had gone to bed early—the graveyard shift. This feeding would come anytime between 3 and 4 A.M. when the baby woke up.

- The final feeding would then go back to the bookend shift, since that person hadn't taken the middle of the night shift. This shift usually came anytime between 6 and 8 A.M.

MM TIP:
According to Dr. Spock, some parents feel very angry with their children for crying, but then feel guilty for feeling angry (are you with me?) and thus the parent is more lenient at night to alleviate the guilt—which can lead to more crying and a vicious cycle. So know that it's okay to be bummed (and angry) if your child cries a lot. But don't feel guilty.

• The next night, they would switch shifts. That way, every other night one either got an uninterrupted night of sleep (the bookend shift) or got to go to bed early and sleep a little late—but had to be up in the middle (the graveyard shift).

There were very distinct advantages and disadvantages to both. On nights when Jen was up in the middle of the night, she truly looked forward to the next night's shift so that she could be the one staying in bed. But then on the mornings she had to wake up early, she looked forward to the graveyard shift the next night, because she knew she'd be going to bed early and getting to sleep in a bit. Alternating made both shifts something to look forward to in a weird, albeit psychotic, way.

The amazing thing about this schedule was that, little by little, the shifts pushed back. Before she knew it, that 3 or 4 A.M. shift became a 5 or 6 A.M. shift. Once Sam was regularly lasting from midnight to 6 A.M., she was able to creep back the midnight feeding to 11 P.M., and so on. While Jack was a bit more trying, I have seen this type of schedule work for many people, so try out some variation of your own.

Response Time

The question that most women have right off the bat is: how fast should you respond to your baby when he cries in the middle of the night? Well, this depends a lot on age, and there are really two theories on this. The first is, if you let him cry and he cries and cries, and then you realize, *wow, he must really be hungry*, and then go to him, he has basically learned that crying gets him food (bad). On the other hand, if you jump and run to him the second he starts to cry, then you are perhaps responding when he may actually put himself back to sleep on his own and was simply making a very common middle-of-the-night noise (also bad). So I would say, use a little bit of common sense. If your baby is typically going about three hours at a time at night between feedings, and it's around that time, then if your infant cries, go feed him. However, if your child was just fed an hour before and he is crying out, give it a little bit of time before you run in—and if you do finally need to go in, try another soothing method before feeding. Sometimes you might hear fussing or you might see your baby stirring—these can actually be normal occurrences during your baby's REM sleep.

If All Else Fails

Okay, so here's the tough love part. In order for your child to sleep through the night, he has to meet certain criteria:

1. He has to be physically big enough to be able to go a long stretch without food.

2. He has to have learned the difference between day sleep and night sleep.

3. He has to have learned how to put himself back to sleep when he wakes up.

Without these three things, you don't have a chance of getting your child to sleep through the night. So if your child is not sleeping through the night, you need to go back and look at the three criteria, and see if perhaps he's missing one of the elements. There is no other way to do it. You must make this work. And you don't want to slack on any of these things (say, rocking him to sleep, but accomplishing the other feats), because then you are simply establishing other habits that will delay your end goal: getting him to sleep through the night.

SIDS and Flat Heads

Okay, admit it. Occasionally, you get up in the middle of the night and go into your baby's room for no other reason than to see if he is still breathing (even when the baby *is* sleeping through the night, you still aren't!). While your reaction is normal, the truth is, the chances of your baby being the one in 1500 babies who succumbs each year to SIDS (Sudden Infant Death Syndrome) is very small.

MM TIP:
Always keep the three-day rule in mind. Any bad habit can be broken with children in three days. Granted, they may be long, tough, torturous days, but you can do it.

MM TIP:
If you're going motherhood alone, I strongly encourage you to enlist a friend or relative to help one night a week. Just getting a little sleep will give you a lot more strength for the other nights.

MM TIP:
Most cases of SIDS occur between ages two and four months, with the majority of cases happening before six months. Coincidentally, six months is about the time when babies begin rolling over on their own, making it next to impossible to keep them on their backs all night. Don't stress about your new little roller, and rest assured you're almost in the clear on the SIDS risk.

MM TIP:
There are many women who, despite all the research, still insist that since their child sleeps better on his tummy, that they will simply run the risk. This is simply not an option. It's far too dangerous. Instead, invest in sleeping wedges and place your child on his side—wedged so he can't roll to his tummy. Also, ask your labor and delivery nurses to demonstrate how they do it.

So what is SIDS, and how do you prevent it? SIDS occurs when a healthy baby, for no apparent reason, simply stops breathing on his own. But there are many things that you can do to decrease your baby's risk of SIDS:

- Put your baby to sleep on his back. Since the American Academy of Pediatrics initiated the "Back to Sleep" campaign in 1994, SIDS cases have decreased 40 percent.

- Use a firm mattress with tight-fitting sheets, and no extra fluffy accessories like pillows, blankets, or stuffed animals that your child may push up against and suffocate.

- Avoid overheating your baby by dressing him too warmly in the crib.

- Don't allow smoking in your home.

- If you're still paranoid that your child may stop breathing in the middle of the night, invest in a monitor that your child sleeps on and detects if they stop breathing. While pricey, it could make you sleep a bit easier.

- Learn CPR so that if your child does stop breathing, you will know what to do.

Of course, all this back sleeping is well and good until your child starts to get a flat head, called plagiocephaly—something our mothers never dealt with, since they put all of us on our tummies. A baby's head has a very soft spot in the back—remember how your baby came out with a bit of a cone head while squeezing through the birth canal? Well, back sleeping for fourteen to sixteen hours a day on that soft spot can cause her head to flatten out. If she sleeps with her head slightly turned, it can be even worse, as it flattens out on one side. Here are a couple of tricks to try and alleviate the problem:

- Have your baby spend time when she is awake on her tummy to relieve the pressure on the back of the head.

- Switch ends of the crib that you put her to bed in. Babies typically turn their heads to look out of the crib, and if you alternate from side to side, your baby's peering out will alternate.

- Buy wedge pillows to secure your child on her side, but not on her tummy.

MM TIP:
Some babies might also develop a bald spot on the back of their head. This is *not* permanent!

If your baby's head doesn't round out by about six months, check with your pediatrician, who may refer you to a specialist. In some instances, babies need to wear a special helmet for a few months to help correct the flat spot.

Three to Nine Months: Sleep Is on the Way

At this point you should begin to be feeling more like a human and less like a zombie—at least I hope so. Your baby should still be sleeping anywhere from fourteen to sixteen hours in a twenty-four-hour period, but now, as many as eight to twelve of them will be occurring—drum roll, please—at night! Thought it would never come, right? And for those of you who aren't quite there yet and still have some middle-of-the-night encounters with your wee one at the beginning of this stage, rest assured that by six months, he'll be physically capable of sleeping much longer. Here's where moms always get blamed: whether he actually *will* depends on if he's learned good sleep habits.

At this age, babies typically need four hours of naps a day broken up into two two-hour naps, one shorter and one longer, or several forty-five minute catnaps. There is really no right or wrong method. However, it is difficult for a child to go too long at this age without sleep, so do not move to one long nap a day at this point. Also avoid any naps longer than three hours, as it can affect his nighttime sleep schedule.

So how do you teach your child the *right* sleep habits?

MM TIP:
If you travel a lot, stay overnight with your child at other houses, or have other people put your child down for bed occasionally, make sure your nighttime rituals are transferable to different situations. For example, choose a book, but let a different person read it to your child occasionally so that she doesn't get stuck in the "only Mommy can put me to bed" mode.

MM TIP:
If your baby is falling asleep while nursing, try doing the nighttime ritual prior to his final feeding so that he is still getting the benefits of the routine. If you are trying to break him of falling asleep during nursing so that he can fall asleep on his own, try giving him a bath after nursing him to wake him up a little, but still keep him relaxed.

- *Set a bedtime and nap times, and stick with it.* Depending on your schedule, a good baby bedtime will fall sometime between 7 and 8:30 P.M. Any earlier, and you'll be up at the crack of dawn. Any later and he's likely to be overtired and not fall asleep easily. (See page 147 on bedtimes.)

- *Start a regular bedtime routine.* Babies thrive on consistency and repetition. It makes them feel safe. So now is the time to set up a routine that you do every night before you go to bed. This can involve a bath, a story, a particular song—as long as it's not overly stimulating it doesn't matter.

- *Establish independence.* If you still have the cosleeper or bassinette in your room, this is a good time to shift your baby to the crib, or at least to the bassinette in his own room. It's also the time to start breaking his dependence on you for falling asleep, if you haven't done so already. Your baby will most likely develop separation anxiety at about seven months, so major changes in bedrooms, cribs, and so on should be accomplished *before* this window of open-mindedness and friendliness closes! Your baby should be falling asleep on his own without rocking or nursing, so that when he wakes in the middle of the night—which, even if you don't hear him, he does three to four times a night—he can put himself back to sleep. If he can't fall asleep on his own, this may be the time to consider a "cry-it-out" approach, such as the Ferber method, which I will explain a little later on. Of course, this is a personal decision based on what is best for you and your baby.

- *Don't mess with the routine.* I promised my husband, and myself, that having a baby wouldn't slow our jet-set life. And it didn't. By the time Jack was six months old he had been to California three times and London once. And then Lilia barely made it down the street until she was one (just kidding). I'm not saying you shouldn't travel with a baby, but I will say it wreaks havoc on their schedule and their routine. If a carefree lifestyle is your thing, go for it—but expect a few sleepless nights. If you're looking for a few more zzz's, better to stick close to home. All kids do much better with patterns. So the best thing to do if you are traveling is to replicate your home life as much as you can. Bring the Moses basket he sleeps in. Bring his blankets and lullaby toy. Whatever pattern you can re-create in the foreign place will bring you that much closer to zzz's. Whatever you do, don't compromise what you wouldn't do at home: have him sleep in the bed with you or suck on the breast all night long. This will only make things worse when you come back home.

Possible Hiccups

Anywhere from six to nine months, your child will begin to sit up, crawl, and even stand on his own. This added daytime activity can cause two shifts in nighttime activity. First, the adrenaline rush of accomplishing these major milestones can cause him to not want to stop practicing these skills at bedtime, making it harder for him to go to sleep. I mean, really, who wants to lie down when you've just learned to stand up? The other thing to happen is that if he practices and succeeds in something like standing and holding on to the crib bars, there's a good chance that he may get stuck and cry out for help. Of course, you will want to go help him get unstuck, but then should encourage him to go back to sleep on his own. Feeding your baby during the night at this point will not help him sleep better, but rather make the problem worse. One thing to pay attention to is whether your baby's increased daytime activities are cutting into feeding times. Keeping on track with meals during the day can prevent babies from having to play food catch-up at night.

Bedtimes

Strangely, babies get in a habit of waking up at the same time almost every day. If their wake-up time is 6 A.M., and you put them to bed at 6 P.M. most nights, if you keep them up later (until, say, 8 P.M.), unfortunately, they'll likely still be up at 6 A.M. Of course, a lot of this can also depend on the amount and quality of sleep they've had during the day. When calculating your child's bedtime, think first about what time you want him to wake up in the morning, and then work back-

MM TIP:
It is not unusual for babies to wake two to three times a night at this point. But their crying out is more out of habit than out of need (a full-term three-to six-month-old baby is more than capable of getting through the night). If you reward the cries with the breast or bottle, the baby will come to expect it. Instead, rub her back or give her a pacifier. Do something else to soothe her and she will begin to be able to self-soothe. Eventually, your child will wake and go right back to sleep on her own, which is the goal.

MM TIP:
If your baby goes down after 8:30 P.M. and begins to wake in the middle of the night, try switching his bedtime back to 8. It's a small shift, but surprisingly he's much more likely to sleep through the night. Go figure.

MM TIP:
If your child is waking too early, try making her first nap of the day later by about an hour.

ward. Calculate the bedtime based on how much night sleep your child is getting at the moment. Just remember, if you choose the 6 A.M. wake up from the beginning, then you will likely be stuck with that time in the future.

Nine to Twelve Months: Too Good to Be True

At this point, your baby should be consistently sleeping eleven to twelve hours at night. These are called the good times. But don't get too comfortable, because if you notice, this section encompasses only about three months. And your child may move to a single nap during the day. Other babies don't move to one nap until eighteen months. It really just depends on how your baby reacts and how much sleep you feel he needs. If you do switch to one nap, though, position it in the middle of the day so that your child never goes for too long without sleep. Also continue to:

- *Have a consistent bedtime routine.*

- *Stay on schedule.* The more defined you are in the schedule for day-time naps, feeding schedules, and bedtime, the easier time you will have getting him to go to sleep—and stay asleep—at night.

- *Have your baby fall asleep on his own.* This means without rocking or sucking on the bottle or breast.

MM TIP:
At this point, allow your child some quiet time in his crib. Don't run in to get him the second you hear a peep in the morning. Let him have a little time to wake up and play alone. This goes a long way to establishing a little independence.

Possible Hiccups

- *Separation Anxiety.* Your baby is much more aware of Mommy and Daddy at this point. This can cause him to wake up in the middle of the night, worried that you aren't there and won't return. While he's likely to calm down when you walk into the room, it's important to not stay there too long, as it can set you back into the baby-cry-you-come cycle of the first few weeks. At this age, they are full-on aware of how to manipulate you! If you haven't done it already, adding a night-light in the room can help remind your child that he is still in familiar surroundings.

- *Teething.* All bets are off when your child is teething. I remember nights when our son would scream out in pain—a cry that you know as a mother is way different from just a normal waking-in-the-night cry. The key to soothing your baby when he is teething is to make sure you aren't establishing a habit. It's fine to comfort for a night or two, but any more than that and it's expected. So try to stick to your schedule as much as possible. And know that sometimes a little dose of infant Tylenol can help quite a bit.

One-Year-Old Sleep Patterns

Your baby may have passed a major milestone—turning one—but he still needs close to fourteen hours of sleep in a twenty-four-hour period. This will be his amount of sleep until he turns two, but how it's broken up will vary from toddler to toddler. Some kids are good for eleven hours at night with a three-hour nap, while others will sleep only ten hours at night but take two naps. It's really less about how much your toddler sleeps and more about how well he functions on the sleep he is getting. By eighteen months, however, most babies—to the chagrin of their exhausted parents—will be down to one nap a day. But think of it this way: if your baby needs only one nap a day, it is because two naps was simply too much sleep and therefore likely would affect his nighttime patterns. So you may be giving up some free time during the day, but it's so that everyone sleeps better at night.

    Just as with an infant, you still need to practice good sleep habits. While the rules are the same, the reasons the rules are important have changed slightly:

- *Stick with that bedtime ritual.* This is more important than ever because now your child will be running around and playing. And if you and your husband both work, the evenings are even more exciting because Mommy and Daddy are finally home to play. It's fine to

MM TIP:
Transitioning from two naps to one can be tough. To bridge the gap, try alternating days: one day have your child take one nap, and the next day have him take two. Also try putting your child to bed earlier on evenings of the one-nap days.

let your child work off that excess energy in the evenings, but make sure you wind things down before bed. Read a book, take a bath, sing lullabies. And follow this pattern every night. Toddlers love consistency, and knowing the routine helps them have a sense of control.

- *Stay on schedule, day or night.* Again, this goes back to the consistency thing. Knowing what to expect out of the day will help your child welcome bedtime. This will become important down the road in avoiding bedtime resistance.

Possible Hiccups

At this age, you could start to encounter a bit of nighttime resistance from your child. This happens when he becomes aware of the impending bedtime and starts to fight you on it, as he would rather stay up and play or simply be with you. Here are a few ways to try to avoid this:

- Make sure he gets plenty of activity and exercise during the day so that he is tired at bedtime and doesn't have as much energy.

- Give your child control over bedtime—here's that control thing again—by letting him have a part in the choices: which PJs he wants to wear, which story he wants you to read. However, never give him choices with unacceptable answers, such as, "Do you want to go to bed?" Make sure the answer is always something you can live with.

- Start to warn your child about how much longer he will be able to play before bedtime, so that it slowly creeps up on him, rather than trying to cut off play abruptly.

- Let him set a fun egg timer and have him help you count down the time until bed.

Big Boy/Girl Beds

MM TIP:
If you're pregnant, move your toddler to a big bed at least two to three months before you're due. That way, your older child will be used to his new bed before he sees a new baby taking over his crib. If the timing doesn't work out, then hold out until the new baby is three to four months old. Chances are the new baby will still be in a cosleeper or Moses basket, and your older child will have time to get used to his baby sibling, making the crib-to-bed transition easier. The big bed just shouldn't seem like a punishment that comes with the new sibling.

Sometime around eighteen months, you may consider switching your child to a toddler bed or a twin bed. Maybe sooner, maybe much later. There is really no reason a baby has to come out of a crib unless a new child is on the way and you need the crib, or if it is dangerous because your child is trying to climb out and is falling. But the good news is, this is not one of those "have to" things. There's no reason to switch out unless there's a reason not to stay.

Here are a few things you'll want to consider:

- If your child doesn't want to sleep in a twin bed, try using a toddler bed, which is much smaller and still has bars on three sides, with a lower guardrail on the front.

- Try a daybed as a larger alternative to a toddler bed, as it has bars on three sides.

- If you go to a big bed first, make sure you add safety rails so he can't roll out of bed.

- Realize that your child now has the ability to be mobile in the middle of the night, so block off stairs or add a baby gate to the door of her room to avoid middle-of-the night escapes. Chances are she'll be able to open the door but may not be able to get past a gate.

Of course, with the big bed comes new challenges with bedtime and waking up, as now your child has the power to get out of bed on his own and come to you. This happened to Jack right after we had Lilia. I made a big mistake by encouraging Marcus to go in and lie down with Jack (I know, dumb). But frankly, I felt guilty with a new baby in my room and Jack on his own. Of course, that made the habit even harder to break, as then he was accustomed to having Marcus in his bed. So here are a few ways to work this out:

- If he gets out and comes to you, immediately walk him back to bed and explain that it is bedtime. Do this as many times as necessary.

MM TIP:
Jen's mom started a fun ritual with her first grandson, Daniel, who started to get up in the middle of the night and want to play once he was in a big bed. When she put him to bed, she'd say, "Don't get up until the sun comes up!" It became a little ritual that they'd say together, and it was something concrete that Daniel could understand. He knew that if it was dark, he needed to stay in bed.

- Minimize contact and conversation when he comes in the middle of the night.

- Do not invite him into your bed.

- Set up a system in which he gets stickers or points for staying in bed all night.

- Leave out a few fun toys for the morning to encourage him to stay in his room for a half hour or so when he wakes.

- Install a baby gate at his door, so that he can see out and call to you but not wander around the house.

- Remember, separation anxiety makes facing the nighttime all the more difficult for young toddlers, just as they're becoming more mobile and verbal and better able to tell you that they don't want to miss out on the action! Stay firm in the face of begging and pleading: calm your child with your voice, from a distance. And above all, don't get angry or sound guilty. Compassionate strength will pay off in the long run.

Staying Until They Sleep

Do not stay in the room, let alone your child's bed, until your child falls asleep. I say this because I've made this mistake not once, but twice (I know, I'm a slow learner). In fairness, I was working a lot and enjoyed cuddling with little ones as we read and they fell asleep. But, clearly, it was more for *me* than for them. And then, of course, they got used to my being there. And then falling asleep took longer. And I would creep out at 8:45, and pray the creak of the door wouldn't wake them up. And it would. And we were back to square one.

So if you do this, know that it's probably not the best thing for your child, as he needs to be able to fall asleep on his own (heard that before, huh?). And it's not the best thing for *you*, as you need to have a semblance of an evening for your own sanity's sake. But if you've gotten into the habit, here's what to do:

- Explain to your child that you're not going to stay in her bed, but you'll stay until she falls asleep. Her job is to fall asleep; your job is to sit in the chair.

- Sit in a chair very close to her the first night, where she can see you until she falls asleep.

- The next night (or a few nights, if you're wimpy like me), stay in the chair for fifteen minutes (or less, depending on how quickly she falls asleep). You can also try moving the chair farther and farther away and toward the door each night, and eventually, sit in the chair in the hall.

- Each night, stay less and less time.

- If she cries and gets out of bed, put up a gate at her door and tell her that it is a reminder to stay in her bed. Let her know that it is dangerous for her to wander around the house alone at night, and that she needs to stay in her bed. You need to help her establish the self-discipline to stay in the bed. It may sound cruel, but this is the best way to do it.

Terrible Twos at Night

Two-year-olds typically sleep for about eleven hours a night, and then have one nap a day for an hour or two in the middle of the day. But unfortunately, this doesn't mean you get a nice, lovely eleven-hour break from parenting. Quite the contrary. On some nights you'll feel like you are back in the baby days. Between the power struggle that can occur at bedtime and the various new sensations your child will have

> MM TIP: Kids spend more time than adults in REM sleep and the deeper stages of non-REM sleep. This means they make more transitions from one sleep phase to the other each night and wake up more often than you do. That's why it's so important that kids learn how to soothe themselves back to sleep.

in the middle of the night—children start to experience and be able to vocalize dreams and nightmares at this age, not to mention the joys of potty training and night walking—this can be a whole new bed game!

Lights Out!

- *"Just one more ____".* This is likely your two-year-old's favorite phrase at bedtime. You fill in the blank: story, hug, snuggle, game, drink, whatever! Try and anticipate these requests by allowing one extra request a night—a little reverse psychology. He'll feel as if he's getting his way, when you know you are really getting yours. But then you must stick to only one request so that they know you mean it, otherwise it will have no validity the next night.

- *Afraid of the dark.* Many children become afraid of the dark at this age, especially after they've experienced their first nightmare. Keep a night-light on, and keep a flashlight on your child's night-stand in case she needs to get up in the middle of the night.

- *Yellow and blue monsters.* Monsters are typically a way for kids to vocalize what they don't understand in their dreams (or they've just watched *Monsters Inc.* too many times). And while there are many cute and tempting products on the market, such as "monster spray," avoid using these tactics. It simply validates your child's fears that monsters actually exist. Instead, explain that there are no monsters in this house (don't try the "monsters are pretend" route, as your child isn't yet old enough to understand such a concept. Then, in the morning, have your child draw the monster, so you can talk about it and confront her fears. Putting it down on paper may help her talk about it. You also might want to think about eliminating scary TV shows, movies, and books.

- *Nightmares.* It's definitely distressing to hear your child crying out in the middle of the night, having just had a scary nightmare. If he does have a nightmare, go to him immediately and talk to him about his bad dream while calming him down. It is important that you don't trivialize your child's fears. Instead, help him confront the fears and realize he's not alone. If bad dreams continue, look for possible stressors in his daily life and try to eliminate them. Most of the experts agree that if your child is truly terrified, it's all right to let him into your bed every once in a while, too.

- *Night terrors.* Children's brains are very active at this point in their lives, creating all sorts of new skills, from walking to talking and everything in between. My son used to do this freaky thing in which he would wake up out of nowhere with a zero-to-sixty scream. When we would go to comfort him, it was as if he were possessed. He would stare at us with a blank look, and nothing would calm his shrill scream for a long time. This is called a night terror. It is caused by stranger or separation anxiety, an image or memory going on in his mind. This is one time in which a little night stimulation is called for. Take him out of his dark room and turn on some lights. Let him see that Mommy and Daddy are there and he is all right. Chances are good that once he calms down, he'll go right back to sleep, as all the crying is incredibly exhausting.

MM TIP: At about age three, Jack seemed to desperately miss me at night and hated the idea that I might leave him. This was undoubtedly triggered by the arrival of his sister. On Betsy Brown Braun's suggestion, I gave him a photo of myself to sleep with at night. I thought she was crazy but asked him if he'd like one (no, not a glossy headshot, thank you). It would sleep beside him and really brought him a great deal of comfort. It's also the same reason younger babies like to have something with them that smells like their mother; it's a nice reminder.

> **MM TIP:** Night terrors usually occur in children aged three to twelve years, with the average age of a child's first night terror being closest to three and a half years—so you probably won't experience these yet! That said, Jen's son, Sam, had them quite a bit at age one. Nightmares, on the other hand, begin to occur closer to ages two or three since the development of language plays a big role in children's sleep patterns.

The Party's Over

Just when you finally get the sleeping and napping down, you may notice that your two-year-old is far less interested in napping. And sadly, you may have to say goodbye to that blissful hour or two when they're asleep and you actually get things done. While most toddlers take a two- to three-hour nap sometime in the middle of the day, others stop napping completely. The American Academy of Pediatrics goes so far as to write, "Unless (your two- to three-year-old child) routinely becomes irritable and overtired from lack of sleep, there's no reason to force a nap schedule on your child." Quiet time may be sufficient (well, for them anyway), and you might want to create variations on the "mat time" that children have in preschool, such as having a parent in one room, one child in another room, other child in another room, and so on.

What the Experts Say

It seems as if there are more books on getting your child to sleep than there are on getting a man to sleep with you (perhaps that's where the problem started), but who has the time to read through all of them? Well, when your child still isn't sleeping through the night at nine months, you'll read anything you can. So I thought I'd save you the trouble and recommend some of the best books I read on the subject:

Solve Your Child's Sleep Problems by Richard Ferber, MD

Catherine, a coworker of mine who has yet to have children, almost went out and got this book after hearing me talk ad nauseum to other new mothers about the pros and cons of "Ferberizing." She soon realized it wasn't some new workout gimmick, but now she's an expert anyway. Richard Ferber, the director of the Center for Pediatric Sleep Disorders at Children's Hospital in Boston, is the author of *Solve Your Child's Sleep Problems*. Ferberizing involves a strategy of letting your baby cry for a set period of time before you comfort her. It has stirred up talk—good and bad—among parents and pediatricians, with opinions ranging from thinking Ferber is a godsend to saying his approach makes babies and parents suffer. Here's a brief overview.

He believes that after a nice bedtime ritual—stories, bath, songs—you should put your child to bed awake, and leave the room. If she cries, wait a certain amount of time—based on the chart in his book and varying depending on your comfort level, how long you've been using the method, and how many times you've checked on the baby that night—before you go back in. When you do go back to her room, Ferber says to soothe the child with your voice but not to pick her up, feed her, or rock her. Then, gradually increase the amount of time between checks. In theory, after about one week, your infant will learn that crying earns nothing more than a brief check from you and isn't worth the effort, and will learn to fall asleep without your help.

While there is some tough love associated with this method, as it's stated above it doesn't seem all that harsh. Well, certain critics (read: moms like me and you) take exception with some issues of his plan. You should be aware of these before you choose this method:

MM TIP:
There are a number of things that can interfere with your baby's lack of sleep, which Ferber acknowledges. Before you Ferberize, make sure feeding habits, pain, stress, or medications are not causing your baby's sleep problems.

- Ferber says not to comfort your crying child at bedtime. You are encouraged not to hold, rock, or nurse your child at bedtime, but you can go in to check on him in limited spurts. Verbal reassuring is allowed, and parents do have an opportunity to see that their child is okay.

- The method advocates letting your child cry—even if she throws up. Lovely, right? Under this method, a baby can cry long and hard enough that she does vomit. Ferber points out, however, that these types of tantrums are tougher on you than on your baby—and don't hurt a child. He encourages parents to calmly clean her up, and then leave her room. If you go to her, she'll learn that crying gets her what she wants.

- Ferber says his method will work quickly and easily for everyone (typically three nights, sometimes seven). Well, pretty much the one thing I've learned being a mother is that *nothing* is foolproof. That said, sometimes expectations are bit high. Many people come to this book as a last resort, and with a stopwatch in hand, they time out their baby's crying fits, only to cave after the first few rounds and then blame the method. Ever confident of his approach, Ferber suggests getting a counselor to help guide you through the process and to reassure you that you're on the right track.

You can start Ferberizing if your baby is six months or older (but hopefully you've been developing good sleep habits before and won't need it). Like most sleep experts, he says that by the time the average infant is three months old, they can make it through the night without a nighttime feeding. And at six months, no babies need a nighttime feeding. He goes on to say that if you're still nursing or giving a bottle in the night at this age, the feedings themselves may be the cause of your baby's wakings because she has become used to them, and her tummy tells her she needs them—all the more reason to begin making a transition.

Healthy Sleep Habits, Happy Child by Marc Weissbluth, MD

This is certainly a softer philosophy than Ferber's, as Dr. Marc Weissbluth, a distinguished pediatrician and father of four, provides a program to ensure the best sleep for your child. It's an easy-to-read, step-by-step regimen that helps you create healthy sleep habits that work within your child's natural sleep cycles. The highlights include:

- Distinguishing between daytime sleep and night sleep, and why both are important to your child

- Coping with all types of sleep problems, from a crying baby to nightmares to bedwetting

- Learning how to get your baby to fall asleep based on his internal clock

- Showing how rocking and feeding are common mistakes parents make when trying to get their child to sleep

- Considering your child's personality when trying to figure out the best sleep cycle for your baby

- Stressing the importance of naps

- Dealing with the unique sleep problems of teenagers—a problem you can look forward to

The Happiest Baby on the Block by Harvey Karp, MD

This method is a great option for all those moms who can't stand the thought of letting their child "cry it out." It emphasizes nurturing and cuddling your baby. Karp is a pediatrician and an assistant professor at UCLA's School of Medicine and his theory is called the Fourth Trimester. He says that after your child comes from the close, confined, and soothing environment of the womb, what you think may be a nice, calm space that you've created at home can actually be as strange, noisy, and wild as a Las Vegas casino. Your baby needs a few months to transition into the world, and Karp recommends ways to do this by mimicking the womb—don't be scared—using the five S's:

- *Swaddling.* A step-by-step method to wrap your child in a blanket, tucking in his arms and legs to make him feel safe and secure

- *Side/stomach positioning.* Proper ways for your child to rest in two positions

- *Shhh sounds.* Calming sounds that mimic the muffled version of your voice in the womb

- *Swinging.* The difference between a gentle rocking versus a shaking

- *Sucking.* The use of a pacifier to satisfy a baby's natural need to suck

The author claims that almost all babies will respond to the five S's (these doctors sure are confident!), although he admits that it can take some time to find the soothing method that works best for your child. Every good theory comes with a controversy, and this one is no different. His suggestion to let children nurse frequently and on demand and his encouragement to use a pacifier have raised a few eyebrows.

The one thing you should realize by now is that you're not alone in your journey of getting a good night sleep. After all, it is the hottest topic of conversation among exhausted new parents, and there seem to be dozens of books out there to choose from. Just develop a plan, and stick with it. And know that all babies (and their parents) eventually sleep through the night.

CHAPTER 6

Baby Care 101 (Because Dressing Them in Cute Outfits Isn't Enough)

Before Jack was born, I thought taking care of him meant a great nursery, a stylish wardrobe, and passing on a love of bath products in case it wasn't genetic. Turns out, that's not really the most important part (sigh). And picking bath products was a lot easier than dealing with cutting tricky nails (let alone dealing with the one that came off in a soccer game), deciphering good mucus from bad, and knowing how to turn my baby into a toddler who could groom himself.

This chapter offers a few helpful tips to assist you in navigating everything from rough bath waters to cleaning those other 1001 small parts, so see what works for you and your little one.

Bath Time

Look, in the beginning, your baby is pretty much wrapped in clean blankets and sterile onesies from head to toe. With the exception of a spit-up here and a poo there, you're not dealing with a terribly soiled child. So there is simply no need to bathe your child every day. Of course, make sure you are doing spot cleaning along the way when you change his diapers, but until he is down on the floor crawling around, two to three times a week is really all you need to bathe your baby.

And while many pediatricians will tell you to avoid bath products and even baby wipes for the first six weeks, unless you or your husband (or other children) are prone to intense skin allergies, it's probably fine to start bathing your child once his umbilical stump falls off; although you may choose to go the sponge bath route for the first several months for sake of ease. But the point is, it's your choice.

Sponge Baths

Until the umbilical cord has fallen off and the circumcision, if any, has healed, a sponge bath is your method of choice. Make sure you have within arm's reach:

- Two or three washcloths

- Baby liquid soap (preferably the pump)

- A towel

- For circumcised little boys, gauze pads with topical ointment

- A clean diaper

While it may seem second nature to sponge bathe a child, there are a few tricks. Keep these in mind:

- Remove all jewelry before bathing your child, as you could scratch him. Take off any necklaces—as your baby will definitely yank it.

- Choose a room that is warm and not drafty. Ideally, the baby will be at your height on a changing table or a counter, but preferably by a sink. Pad the surface well with a towel.

- Strip your baby down to his diaper (remember, your baby is armed and dangerous down there, so don't leave yourself exposed) and start cleaning the least dirty areas first: the face, neck, and hands. Take a warm wet washcloth and add a little soap and wash these areas. Then rinse the washcloth and wipe the soap off the baby. Don't forget behind the ears!

- Next go for the arms, tummy, and back. Don't forget all of those yummy folds of skin. Make sure you rotate the cloth to clean sections as you go. Once you are done with the upper body, dry and dress your baby's top half before continuing on to the bottom.

- Move on to your baby's feet and legs next.

- When you're ready to clean the baby's genitals and bottom, switch wash cloths and remove the diaper. To make sure your baby stays warm, cover exposed areas that you aren't washing with a towel as you go. On girls, always start at the genitals and work backwards to the bottom, as the bottom is the most dirty, and working the other way around could lead to a urinary tract infection. Make sure you spread the labia and clean with soap and water. If you see a white discharge, this is totally normal. Don't try to scrub it away. For boys, make sure you get in all the crevices, but don't try and retract the foreskin of an uncircumcised penis.

- If your son has been circumcised, carefully dry the penis, dab a little antibiotic ointment on the tip, gently place a piece of gauze over the ointment (no need to wrap it), and then diaper your baby. The ointment helps the penis heal more quickly and make sure the open wound doesn't stick to his diaper. The gauze stays saturated with the ointment while the diaper soaks it up.

- When you're done, wrap your baby up in a nice warm towel. Dress your child and you're good to go.

Bathtub Baths

As soon as that umbilical stump falls off, your baby is ready for a bathtub bath. Most moms won't want to use their regular-size bathtub for a teeny-tiny baby and therefore opt for a baby bathtub. Certain tubs actually fit nicely into a sink, which is a bonus as then they are hip high. I personally found that just using the sink was the easiest way to go. Totally up to you. The most important rule for baths: never leave your child! It takes only a second for an accident to happen. Have everything you need right there, and don't let go of an infant—especially if he is not sitting up on his own yet.

- Always run the bathwater before the baby is in the tub, as sudden temperature changes can occur. Test the water first to check for temperature. Babies typically prefer a bath that is cooler than what adults prefer. Lukewarm is just right for them.

- Fill the tub to only cover part of the baby's body (about up to his belly button), not all of it.

- Place a wet washcloth or towel on the bottom of the sink or tub if there isn't already a skidproof liner. This will help keep your child in place.

- Gradually place the baby in the water, feet first, with a tight hold on her. Water can scare babies, so you want to make sure you have a good grip in case she startles. If she screams uncontrollably, take the baby out, go for a sponge bath, and try again in a few days.

- Wash your baby in the same order as in a sponge bath, starting with face, neck, and hands, and then moving on to the legs and genitals. Rinse.

- Shampooing your baby's hair is necessary only once or twice a week, unless he has cradle cap (see page 167). Save this for the end of the bath to prevent too much heat loss from his wet head. Wet your baby's hair using a gentle spray, a little cup, or simply a wet washcloth. Use just a drop of shampoo or baby soap, and rub to

MM TIP: The first time you give your child a bath in the tub, do it without soap. Babies are slippery enough when wet. Add soap and she may just glide out of your hands. Once you're comfortable, then add a little lather. If you're still having trouble keeping a grip of her, wear a pair of thin cotton gloves when you bathe your baby. You may feel silly, but having a good hold is worth the fashion faux pas (and the gloves can become the washcloth).

create lather. Hold the baby's head and rinse with the spray, cup, or wet cloth.

- Wrap your baby up in a towel.

Best Bath Time

Avoid giving your child a bath right after dinner, as it can upset his tummy and cause him to spit up. As for time of day, it really depends on your baby. A lot of moms insist that the bath soothes their child, and is a great prebed ritual that helps their child wind down. Makes sense, right? Well, my son got so excited over the bath and would splash around so much that he ended up as wound up as a cuckoo clock, so we had to switch his bath to the middle of the afternoon. Test out both times with your child and judge for yourself.

Switching to a Big Tub

As your child gets older and can sit up on his own, bathtub baths will likely be the next step. Try putting your child in a plastic laundry basket inside the tub to ease the transition period and keep your child and his toys contained. Also, as your child gets bigger, you may find that shampooing becomes a constant struggle at bath time. Many children don't want to hold their head up for you to be able to rinse. One trick a friend of mine discovered was to put a funny picture on the ceiling of the bathroom, and when it was rinse time, she simply had her child look up at the picture. You can also try using a spray

> **MM TIP:** Face your child away from bath nozzles and faucets, and, if you can, cover them with a washcloth during baths so that they don't look like fun toys to play with. Always turn the hot water off first when filling the tub so if your child accidentally turns on the water, cold water will come out of the tap first.

nozzle (if it doesn't terrify your child), or you can buy one of those nifty shampoo visors that protect their eyes while still leaving the hair exposed for rinsing (if they'll wear it).

Little Kid Bath Activities

Baths can soon become a fun playtime ritual for your child as he gets older and is more comfortable with the water. Still, never leave the room when your child is in the tub, as this is simply a recipe for disaster. It only takes a few seconds for your child to drown. Okay, so enough of the morbid stuff. Here are a few of fun bath ideas:

- Buy soap crayons for the tub for your child to be able to write on himself or the bathtub walls.

- Get a watering can to use for rinsing shampoo and soap.

- Add colored water tablets to the bath (but avoid the red one, it's a little freaky).

- Use squirt guns in the bathtub.

- Give your child paint brushes and shaving cream to paint on himself.

MM TIP:
If you can't get your child to stop splashing, put only a little bit of water into the tub. Let your child know that more water will not return until he stops splashing.

Sometimes the biggest problem with a little one who loves her bath is getting her out of the tub. Try setting a timer when there is five minutes left in the bath so that your child knows exactly how much time she has. Or allow your child to stay in the tub until the last drop of water drains out, but she must get out as soon as the water is gone. This is something she can see and may help her understand the time limit.

If Your Child Is Terrified of the Bath

As in general with children, don't force the issue. If he is really upset, take him out, try a sponge bath, and try again another day. To build up his tolerance:

Store bath toys in a mesh bag that you can hang in the shower to dry. Run plastic bath toys through the dishwasher on a low heat setting once a month to get rid of soap scum and mildew.

- Keep baths short.

- Don't expose him all at once. Try bathing him with a shirt on so his top remains warm until the last minute.

- Avoid using bubbles. Babies get freaked out sometimes if they can't see what they are sitting in. Clear water may be better.

- Introduce your baby to splashing. Once he learns this fun game, he will likely enjoy his bath.

- Give your child a bath toy to distract him, and save that special toy just for baths.

Caring for Those Other 1001 Small Parts

Okay, so you've accomplished the bath. I hate to say it, but you're only about halfway through with the baby grooming process. They've got all these other little parts that need to be tended to. Kinda makes my beauty ritual look low-key! Here's your primer from head to toe.

Eyes

Use clean, damp cotton balls to clean off your baby's eyes, but only when they appear to need it (dirt or food around the area, or sleepy sands have built up). Use a different cotton ball for each eye, so as not to spread disease from one eye to another, and wipe from the inside out. If you find that your child has an excess buildup of dried tears or yellowish-milky discharge, try dropping a few drops of breast milk in his eye, and then rubbing gently (note: this does not work with formula.) If it still hasn't cleared, contact your pediatrician, who will likely give you a prescription.

Umbilical Stump

Okay, so this was probably one of the things that freaked me out the most. Their umbilical stump is, well, pretty nasty. It's black and crusty, and eventually falls off (gross!). But the good news is, you really don't have to do much to it but stay away from it. Used to be that doctors thought you should clean it off with alcohol on a cotton swab to help it heal faster, but recent studies have proved just the opposite. Here's what you should do:

- Fold your baby's diaper down so that the umbilical stump is exposed to air and not rubbing on the diaper. Certain brands even make diapers with the umbilical part cut out.

- Skip baths and make sure the navel area stays dry when doing sponge baths. If the navel starts to ooze or has a nasty smell, call the doctor. That said, my son's umbilical stump started to ooze and smell, and I called the doctor and he said it was perfectly normal. Sure enough, it fell off the next day and was fine.

Cradle Cap

This is basically like a bad case of dandruff. Many babies have it when they're born, and it usually goes away within a month or so. Here are some ways to speed it along:

- Wash your baby's head with a dandruff shampoo, but be very careful to avoid his eyes.

- Brush his scalp with a soft brush to try to loosen the flakes while you shampoo.

- Rub his scalp with Vaseline or other oil product such as baby oil or even vegetable oil.

Hair

As I said above, avoid using shampoo every day on your child, and follow the washing instructions outlined earlier. Obviously, brush or comb your child's hair as well. But what about that first haircut? Many children are terrified of a stranger coming at them with a pair of scissors—something you've no doubt explained is dangerous. Try a few of these tips to make the first cut not so deeply scary:

- Role play at home. Create a fun at-home version of the barbershop for your child to play with a teddy bear or doll. Make it complete with a towel, comb, brush, and children's safety scissors (which he likely won't be able to use properly anyway). Let him play and get comfortable with the ritual.

- Explain that his hair will grow back, and it doesn't hurt when it is cut. Perhaps even take him with you while you get your hair cut—but avoid taking him on a lengthy highlighting or coloring trip.

- Look for a kid's barber. Many come with fun chairs to sit in and video screens at every station. The people who work there will likely be a lot more patient with your little one's resistance.

- Avoid the shampoo. Having to lean his head back to wash backwards in a sink is not only uncomfortable but terrifying for a little one. Use a few spritzes of water and call it a day.

- Pick a time in which your child is in a good mood, not tired or cranky.

Penis

No, this is not the section where I tell you how to get your sex life going again with your husband (see chapter 2). If you are like me, when I had a little boy, I had *no* idea what to do with his penis to clean it. Sure, I've been around a penis or two in my life, but never was I responsible for one, nor had I been around one so small. Well, it's really quite simple. For a circumcised one, leave it alone until it heals. Short of putting a little antibiotic ointment on it and covering it with gauze, really just let it be until it heals (which is remarkably fast—about ten days—by the way). As for a noncircumcised penis, you may have heard stories about needing to forcibly retract the foreskin (ouch!) and clean under it with cotton swabs and antiseptics. Well, not only is that now deemed unnecessary, but it's even considered harmful. Once the foreskin has separated, you can retract it occasionally and clean under there, but don't stress about it. This is one of the things your pediatrician will have an eye out for and will let you know in plenty of time if there is a problem.

Ears

You've probably heard your grandmother say, "Never put anything smaller than your elbow into your ear." Well, most doctors would agree. While it's fine to clean the outer ears with cotton swabs, cotton balls, or a warm washcloth, never stick a Q-tip into the inner ear canal. You are likely to push the wax back further, thus inhibiting the ear's natural tendency to self-clean and rid itself of earwax. If wax is really building up, ask your doctor to take a look at the next visit.

Nose

Same pretty much goes for noses. Don't try to get things out of the inside of the nose with cotton swabs, rolled up tissue, or your fingernail. Wipe the bottom of the nose if it's running, and if your child has a lot of mucus due to a cold, use a nasal aspirator to remove it. Remember to squeeze the air out of the aspirator, then insert it into the nose and release the pressure on the bulb to suck the mucus out.

Nails

With all that calcium from breast milk and formula, it's amazing how quickly your baby's nails will grow. And all your baby will want to do is rub at his face, which will mean weeks of scratches if you don't trim back. We actually bought these special baby mitts for our son, who each morning looked as if he'd been in a fight with our cat. And while trimming a baby's nails isn't exactly difficult as they are soft and easy to cut, getting a baby to sit still for the procedure is another thing altogether. If your infant is a heavy sleeper, that's the perfect opportunity to trim away. If not, try having your husband or friend help out so that one of you can hold the baby's hand steady while the other one trims.

- Always use special baby-size nail clippers, which have a rounded tip and will make for a more accurate cut.

- Press the finger pad down and out of the way to avoid nipping the skin as you cut.

- Try cutting nails after the bath, when they are softer and easier to cut.

- Always trim toenails square (to avoid ingrown toenails) and fingernails round (to avoid scratches).

Teeth

Your child has a tooth. So cute! What fun! So now you're supposed to brush it? I know, it sounded a little ridiculous to me, too. But here's the thing. Those bottles of milk and eventually that fruit juice that you may decide to give him, coupled with a long nap or night of sleep in which saliva production is slowed, equals potential disaster on those little choppers. And while you may think—I know I did—well, they're going to fall out in a few years anyway, consider this: the teeth they have now hold the place for the teeth they will have permanently, and decay and loss of these teeth early can deform their mouth later on (not to mention cost thousands in braces!). It can also affect speech development along the way. The other reason to start brushing now is that it sets up a habit of good dental hygiene early on. Here's how to do it:

- Wipe your baby's teeth and gums with a clean damp cloth or wet gauze pad, or use a wet finger brush—this is a rubber tip that fits over your finger and has a little bristly end to it.

- Brush after they wake up and right before bed (after the last bottle.) It's also good to do after mealtime, but as long as you do it twice a day, you'll be fine.

- Because children tend to swallow toothpaste rather than spit it out, you should let your child only use about a pea-size drop of toothpaste, whether it's fluoridated or not. Swallowing too much fluoridated toothpaste over time can lead to fluorosis, which causes white spots on their adult teeth.

- Move on to a baby toothbrush as molars come in, and encourage your child to do it himself if he wants to. This will set up a nice ritual that's good for him, too.

- It's a good idea to let your child brush his own teeth as soon as he is able so that he can feel some independence, but recognize that he won't do as good a job as you will. Consider brushing your teeth together and then "checking" for spots you missed on each other and finishing the job.

> **MM TIP:** If your baby screams when you try to first brush his teeth, wait a few days and try again (another reason to start with that first tooth—it may take a few weeks for this ritual to kick in). You could get some resistance, especially if he is cutting another tooth. I always found it best to get him giggling first, and then brush his teeth. He thought it was a game and laughed at the tickly bristles.

> **MM TIP:** Most toddlers won't have the coordination needed to brush their teeth until about the same time they've mastered using a knife and fork.

MM FAVE: First Teeth Baby Toothpaste with Infa-Dent Finger Toothbrush kit. The toothpaste is apple-banana flavor with milk enzymes and is fluoride free and safe to swallow. Made by Laclede, www.laclede.com.

MM TIP: Cavities can actually be spread by bacteria like an infectious disease. Resist the temptation to lick/use a spoon and then share it with your baby.

MM TIP: Many pediatric dentists won't charge for a first visit, especially if it's used to informally introduce your child to the office and equipment in a nonthreatening way. Ask around.

MM TIP: I've said it before: never let your child go to bed with a bottle. The sugars in formula or juice cause enamel erosion, otherwise known as bottle teeth, which can cause the teeth to fall out or need to be pulled prematurely.

Teething

What can I say about teething? It's one of life's great mysteries. For some babies, it's a piece of cake. For other babies, it's utter hell. And, of course, it's tooth by tooth. So if your child isn't screaming about his first tooth (which is usually one of the bottom two center teeth) wait a week or two, because he might be screaming about the next one. All of this fun can begin as early as three months, but for most, it's around seven months. Like all things baby, it's not an exact science. Jack didn't cut his first tooth until five months, while Lilia cut hers at three months. This is one of those hereditary things, so find out when you and your husband cut your first teeth.

There are certain telltale signs that your child may be cutting a tooth. It's good to recognize these signs, because it's very easy to mistake your child's discomfort with him being sick. That said, a lot of these signs are really similar to what you'll experience if your child has a cold or an ear infection. If you're really unsure, you can always check with your doctor.

- Drooling (perhaps coupled with a rash on the chin or face from excessive drool).

- A little cough. Teething causes excessive saliva (hence the drooling), which can cause your baby to cough or even gag.

- Diarrhea. Because diarrhea can also be the sign of something much more serious, be sure and report it to your doctor if there are more than two loose stools.

- A runny nose that is clear instead or yellowish or green.

MM TIP:
If your child gets a rash from drooling during teething, wipe the drool off with a cloth, then smooth Vaseline on her chin before a nap or bedtime to protect the skin from further irritation.

MM TIP:
If your child seems to drool endlessly, a great trick to stop the drooling is to have your child drink primarily out of a straw for three months. The puckering action will strengthen their lip muscles, which will cut down on the drooling significantly.

> **MM TIP:** Teething pain and symptoms can precede the actual appearance of a tooth by as much as two or three months! So just because you can't feel a tooth popping through doesn't mean your child isn't experiencing teething pain.

- Loss of appetite.

- A low-grade fever (under 101°F rectally). Call the doctor if it persists for three days, and treat as you would a normal fever (with baby Tylenol).

- Your baby is cranky and irritable.

- Your baby tugs on his ear or rubs his cheeks a lot. Be careful with the ear pulling, though, as it can be a sign of an ear infection.

- Sticking his hand or any object in his mouth repeatedly, and biting down.

- Waking up from naps and at night when he normally doesn't.

Relieving Teething Pain

Almost every grandmother in the world has a home remedy for teething. Some are great, others I would definitely avoid (like the old bourbon on the gums). Here are some of the more popular ones:

- Cold or frozen teething rings or teething toys

- A frozen washcloth (wet a washcloth, roll it up, and freeze overnight)

- Cold food such as applesauce or yogurt

- Homeopathic teething tablets, sold at most drugstores

- A clean toothbrush

- A firm rubbing of their gums with your clean finger

- Ice water in a bottle

- A frozen seedless bagel

- A frozen banana (although very messy)

- A thick, chilled carrot, but only for the first few teeth, as carrot pieces can choke a baby

MM TIP:
Take your child for his first dentist visit sometime between ages one and three, depending on when his teeth are coming in. The American Association of Pediatrics wants your child's pediatrician to check their teeth at every visit after age six months. If problems were identified, your child would then be referred to a pediatric dentist. If everything looked good, routine dental checkups would start at age three. But the American Dental Association wants kids to be seen by a pediatric dentist as early as six months after the first tooth appears. The answer is some place in the middle, as long as teeth are getting brushed regularly. The important thing is careful preparation for the visit, with age-appropriate books (starting at about age two and a half) and upbeat, positive descriptions of the visit.

I used Hyland's
Homeopathic Teething
Tablets
(www.drugstore.com.) Both
Lilia and Jack loved, them
and they seemed to help.

Babies rarely get *all* of the
teething symptoms at
once. So if it seems a little
too intense to be teething,
chances are it's something
else. Also keep in mind
that teething causes
sporadic pain, not constant
like a cold or an ear
infection.

- Baby Orajel rubbed on the gums

  - *Note:* Although a topical analgesic is basically safe, some pediatricians don't recommend it as if you use too much it can numb the back of the throat and possibly decrease the baby's gag reflex and in rare cases, babies can be allergic. Some also say the numbing sensation may be more uncomfortable.

- If all else fails, try a little infant Tylenol. Check with your doctor for dosage.

That Doesn't Look/Feel/Sound Right!

Okay, so you're probably thinking, *Oh, great. How am I ever going to know if it's teething, or if my baby is really sick from a weird cold or virus?* Well, you have to use your gut. When Jen's son Sam was seven months old, he got a low-grade fever. She didn't want to be "that mom," so she passed it off as teething. Then he got a runny nose and was tugging on his ear. Still, she thought, all reasonable signs of teething. By the third day, he was crankier than she'd ever seen him, so she finally whisked him off to the doctor for a checkup. She was going to feel like an idiot had it simply been teething, but it turned out he had a vicious ear infection and needed antibiotics.

Frankly, I know very few mothers who aren't in constant fear that something is potentially wrong with their child—from birth until, well, does it ever end? And never is that more true than when your baby gets his first cold or earache, or you think he has allergies, or he falls on his head. Or in my case, when I saw my husband fall down a flight of stairs with Jack in his arms. Nothing quite like seeing your nine-month-old with a full leg cast to make you a little protective. (He's fine now. Really.)

So whenever friends ask me if they should call the pediatrician, I always answer with a resounding "yes!" for two reasons: First, I don't really care what my doctor thinks of me. If I'm the most nagging mom in the office, it really doesn't matter. I don't have to hang out with him socially. I just have to make sure my child is okay. That is my primary job. Second: could you ever really forgive yourself if something were terribly wrong and you *didn't* call because you didn't want to bother the doctor? Hello? That's his job.

I'm not suggesting you become a total hypochondriac. Use your head first. Check out my list of what's normal and what's not. Cross-reference with your favorite baby medical books. But never be afraid to call the pediatrician when in doubt.

Here's the thing. Your first medical crisis—small or large—will most likely happen after regular doctor's office hours. So to help you navigate what is an emergency versus what is simply in need of attention when the office opens the next day, I've made two lists for your reference.

Get Help STAT!

Call the doctor—even in the middle of the night—or go to the emergency room if:

- Your baby is under two months and has a fever higher than 100.2 °F.

- Your baby is over two months and has a fever higher than 105 °F.

- Your baby is having a convulsion (stiff body, eyes roll back, arms and legs flail).

- The baby is crying inconsolably, way beyond colic, and winces when touched or moved.

- Your baby is not responsive in any way or has gone limp.

MM TIP:
It's inevitable that his first real sickness will come in the middle of the night or on a weekend. So the best time to ask your doctor about what to do when your child gets his first fever is *before* your child gets his first fever.

MM TIP:
One important thing to find
out perhaps even before
your baby is born (or
shortly thereafter) is the
phone number and the
address of the closest
twenty-four-hour
pharmacy. That way you
won't find yourself hunting
it down one Saturday night
at 3 A.M. while your baby is
screaming.

MM TIP:
Calling the doctor in the
middle of the night can be
traumatic. Any time you
call the doctor, be
prepared by having a pen
and paper, and know your
baby's age, weight,
temperature, symptoms,
and the twenty-four-hour
pharmacy's phone number.

- You see purple spots on his skin anywhere.
- The baby is having trouble breathing.
- Her neck is stiff and she resists having it pulled forward toward her chest.
- Her fever follows exposure to intense heat (a hot day in the sun or being in a hot car).
- Unusual bleeding.
- Heavy vomiting.
- Glassy eyes.
- Your gut tells you something is wrong even if you can't pinpoint it.

Get Help When It's Practical

If you notice the following in your child, seek medical attention as soon as you can, but there's probably no need to rush your child to the hospital or call in the middle of the night. If it's Friday night and the office will be closed all weekend, then you should call the doctor over the weekend in the daylight hours.

- Your baby is between two and six months old and has a fever over 100.4°F but under 105°F.
- Your baby is older than six months and has a temperature over 102.6°F but under 105°F.
- Your baby is showing signs of dehydration (dry diapers, dark yellow urine, very few tears, dry skin or lips)
- The baby seems out of sorts:
  - Overly cranky
  - Excessively sleepy
  - Unable to sleep

- Sensitive to light

- Not eating normally

- Pulling at ears

- A low-grade fever of a few days suddenly spikes.

- A child with a cold of several days suddenly gets a fever (usually a sign of a secondary infection, such as an ear infection).

- The baby has a fever, but it is not brought down by infant Tylenol.

- A fever for more than twenty-four hours with no other signs of illness.

- A low-grade fever for more than three days.

- Diarrhea for more than two movements or constipation for more than five days.

- Yellowish green mucus in a runny nose. (Doctors actually know now that green and yellow mucus is an indication of how much inflammation is present in the nose/nasal passages. It isn't an accurate predictor of whether a bacterial infection is present.)

- Coughing.

- Skin rashes.

Temperatures

The old feeling the forehead method is incredibly unreliable in diagnosing a fever, although it can do a lot to disprove a fever (if it is cold, you are likely fine). That said, the most surefire method to tell if your baby has a fever is using a rectal thermometer (nonmercury.) Lubricate the tip of the thermometer with Vaseline, and with your child on his belly over your lap, spread the buttocks with one hand and gently insert the thermometer with the other about an inch deep. Be careful not to force it. Try and distract your baby by singing a favorite song or

MM TIP:
It's important to know that fevers are actually a *good* response for a child to have, as it shows that their bodies are fighting off an infection. The reason doctors treat fevers is because they can make kids uncomfortable and prevent them from drinking enough and sleeping enough.

MM TIP:
Some mothers and doctors advocate alternating Tylenol with Motrin as a way to reduce fever. Although this works for some, it won't work for all (Tylenol breaks Lilia's fever in a minute; Motrin doesn't for some reason). Also, you should be very careful about dosages, as some medicines are to be given every six hours and others every four. Unless your doctor strongly recommends it, I'd suggest finding the one that works best and sticking with it.

MM TIP:
Infant medicines are more concentrated than children's. So don't try mixing and matching for different ages.

talking in a slow calm voice. Hold the thermometer in until it beeps and then remove.

Ear thermometers are a lot less uncomfortable for your child and fast. But they're trickier to use correctly and you may not get a consistent reading if you don't use it properly. The first few times I used one on my son, I was convinced he was actually a reptile, as his temperature was always about six degrees lower than it should be (he was fine, the thermometer was not). Underarm thermometers tend to be a bit more accurate but take a bit longer. Because of that, some pediatricians will still want you to take your child's temperature with a rectal thermometer before bringing him in. In fact, fevers are the number one reason pediatricians get called. So if they don't sound as alarmed as you feel, you can't really blame them.

If you meet the standards above for calling your doctor, then by all means do. If not, and you just want that fever to break, give these methods a try:

- *Keep her cool.* Bundling your feverish child with blankets and clothes will only overheat her. You should dress her lightly, and if it's summer, leave her in just a diaper.

- *Increase fluids.* I always found this the hardest thing to do, as my son never seemed to want to drink anything when he had a fever. For younger babies, increase breast milk or formula feedings. When my son was a bit older, I would put a little apple juice in his water to make it a treat (since he wasn't used to getting juice), and it helped a bit.

- *Give fever-reducing medicine.* Always check with your doctor first on whether to give and the dosage. If your baby is suffering from heatstroke, you do not want to give acetaminophen or aspirin, so it is very important to check first.

MM TIP: A regular teaspoon rarely equals a measured teaspoon, so always use an oral, medical syringe to measure amounts for administering medicine. You can also find great pacifiers which are designed to administer medicine.

Ear Infections

It seems as if some children are simply prone to ear infections and get one a month, while others can go their entire childhood without experiencing one. They are typically more common in the winter, but some children get them year-round. And if your child gets a few of them, he is more likely to continue getting them. Jack had about ten before he turned two. Lilia has had one to date (although having written that, inevitably she'll get one tonight).

The bad news is that young children are particularly likely to get ear infections because their eustachian tubes (ear canals) are horizontal and short (about a half inch). The good news is that as they grow, the tube typically becomes more vertical and triples in length, so fluid drains more easily. As such, most children will outgrow even frequent ear infections by about the age of three.

The symptoms can, but don't always, include:

- Ear pain, if your child can vocalize it, or tugging at the ear if your child is too young to speak

- Pain when sucking or drinking, or when lying down

- Fever ranging from moderate to high

- Runny nose and congestion

- Nausea

- Loss of appetite

Of course, to make matters even more confusing, sometimes children can have an ear infection with no symptoms at all. The only way to know for sure is to have your doctor check your child's ears. If there is an ear infection, he will see that the middle ear is inflamed and bright red. At this point, your options are to either wait it out or to give antibiotics or possibly eardrops. Your doctor will help you make this decision. You can also try local, dry heat to the ear, such as warm water in a hot water bottle.

MM TIP:
If your baby or toddler is prone to ear infections, don't let him drink from a bottle lying down. This may cause more fluid in his ears. Also, consider getting rid of the pacifier. A Finnish study showed that 25 percent of all ear infections in kids under the age of three were associated with pacifier use.

MM TIP:
If your child has recurring ear infections, your doctor may suggest tubes in her ears or removing the adenoids to reduce the problem. There are, of course, risks to any medical procedure, so be sure to consult your doctor.

Sore Throat

These are tough to recognize in a baby, as they typically can't vocalize what pain they are feeling, but older kids will come out and tell you. To find it with a baby, look for the other symptoms:

- Moderate fever (101 to 103°F)

- Fatigue

- Difficulty or unwillingness to swallow

- Fussiness and irritability

- Throat appears red and tonsils are enlarged

The cause of a sore throat can range from a variety of viruses to allergies to smoke in the air. Here are some things you can do to ease the pain:

- Check with your doctor about giving acetaminophen.

- Give your child cold, nonacidic food like Jell-O. Avoid milk products, which cause phlegm.

- Let your child suck on a Popsicle, or make more nutritious popsicles of your own with apple juice.

- Pour fruit juice over shaved ice for your child to eat.

Congestion

This is pretty much the easiest thing to diagnose in your child. You will notice that his voice (or babbles) take on a different tone, you may hear him breathing more heavily, and will likely see a lot of unpleasant activity around his nose (read: yellow and green boogers! Yuck!) Here are a few tips to relieve it:

- Add a humidifier to your child's room.

- Take your child into a bathroom with you, close the door, and run the shower on the highest temperature possible to steam the room for a good fifteen minutes. Make sure there is no danger of the hot water splashing on your baby. Change your child into dry clothes when you get out of the bathroom.

- Clear your baby's nose using a nasal aspirator.

- Elevate your baby's head in the crib by putting a few books under the head end of the mattress.

- Spray saline drops into your child's nose about fifteen minutes before feedings to help clear the passageway.

- Increase the fluids your child drinks.

- Check with your doctor about using a decongestant or medicated nose drops.

MM TIP:
Breast-feeding mothers can also try a few drops of breast milk in the nostrils to help loosen things up: the breast milk itself helps fight infections and the warmth is an added bonus.

MM TIP:
The side effect to a runny nose is the weeks of chafing and chapping around the nose area. Unscented baby wipes or a soft burp cloth are much softer on your baby's nose than tissue. Also, use petroleum jelly around the nose area to seal in the moisture.

Diarrhea

The good news if you're breast-feeding is that diarrhea is very uncommon in babies who are drinking breast milk, as there seem to be certain substances in breast milk that destroy the microorganisms that cause diarrhea. But unless you are planning to breast-feed for life, you will likely have to deal with this sooner or later.

There are many reasons a child can get diarrhea, ranging from a virus (typically rotavirus), bacteria, parasites, teething, reaction to certain food, too much fruit or juice, or a reaction to antibiotics. You will know right away if your child is having diarrhea from an increase in frequency and amount, with perhaps the lovely addition of mucus or blood in the stool. As if changing a diaper weren't fun enough on its own.

- Make sure your child gets plenty of liquids (at least two ounces an hour).

- Continue feeding your baby, preferably bland, starchy foods (mashed potatoes, banana, rice, pasta, rice cereal, or dry white toast).

- Limit dairy products.

- Change your baby's diaper often, and apply a thick layer of barrier cream when you do change her to avoid diaper rash.

- Check with your doctor before giving antidiarrhea medicine, as some can be very dangerous for babies.

- In severe cases, a baby may need to be hospitalized to regain bodily fluids, so make sure you check with your doctor if your baby has diarrhea.

- For toddlers, for the first day, make water the main fluid. Don't give fruit juices, as they make diarrhea worse. Starchy foods such as bread, rice, crackers, carrots, bananas, and applesauce are good options. Also, saltines or pretzels are good, as they have sodium (which will help them retain fluids). On the second day, if he won't eat any solids, try some milk. Also consider Pedialyte juice or pops.

Cuts

MM TIP:
If a small cut does not stop bleeding after ten minutes with some direct pressure, you may be dealing with a more serious cut, so call a doctor.

MM TIP:
If the cut is on your child's face, and will likely leave a scar, call your doctor and see if they can refer a plastic surgeon, as it may be worth having a stitch or two.

If your child somehow cuts himself seriously, plan on taking him immediately to the doctor. In the meantime, apply direct pressure to the wound with a diaper, burp cloth, maxi-pad—basically, anything that is absorbent. Also, try to keep the wound elevated above his heart. For all other minor cuts, follow these guidelines:

- Wash your hands first.

- Wash the cut area with soap and water. Make sure you run the cut under running water to flush out any dirt.

- Encourage your child not to stick the wound (such as a cut finger) in his mouth, as this can transmit germs to the wound.

- Apply an antiseptic solution or antibacterial ointment to the cut.

- Put on a nonstick bandage.

MM TIP: If skin has been broken, then exposure to tetanus is a possibility. So always check to be sure his tetanus immunizations are up to date and watch for any swelling, reddening, or oozing, which could indicate an infection.

MM TIP:
Have a red washcloth in the house to use in case of cuts. Blood on a white washcloth will likely freak your child out at an already scary time.

Blisters

Blisters are a bummer, but you should gently bandage them with a Band-Aid, but with no ointment. Once it breaks (and *don't* break it yourself), treat it as you would a cut.

Burns

There are all types of burns, from sunburn to chemical burns to electrical burns to burns from a hot flame. Let's just hope the worst you ever have to deal with is a sunburn. Here are some basic rules of thumb for various burns.

Minor Burns from Heat

If it involves a limb, immerse the burn in cool water, and if possible, cool running water. If the part is not immersable (such as the face), then use a cool compress between 50 and 60 °F for about half an hour. Keep an aloe plant on hand to soothe the burn. Do not use butter, toothpaste, egg white, or any other old wives' tale substance on a burn, as it could cause infection.

Major Burns from Heat

First, call 911 and get them on their way. Then, gently remove any clothing from the area where the burn took place, making sure that it doesn't stick to the wound (if it does, leave it alone; you could do more harm than good). Get a cool, wet compress and apply it to the burn area (if, God forbid, your child is burned all over, apply the compress to only 25 percent of the body at once). Do not apply pressure to the burns. Also, don't use ointments, butters, or oils. If your child is conscious and his mouth isn't burned, give him water or other liquid.

Chemical Burns

If a baby gets into a caustic substance, such as lye or acid, she could suffer either a topical skin burn, or perhaps even an inhalation burn. Call 911 or the Poison Control Center (800-222-1222) immediately. If there is any dry chemical matter on your baby, carefully brush it away from her skin and remove clothing that has the substance on it. Rinse the skin with lots and lots of water. If your child is having trouble breathing (meaning they've inhaled the fumes), get immediate medical attention. Also, bring the container with you to the phone; it helps the Poison Control Center if you can read ingredients off the label.

If your baby swallows something you think is poisonous, try to get him to spit out any in his mouth. Call 911 and be sure to keep the container to identify what the ingredients are. Do not make your child vomit as this could injure your child if the substance is a strong acid or strong alkali, as it would burn being brought back up. Also call the American Association of Poison Control Centers at 800-222-1222 to be automatically redirected to your local Poison Control Center.

Electrical Burns

Your first instinct is going to be to grab your child away from whatever electrical device is shocking him—which is sadly the worst thing you can possibly do. If you have time to disconnect the power, go for it—but that usually will take more time to access than you have. Instead, grab a nonconducting object like a wooden broom handle, a large book, a cushion, or even a chair, and try to separate the source of the electricity from your child. Just *don't* use your bare hands or you could both become victims. If your baby is not breathing, start CPR immediately and have someone call 911. Electrical burns must be evaluated by a doctor, so head to the ER, ASAP.

MM TIP:
Because of the seriousness of CPR, I am not going to give instructions on how to perform. However, I strongly recommend that you and anyone who is regularly with your child, take an infant CPR class. You can find a local site by visiting the Red Cross website at http://www.redcross.org or you can ask your pediatrician for classes in your area.

Sunburn

If your child gets a sunburn, apply cool wet compresses to the various sights of the burn for fifteen-minute increments, several times a day. You want the compresses wet to add moisture back into the skin. In between compresses, apply aloe vera gel to help cool the site of the burn. Avoid putting Vaseline on a burn, as it seals out air, which a burn needs to heal.

Bumps and Bruises

These are inevitable. And if your kids are as active as mine, you'll wonder why social services hasn't come banging on your door to investigate all of the bruises. The best remedy is some sort of cold compress like an ice pack wrapped in a towel. I found a cute little stuffed bunny that holds a plastic ice cube that you keep in the freezer called a boo-boo bunny, which may make the fear of an ice pack a little easier. If the bruise is a head injury or appears out of nowhere, call your doctor.

Some simple rules are:

- Anyone under the age of six months should be seen right away.

- Anyone, at any age, who had any loss of consciousness should be seen right away.

- Anyone with major bleeding or any open/split skin should be seen right away.

- Anyone who's vomited three or more times should be seen right away.

- Anyone with swelling greater than the size of a fifty-cent piece should be seen right away.

You can always discuss specifics with your doctor.

MM TIP:
A good rule of thumb is that head injuries are typically more serious if the child has fallen from a height equal to or greater than his own height onto a hard surface. Side blows are more serious than a blow to the front or the back of the head.

MM TIP:
Just as in labor recovery, a bag of peas makes a great ice pack, as it can mold to pretty much any shape.

Nosebleeds

Contrary to popular belief, you should not have your child tilt his head back when he has a nosebleed. This could cause him to swallow blood, which could then cause him to throw up. Instead, have your child lean his head forward (place a towel on him if he's wearing something you want to protect). Do not stick anything up his nose, but do pinch the soft part for about ten minutes to try and stop the bleeding. If the bleeding doesn't stop after ten minutes, call a doctor.

Bee Stings

MM TIP:
Benadryl now comes in (relatively) good-tasting chewable tablets. Sometimes these are a lot easier for children to swallow.

Nothing will make your child hate the outdoors more than a bee sting. There are approximately one million bee stings each year in the United States but only 1 percent of people who are stung will have a generalized reaction (slightly red and a bit itchy). Should your child get stung, don't try to squeeze the stinger out. Instead, take a credit card and scrape it along the stinger to coax it out. Apply ice to help the pain. You should watch for any difficulty breathing, or any tingling or swelling of the lips or mouth. If these are seen, give a dose of Benadryl and call the doctor immediately. Benadryl won't prevent the local swelling that occurs with insect bites and bee stings, but it will help with itching and can be lifesaving in the case of a severe allergic reaction.

Splinters

If your child gets a splinter, there are a few things to try. If it's on the surface, try using a piece of Scotch tape to painlessly remove it. Another is as with a bee sting to scrape a credit card across it (who knew a VISA was so versatile?). If that fails, soak the splinter in warm water to try to bring it to the surface and soften the skin around it. Some splinters will work themselves out and can be left on their own. Watch for redness, swelling, yellow pus, or tenderness at the site.

Hiccups

Hiccups are common and normal in infants and usually bother the parents more than the baby. You can try just having babies take a sip of water. The exception is that babies really don't like hiccups when they're trying to eat: if your baby hiccups when eating, try feeding him when he's less hungry or more calm and take breaks to let him rest and get burped.

Hiccups in older kids can be really uncomfortable, however, and you can try these methods to alleviate them:

- Have them lie down.

- Pull on their tongue with your fingers.

- Have them try to drink from the "wrong side" of a cup.

- Have them quickly swallow a teaspoon of dry granulated sugar.

Vaccinations

Hopefully, aside from the above maladies, the only reason you'll have to visit the pediatrician is for your kids' monthly and eventually annual checkups (okay, so I'm an optimist). These days, your kids can pretty much get vaccinated for everything. Remember that awful itching of chickenpox? Our kids probably won't have to experience that. Many diseases our parents suffered through are now a shot away from being obsolete.

Of course, with every bit of prevention comes a heck of a lot of controversy. And, ironically, vaccinations aren't immune. The most recent controversy has to do with claims that traditional childhood vaccinations can cause autism. In the late 1990s, some parents started blaming thimerosal (a mercury-based preservative used to prevent contamination from fungi and bacteria in countless vaccines) and the triple vaccine (against measles, mumps, and rubella, otherwise known as MMR) for causing autism in their children. The media hype, coupled with activists' urging, convinced pharmaceutical companies, federal public health agencies, and the American Academy of Pediatrics to agree to reduce or eliminate thimerosal from vaccines as a precautionary measure.

But studies have shown that the small doses of vaccines are not toxic enough to do any damage, and there are very few studies that prove a solid case *against* vaccinating children. On the contrary, there is an overwhelming amount of literature from many reputable medical organizations that indicate that childhood vaccinations are *not* associated with autism, and most experts urge parents not to forgo vaccines in trying to protect their kids. All this said, definitely consult your doctor about the risks and benefits of vaccinations so you can then make an informed choice for your child. Some good questions to ask include:

- What is the risk or probability of my child getting the disease?

- What are the health consequences if my child doesn't have the vaccination and contracts the infection?

- Is the immunity provided in the vaccine solid and long lasting?

- Are there any alternatives to immunization, and if so, are they safe and effective?

A famous study exonerating the MMR vaccine comes from Denmark, where investigators looked at the health records of every child born from 1991 through 1998, which equaled more than 537,000 children. There was no difference in the autism rates of children who received the MMR vaccine and those who did not.

It is not against the law to not vaccinate your child, but rules and regulations vary from state to state, and in certain states, restrictions might be placed on families whose children are not vaccinated—for instance, children may not be able to enroll in school until they are vaccinated. You can contact your local state health department to find out the guidelines (www.immunize.com). Should you decide to vaccinate your baby—which I certainly did and strongly suggest you do, too—here is what the normal vaccines will be as well as a "typical" schedule would look like, as many pediatric offices will schedule immunizations slightly differently, and schedules often change as current recommendations change.

What the Heck Are All These Shots For?

Hepatitis B

Protects against hepatitis B, a viral illness that can damage the liver and sometimes lead to cancer. It can be passed from a mother to her baby at birth, or it can be spread via sexual intercourse or via infected blood. Side effects of the vaccine include fussiness and soreness/redness/swelling at the injection site. Hepatitis A is a viral infection that causes fever, fatigue, nausea, and loss of appetite (ask your doctor if vaccination is recommended in your part of the country).

Hib

Protects against *Haemophilus influenzae* type B, a bacteria that can cause meningitis (an infection of the tissues surrounding the brain), epiglottitis (an infection in the throat that interferes with breathing), or pneumonia. Side effects include soreness at the injection site and a low-grade fever.

Chickenpox

Protects against chickenpox, a viral illness that can cause severe infections in certain children, including babies under the age of one, adolescents, children with weakened immune systems, or children with asthma or eczema.

MMR

Protects against three diseases: measles, mumps, and rubella. Measles is a viral illness that causes respiratory problems including pneumonia and sometimes encephalitis. Mumps is a viral illness that causes swelling of salivary glands and can rarely cause dangerous cases of meningitis (an infection of the tissues surrounding the brain) or encephalitis (an infection of the brain itself). Rubella is a viral illness that causes rash and fever in most children but that is most dangerous to pregnant women and their unborn babies. Basically, you really don't want your baby getting any of these. Side effects of the vaccine begin to show up seven days following the injection and include a low-grade fever, a mild rash, and swollen lymph nodes.

IPV

The inactive polio vaccine protects against polio, a viral disease that paralyzes muscles. Side effects include soreness at the injection site.

DPT

The DPT vaccine protects against three illnesses: diphtheria, pertussis, and tetanus. Diphtheria is a bacterial illness that affects the throat; one out of every ten people who become infected will die from it. Also known as whooping cough, pertussis is a dangerous respiratory infection: one out of every 100 babies under the age of two months who gets it dies from it. Tetanus is a dangerous illness caused by a bacterial toxin that causes muscles to have severe spasms; two out of ten people who get tetanus will die from it. Side effects include a low-grade fever (less than 102°F), redness at the injection site, and irritability. None of these should last more than forty-eight hours.

PCV$_7$

The PCV$_7$, or Prevnar, vaccine protects children against the bacterium *Streptococcus pneumoniae*, which can cause meningitis, pneumonia, and ear infections. It is the leading cause of bacterial meningitis in the United States, and the invasive form of this disease is responsible for about 200 deaths each year among children under five years old. Side effects of the vaccine may include redness and soreness at the injection site, a fever that sometimes rises to 102°F, and fussiness.

TB

The TB test is a skin test that detects a tuberculosis infection. Tuberculosis is a bacterial disease that most commonly causes pneumonia, but can also cause infections of the spine and brain. Because the disease is spread easily between people sending time together in close quarters, most children will need this test before they begin school. In states where infection rates are higher, your child might be tested as early as age one.

Vaccinations Month by Month

Birth
- Hepatitis B

One Month
- Hepatitis B

Two Months
- DPT
- IPV
- Hib
- PCV7 (pneumoccocal conjugate vaccine)

Four Months
- DPT
- IPV
- Hib
- PCV7

Six Months
- DPT
- Hib
- PCV7

Nine Months
- Hepatitis B

Twelve Months
- MMR
- TB
- Chickenpox (optional but recommended)

Fifteen Months
- Hib

Eighteen Months
- DPT
- IPV

Twenty-four Months
- TB
- Hepatitis A (optional but recommended in certain parts of the country)

Preparing Your Child for Shots

The good news is that Lilia has been sick so rarely that the only time she goes to the doctor is for her shots. The bad news is, she now knows she's getting a shot and screams from the moment we enter the waiting room until we leave. Here are a few strategies to help kids deal with shots:

- An appropriate dose of infant Tylenol can be given prior to the visit to help alleviate side effects or pain.

- Age-appropriate story and picture books can be used well in advance of visits, and discussions about parents receiving their vaccinations can be held in a positive way (i.e., "I remember going with your grandmother to get *my* shots before kindergarten. I was so proud that day! I wonder if we should do something special that day, after all, you're getting *so* big and strong and your shots are going to help make you stronger!").

- Local anesthetics such as EMLA cream have been used to successfully reduce the pain of needle insertions and injections. However, their use has not yet been studied in the context of immunization efficacy, and their use prior to vaccinations should therefore be postponed.

- If all else fails, I'm a big one for bringing a treat with me or a new toy as a great distraction for after the shot. I know, don't reward with a treat, but come on, this can be an exception.

Many Mini-Milestones

Clearly, your pediatrician will also be looking for a lot of advancements in your child's development during all of these visits. To help you keep track on your own and mark the progress of your child—for things the doctor will be looking for and beyond—I'll be walking you through the many mini-milestones in your baby's life. Now, let me just preface this with the comment that this is the part of the book that will absolutely cause you the most anxiety and tension. I know this because while writing this, I was hyperventilating at the fact that neither Jack nor Lilia hit any of these milestones when "most children did." Some they hit earlier, a lot they hit later. That is perfectly normal.

Here's the thing: all children develop differently, and it doesn't mean that your child is bound to be a high school dropout while your neighbor's will be a Rhodes Scholar because he could hold a fork sooner. This is simply a guide to keep in mind and help you monitor what you may need to work on, or for what you can pat yourself on the back. (After all, as moms we typically take full credit for stuff like our kids walking and waving, right? I mean really, we gave birth to them, so we get credit, right?) And honestly, with a lot of this stuff, there is nothing you can really do to hurry your child along. You must wait and let them hit their milestones when they are ready. Dang.

What to Expect Developmentally and When

Should be able to:

- Visually track objects in front of her

- Begin to lift head when lying on her stomach

- Respond to loud noises and startle

Might be able to:

- Turn head from side to side

- Smile

Should be able to:

- Smile as a response to your smile

- Respond to noises by startling or crying

Might be able to:

- Follow objects with eyes

- Lift head with more control or even be able to hold it upright

- Make cooing noises or vocalize in some way

- Raise chest when on her belly, supported by her arms like a push-up

Should be able to:

- Lift head easily

- Follow an object 180 degrees from side to side

Might be able to:

- Laugh
- Bring both hands together
- Grasp an object like a rattle
- Roll over, first from belly to back, then the other way around
- Coo and squeal and notice she can make that sound
- Turn in the direction of a familiar voice
- Make razzes with her mouth

Four Months

Should be able to:

- Lift her head ninety degrees when on her stomach
- Laugh
- Smile spontaneously and smile back at you when you smile

Might be able to:

- Hold her head steady when upright
- Reach for an object
- Bear some weight on her legs when held upright

Five Months

Should be able to:

- Hold her head steady when upright
- Support her chest upright when on stomach with her arms pushed up like a push-up
- Reach for an object
- Squeal in delight
- Turn over, first from belly to back and then from back to belly

Might be able to:

- Grab objects and bring them to her mouth
- Sit without you supporting her
- Bear some weight on her legs when held upright
- Object if you take something away that she wants
- Go after a toy out of reach
- Babble

Six Months

Should be able to:

- Keep her head level with her body when you pull her from lying to sitting position
- Say vowel–consonant combinations like "ah-goo"
- Sit up unassisted
- Bear some weight on her legs when held upright

Might be able to:

- Stand holding on to something or someone
- Work to get a toy that's out of reach
- Feed finger food to herself

Seven Months

Should be able to:

- Coo or babble in reaction to something good
- Smile a lot when interacting with happy things
- Finger-feed herself

Might be able to:

- Creep (sort of like an inch worm), a precursor to crawling
- Start to respond to games like peek-a-boo
- Pass an object from one hand to another

Eight Months

Should be able to:

- Turn in the direction of a voice
- Look for a dropped object

Might be able to:

- Crawl
- Make more sounds
- Pull up to a stand when holding on to large objects
- Have a new fear of strangers
- Say "mama" or "dada" indiscriminately

Nine Months

Should be able to:

- Pull up to a standing position from a sitting position

Might be able to:

- Cruise (walking while holding on to objects)
- Go from lying down to sitting up and from sitting up to standing up while holding on
- Clap hands and wave bye
- Understand "no," but not necessarily obey it
- Stand alone

Ten Months

Should be able to:

- Stand holding on to someone or something
- Say "mama" or "dada" indiscriminately
- Object if you take a toy away that she wants
- Cruise

MM TIP:
Many mothers rush out and buy their child shoes with thick soles and lots of ankle support at this point, feeling as though they need this in order to walk. And although that used to be popular belief, pediatricians today urge you to keep you children barefoot (or if it's cold, in soft-soled moccasins or socks with rubber bottoms) so that their feet and ankles develop the strength to hold your child on his own.

Might be able to:

- Hold her own bottle
- Point to something she wants
- Roll a ball back to you
- Pick up objects with thumb and forefinger

Eleven Months

Should be able to:

- Sit from a lying down position
- Understand "no," but not necessarily obey it
- Pick up objects with thumb and forefinger

Might be able to:

- Stand alone for short periods of time
- Say "mama" and "dada," and actually know who is whom
- Expand her vocabulary to one word beyond "mama" and "dada"
- Go up stairs on all fours and come down on belly

Twelve Months

Should be able to:

- Walk while holding on to bigger objects
- Use gestures to get what she wants

Might be able to:

- Walk alone
- Drink from a cup
- Have complete conversations in her own baby language
- Respond to commands without gestures
- Take things like large Legos apart

Thirteen Months

Should be able to:

- Pull up to standing from sitting
- Easily get into a sitting position
- Clap hands
- Make her needs known in some way other than crying

Might be able to:

- Place an object inside a container
- Stand by herself
- Imitate activities and words
- Put objects into proper places like large puzzles, although typically not in the right places

Fourteen Months

Should be able to:

- Wave bye-bye
- Stand by herself
- Respond to commands without gestures
- Call Mama and Dada by the correct names

Might be able to:

- Bend over and pick up objects and place them inside another object, such as a bucket
- Pull herself up steps

Fifteen Months

Should be able to:

- Walk by herself

Might be able to:

- Follow basic commands
- Name a few items
- Drink from a cup
- Understand the meaning of "no"
- Scribble
- Point at an object she wants

Sixteen Months

Should be able to:

- Scribble
- Imitate activities

Might be able to:

- Use two words together

Seventeen Months

Should be able to:

- Use two words together
- Drink from a cup unassisted

Might be able to:

- Walk up steps
- Build with blocks or cubes
- Remove a piece of clothing
- Throw a ball

Eighteen Months

Should be able to:

- Use three or more words at a time, but not make full sentences (which is really around twenty-three to twenty-four months)

- Point at what she wants

Might be able to:

- Run

- Use fingers and hands more proficiently

- Recognize wet and dirty diapers

- Use a spoon on occasion

- Point to a body part when asked

Nineteen Months

Should be able to:

- Run

- Use fingers and hands more proficiently

- Recognize wet and dirty diapers

- Use a spoon on occasion

- Point to a body part when asked

Might be able to:

- Walk up steps

- Identify pictures by pointing

- Name body parts

Twenty Months

Should be able to:

- Combine words

- Dump an object by imitation

Might be able to:

- Speak and be understood about 50 percent of the time
- Use fifty or more single words
- Pretend play

Twenty-one Months

Should be able to:

- Use a spoon by herself more frequently
- Run with confidence
- Build a tower of two cubes or blocks

Might be able to:

- Kick a ball
- Brush teeth with help

Twenty-two Months

Should be able to:

- Go up and down steps walking
- Use six words together

Might be able to:

- Build a tower with four cubes
- Follow a two-step command without any gestures such as, "Go to your room and get your shirt, please"
- Wash and dry hands

Twenty-three Months

Should be able to:

- Kick a ball

Might be able to:
- Combine words to make a sentence
- Put on a "simple" article of clothing

Twenty-four Months

Should be able to:
- Climb
- Understand the word "no"
- Take off an item of clothing
- Handle a spoon and a cup well
- Sit still (temporarily) to listen to a story with pictures
- Actually interact with children while playing, rather just play side by side

Might be able to:
- Throw a ball overhead
- Identify an item in a picture by naming it
- Jump

Twenty-five to Twenty-seven Months

Should be able to:
- Use fifty or more words
- Combine words to make a sentence
- Follow a two-step command without gestures, such as, "Go to your room and get your shirt please"

Might be able to:
- Use prepositions such as at, by or with
- Have a conversation with two or three sentences at a time

Twenty-eight to Thirty Months

Should be able to:

- Dress herself with one item of clothing
- Jump
- Name at least six body parts
- Identify pictures by pointing

Might be able to:

- Identify several pictures by naming
- Draw a line if one has been drawn to copy
- Balance on a foot for a short period of time
- Identify a person other than Mommy or Daddy by name

Thirty-one to Thirty-three Months

Should be able to:

- Brush her teeth assisted
- Build with six blocks

Might be able to:

- Identify colors
- Count to one

Thirty-four to Thirty-six Months

Should be able to:

- Wash and dry her hands by herself
- Identify a friend by name
- Throw a ball overhead
- Speak and be understood most of the time
- Use prepositions

Might be able to:

- Use two adjectives
- Put on a T-shirt
- Explain the use of two objects
- Draw a circle if one is drawn for her to copy
- Make a bowl of cereal
- Dress without help

Okay, so don't go nuts with this list, since, as you can see, there is a huge range from when a child *may* be doing something to when they *should* be doing something. And even the shoulds will likely come later in some cases. This is more of a general guide. If at any time you are concerned about your child's progress, consult with your pediatrician or a child development specialist—and chances are, they will let you know your child is perfectly fine!

CHAPTER 7

Teach Your Children Well . . . Or Else
It's Hell

At this point, you may think the hard part is over. After all, you've survived getting your child to sleep through the night (for the most part), and you're likely on a roll with the food stuff, too. She's probably walking or about to start. I mean really, she barely comes up to your knees, so how hard could this be? But when your toddler is in the middle of Tom's Toys throwing a tantrum, yelling and screaming on the floor over a Wiggles figurine that only five minutes before she had no idea even existed—and every eyeball in the joint is on you—you may realize that the hard times have only just begun.

But perhaps the trickiest part of dealing with a toddler is learning how to speak to him and, more important, understand what he is trying to say (which can range in anything from a grunt to a scream to a giggle to a whine to a few words strung together to complete sentences). And just when you think you've mastered what they're all about, they grow and change completely. One childhood development expert explained to me that comparing a one-year-old and a two-year-old is like comparing peanut butter and asparagus. The two simply have nothing in common. So before I can let you in on *how* to communicate with your child, it's important that I first introduce you to *who* your child is likely to be at various ages.

Hi, My Name Is Mommy, and You Are . . . ?

With all things children, you may find that your child is slightly ahead or behind on this curve in terms of his or her developmental stage (and don't panic, "behind" here has nothing to do with whether he'll become the valedictorian eighteen years from now). But for the general population, these descriptors will ring true.

Birth to Fifteen Months

For the most part, babies are still infants until about six months of age, and then there is a period from about six months to fifteen months when your child is no longer an infant, but not quite a toddler. And while children are born with a very specific temperament and begin to exhibit signs of that personality after only two months, it isn't really until this stage that they exhibit signs of becoming a person. They will accomplish many things by fifteen months: sleeping through the night, sitting up, crawling, walking, learn to use their hands to pick things up, utter a few words, and so on. But very few are able to actually comprehend behavioral modifications prior to this point. Now this isn't to say that you can simply ignore bad behavior or not expect good behavior. Quite the contrary. Babies are constantly imprinting from the moment they start breathing. They won't necessarily remember, but everything you do from day one starts to put together the very important pieces of your child's behavioral foundation. Around nine months to a year, they start to be aware of what is going on and need limits. They are trying to experiment and their boundaries are expanding. It is our job to be the one most in control (which is ironic, as you're probably feeling quite out of control).

Fifteen to Twenty-one Months

Children may begin to exhibit signs of being a toddler when they start walking, or trying to do things for themselves, but for most children, full toddlerdom doesn't kick in until about halfway through their first year. The typical fifteen to twenty-one-month-old:

- Stumbles his way through the world as if he was thinking with his feet.

- Typically does just the opposite of what an adult would find logical.

- Has trouble with the fact that he can't do what he wants: he falls when he wants to be standing, he can't grab objects that he wants to hang tight to. His motor skills are there at times and simply aren't at other times.

- Doesn't have the language skills to express what he's feeling, even though the feelings exist in his mind.

- Is frustrated by his lack of skills and frustrated by his parents' inability to understand him. Life is a challenge.

Twenty-two to Twenty-seven Months

Around the time a child turns two, life gets a bit better for her (and subsequently better for you). Her motor skills have improved, and therefore she is much more sure of herself. She is also calmer emotionally. Here is what to expect:

- She can walk, run, and climb with greater skill and assurance.

- Language skills have improved, so she can express herself better and people can understand her.

- Her needs appear to be bit lessened, because she can express herself by either saying a few words or pointing to things. It makes the intensity of her desires seem less because it simply isn't so frustrating for her to get what she wants. So, often, a two-year-old seems happier than an eighteen-month-old.

- A two-year-old can be emotionally more chilled out, and therefore her mood swings are fewer. Anger and disappointment are there but aren't as strongly felt.

- Most two-year-olds are loving little people to be around.

Twenty-eight to Thirty-six Months

Just when you got used to your lovely little two-year-old, get ready for the next stage. It isn't until about two-and-a-half that the "terrible twos" really kick in. I guess it just sounded better than the terrible-two-and-a-halves. This age is distinguished by incredible extremes. Children at this age go from zero to sixty in a second flat. Some things you will notice in a two-and-a-half year-old:

- Exploration mode kicks back in. This helps him become aware of the choices available to him.

- Routine is very important. He will be incredibly thrown off if things are altered in any way. This can be something as simple as Daddy coming home through a different door than the one from which he left.

- You will be amazed at the elaborate rituals your little one creates for himself such as kissing ten dolls in the exact same order, every night.

- Timing becomes important. This is not literal clock time, but event timing. If he always has lunch when he gets home from play group, but play group gets out early, chances are your two-and-a-half-year-old will still want lunch right then.

- He will bounce back and forth between choices. As soon as he's made up his mind, he is likely to choose the other alternative. Sounds like me at a sample sale, so how can I be mad at him?

- Exaggerated habits kick in. Thumb sucking increases. Sometimes stuttering can start (the brain is working faster than the mouth). All the more reason to try and modify behaviors as they come up.

- "No," "I," "Me," and "Mine" become favorite words.

It's incredibly important to realize that while not all children will go through the exact timing, or the extremes of the behavior above, it is pretty standard. And these behavior swings from easier to harder and back again will go on for much of childhood, usually in about six-month cycles.

MM TIP:
Dealing with a two-and-a-half-year-old can be *very* trying on your nerves, with the mood swings, the temper tantrums, and the impossibility of deciphering what they actually want. It is highly recommended that you don't take it all on yourself. Get an aunt or a grandmother or a friend or even a neighborhood kid (as a mother's helper) to come twice a week, or put your child in a nursery school for a few hours. (And here you thought nursery school was only for the child.)

Communicating with Your Child

Okay, great, so I have the kid nicely psychoanalyzed in a month-by-month guide, pointing out that basically, you're in for a few years of stress and confusion. But how do you actually *deal* with your child?

Well, there are many theories on the best way to react and talk to your child. Some methods are more radical, while others are a bit more laid back. My personal beliefs fall somewhere in between. And while I get into detail about the various child development philosophies at the end of this chapter (and I encourage you to explore these on your own), the following are some basic tenets as to how you might want to approach your little one from birth.

MM TIP:
Narrate and explain things that are going on around him and to him. If you are about to use a cold wipe on your baby's bottom, give your baby a bit of a warning: "This might be cold." If you're closing the car door, let him know, "This will be a loud sound." Not only does it help teach your child about the things around him and give you something to talk about, but it also establishes a bit of trust from the beginning.

- *R-E-S-P-E-C-T!* To me, the most important thing that I've learned is that babies, toddlers, and children respond far better if you give them the respect you would another adult, rather than treating them like a doll baby—from the beginning. I'm not implying that you should carry on full conversations and expect your fifteen-month-old to respond in kind, but know that your child is probably taking in far more than you think she is. Always assume that your child gets it. Case in point: one of my greatest regrets is the lack of respect I feel I gave to Jack. When Jack was born I assumed he was a baby and I was an adult and that he understood me as well as I understood him—which was barely at all. I assumed communication would come when he started talking. The truth is that he was watching, learning, and listening from the start. And although he was a late developer verbally, it was clear he knew far more than I had given him credit for. Having learned from my "mistake," with Lilia I assumed she understood everything from moment one, and (I feel) treated her with more respect from the start. Although I don't like to say some babies are easier or harder than others, it did seem that she "understood" more because I helped walk her through it.

- *Don't try to be mommy the savior (err, controller).* You may think that as the mommy (or daddy) your job is to protect your child from every harm, unhappiness, and frustration that may face her. Well, guess what? You can't. And you shouldn't. Life *isn't* about being happy all the time, and trying to keep your child from every hurt and disappointment is likely to make her more reliant on you and less able to function in the real world. The more you rush in to help her finish a task or swoop in to comfort a boo-boo, the less she will feel the need or the confidence to do it herself. She must learn to tolerate disappointment. If she isn't given a chance to swing through it, she may never be able to handle it.

- *Focus on your baby or toddler.* No, I don't mean all day every day. That's not possible and not realistic. But when you are with your child, really *be* with him. This is what many books and pediatricians refer to as "quality time" or "emotional time." Try not to constantly be on the phone, doing e-mails, or focusing on something else. Keep your eyes and mind on the child.

- *Maintain predictability.* Having your child know what to expect in routines can really help a baby or toddler gain comfort in a situation. And while we can't (and shouldn't) stop change, predictability in small things (like your daily routine) can help make bigger changes easier to deal with.

- *Validate her feelings.* Let your child know that her feelings and emotions are important. If your child is screaming and crying over a toy's being taken away, don't just ignore it. Rather, say to her, "I know you are upset, and that is okay, but we need to leave for play group and you can play more there." Give your child a safe haven to express herself emotionally and let her know that you are there to listen.

- *Remember that a toddler is learning the rules of the road.* She isn't born knowing not to throw food off the tray, or not to throw a baseball in house. She will test limits to see what those limits are: *Does no always mean no? Is it sometimes no, but sometimes yes? What about today? Is no still no?* They are in constant learning mode, interacting with their environment. And they will challenge you, because they go about it in a way that is totally counterintuitive to how you or I would go about doing things. But if you keep in the back of your

MM TIP:
When your child falls down or bumps his head or gets his finger caught in a drawer—and yes, all of these things will happen—don't let out a huge gasp the second it happens (hard as that may be to do). Wait a few seconds and see what your child's reaction is to the incident. Often, the tears come, in part, because you've made an issue over it when, if no one were making a fuss, your child might have just coasted on through the boo-boo. On the other hand, don't swoop in and immediately say, "You're okay." This only discounts what your child may be experiencing—whether physical or emotional—and teaches him not to trust his own feelings. Rather, tell him that you understand and that the incident must have been scary or painful, or whatever other adjective fits.

MM TIP:

Wow, I'm feeling pretty holier than thou with all my fancy advice. Please remember that these are guidelines and none of us are (or will be) perfect. So if you bend a rule, be honest with your child. Say, "I know I let you watch an extra hour of TV yesterday. I did it because I was really really tired. And I shouldn't have done it. Moving forward, we're only going to watch thirty minutes each day." Ignoring the "broken" rule may make your child more likely to think he can get you to change your mind.

MM TIP:

• **Remember to limit choices**. A toddler is taking in the world at rapid speed, having thousands of new images bombarding him every day. When you are giving your child a choice, limit it to two things: the swing or the slide, playing inside or playing outside, pancakes or waffles, sneakers or sandals. Not only will you be giving your child some power and control (which can sometimes avoid a tantrum) but you will keep from overwhelming him.

• **Measure your own expectations**. In order to choose the best course of action, you have to first look at the developmental stage your child is in. You should have far fewer expectations of a frustrated nineteen-month-old than a calm and happy twenty-four-month-old. And at the same time, something your twenty-six-month-old was able to handle and grasp may be impossible for her to comprehend a few months later when her stage has shifted again.

• **Establish limits and boundaries early on and be consistent**. Well, at least I'm being consistent in talking about *this*. You can choose to be "permissive" or "strict." It's up to you. But whatever you decide, you *must* stick with your choice. Clear limits (as I mentioned) are probably the best thing you can give a child.

head that your job is to teach them, rather than to punish them, this mantra will go a long way. Every time your child does something that makes you go *What?*, before you say no and yell, ask yourself, *What is my child trying to learn/explore/discover here, and how can I teach her?*

Creating Independence

Although this topic really goes with the above list, it's so important that it deserves its own section. Helping your child achieve a sense of independence is likely to help in everything from her play time to separation anxiety.

• *Babyproof so your baby can explore.* Although I talked about this in chapter 3, to develop independence, your child should be free to test limits and explore her surroundings without you hovering. All the more reason to make sure your home is toddler safe. This will also cut down on the number of times you have to say "no" when she is perilously close to danger. Also have lots of safe fun stuff around. This will give her a little more autonomy, without giving you a heart attack.

- *Let your child be the leader.* While it's important for you to set limits, it's also important for your child to feel a sense of control over her decisions—even if it seems ridiculous. If your two-year-old wants to wear a wool poncho and Ugg boots in ninety-degree heat in June, let her. You may be cringing about what your neighbors think, but at some point she'll get overheated and figure out for herself that a tank top makes more sense. By letting her come to that decision on her own, you give her the chance to learn and grow— and hopefully chalk that up to a "don't" page in her fashion memoirs.

- *Walk her through it, but then let her do it on her own.* Being able to do a good job is paramount to a sense of independence and accomplishment in your toddler. But often, she'll need a little guidance along the way. Break the actions down into individual tasks, and walk her through it (first put the toothpaste on the brush, then wet it with water). But be careful not to give too many directions at once—remember two directions in a row is plenty at this age. Then step back and watch how she does it on her own, and give her lots of praise for the effort. More on praise later in this chapter.

- *Let her help.* When your toddler sees you doing anything vaguely interesting—cooking, cleaning, organizing your shoe collection— she will likely want to get in there and help. Look for any possible (safe) way that she can assist you. She may not be able to help you hang up clean clothes, but she can certainly help put the dirty ones in a basket.

- *Hold back.* If you've assigned a job to your toddler, let him see it through, even if it takes him twice as long as it would you (this will likely drive you insane, so make sure you have the time before you suggest it). This could mean that it takes him twenty minutes to put all of his books back on the shelf, but in the end, he'll feel like he's really accomplished something for himself.

Discipline

Okay, so you're treating your child with respect, you're giving him choices—heck, you've devoted half your house as a safe place—so you should be in the clear of tantrums, biting, or hitting, right? I wish. Every child will go through "difficult" stages, pushing their limits and wanting to know how to behave.

But discipline with children is a strange thing. For many of us, our parent's idea of discipline was sticking us in a corner, taking something away from us, or even giving a good spanking. And while we'd like to think we've evolved way beyond that, many parents are still perplexed as to what exactly to do when our kids don't behave. We tend to think that we need to punish our children in order for them to understand what is right. And what we really want is for our children to learn "right" and "wrong." But simply put, there is no *learning* in punishment. And in fact, the Latin root for *discipline* is "to learn," not "to be punished." Keep this in mind because the key with a toddler is to teach them so that they know right and wrong, rather than to simply punish them for guessing the wrong action or behavior. And since children are imprinting from birth, it's a good idea to start the learning process from day one. While a six-month-old may not get what you are trying to teach her the way a sixteen-month-old will, it is a good habit to get into for both you and your child. Here are some approaches to discipline.

Saying "Yes" Instead of "No"

The key to living with a toddler is to try to set limits and boundaries *before* the bad behavior occurs. Obviously, this is a lot easier said than done, as most of the time, you can't even comprehend what sort of ridiculous thing your little one will get into. But discipline will come best if your child can self-discipline. You do this by saying "yes" as often as possible, instead of "no." Redirect and tell them what they can do rather than what they can't do. For example, if your twenty-five-month-old is throwing the ball in the living room, you whisk

MM TIP:
Every family will have its own unique set of family rules. Some families are more patient, while others are more lenient. But most families don't start limits until problems arise. Oops, Johnny is standing on the table, we better set limits. It's actually best to set limits up front, before the behavior even starts. It's kind of like establishing your limits with your husband about how long you're going to let the baby cry *before* it's 2 A.M. and you're bleary-eyed. Set household rules that you can live with before the behavior is an issue.

your child to the yard and say, "You want to throw the ball? Let's go outside, we don't throw the ball inside the house." Can't go outside? Give them a bean bag or ball to throw into a laundry basket. Be creative, just redirect. This way your child has learned the proper behavior, while getting a lesson about what is improper—all the while enjoying the activity that she wanted to do. Added bonus, you avoided using the word "no."

Obviously, it's unrealistic to expect that you *never* use the word "no." In fact, "no" is probably one of the first words your toddler will learn—it's just so darn easy to say. It's just best to avoid using it when possible, so that when you really need it, it is all the more effective.

Also keep in mind there are times when this technique doesn't work. Toddlers are all about learning limits, and even if you redirect their behavior, they want to do what they want to do. Depending on the age of the child, you could say, "I know you want to do this, but we need to do that." If they kick and scream, then put them on the ground and let them have a tantrum. Let them be pissed. It's all a part of them expressing their emotions (and don't worry, I have tips later on dealing with that tantrum!).

Teaching That Actions Have Consequences

This is another great way to "discipline" your child. Your child needs clear consequences for her behavior. If she throws her food, it means she's done, so you remove the food. If she wasn't done, she will quickly learn that throwing food made the food go away. While an older child may pick up on this quickly, a younger child may have to deal with it several times before it sets in.

Then, as explained above, you redirect her behavior. She wants to throw something, so you give her a ball and let her throw the ball. You say, "Balls are for throwing, food is not." Of course, it may take a fifteen-month-old 150 times to learn this, while a twenty-four-month-old will get it in two throws, but the point is, her actions had consequences (she lost the food) and her negative behavior was redirected into something positive.

MM TIP:
Make sure you pick a consequence to your child's action that *everyone* can live with. If your child is acting up before you were supposed to go meet another family with kids, don't take away the meeting if it was something everyone was really looking forward to. Instead, find a suitable consequence for your child that won't be such a bummer for the rest of you. If your child was throwing a toy across the living room, take the toy away since he couldn't play nicely with it. This type of deliberate acting out will start somewhere around eighteen months to two years.

It's also important to make sure that actions have related consequences. Taking TV away for throwing food is a completely unrelated consequence. Taking food away at that meal for throwing food makes a ton more sense.

Time-Outs

Simply put, time-outs are as *out* as chandelier earrings. Okay, fine, they seem so effective on nanny shows, but you have to look at who is giving the message. That nanny in the show is a virtual stranger to these children. Kids tend to take direction from a stranger much more seriously than they take direction from someone they know and see every day. Quite frankly, getting a stern reaction from a stranger scares the bejesus out of most kids. (Quite useful, in fact, to employ if your child is misbehaving in the grocery store. Have a clerk ask your child to not throw lemons and he will likely stop immediately.) Also, the behavior may be extinguished at that moment, but a time-out doesn't do anything to change the long-term behavior. Think about time-outs the way you would the cabbage soup diet. Sure, you can subsist on cabbage soup for a week and drop a few pounds, but it really does nothing for long-term weight loss the way modifying your eating habits (or in your child's case, their behavior) will.

So basically, time-outs were created to give parents a break so that parents didn't pick up a child and throw him against the wall. But from the perspective of a child, here's what happens. You are upset with your child. You give him a time-out to go sit in the other room for a set amount of time. We already know that a child doesn't understand real time, but only *event* time (flaw one). You tell your child to think about what he's done. He typically doesn't understand what he has done, and even if he does understand, he probably doesn't know why it is wrong (flaw two). So he sits in the chair and thinks about how mean his Mommy is. It goes something like this:

Wow, Mommy is mean. She put me here when I want to be there with everyone else. Yes, Mommy is mean. Oh, but look, there's my fire truck. That's pretty neat. I like fire trucks. It's red, that's a pretty color.

As you can see, he's not exactly thinking about what you intended him to think about. He is just being banished. All it teaches kids is that someone that is bigger than you can make you do something you don't want to do. In the end, this is a horrible lesson. It is much better to give a yes alternative to the no behavior they were doing, or teach them that their actions have consequences. Here are a few other consequences he will likely be able to learn from:

- Anytime your child does something bad that causes him physical pain, consider the pain his consequence. He climbed on a table and fell off and cut his arm. The pain is his "punishment." Point this out to him. Not that it is "punishment" but that that is what happens when we do things we've been told not to.

- If he has really hurt someone else—hitting, shoving, biting—make the consequence be that he has to make the other person feel better. He can't go outside and play, he has to bring his friend/brother/sister treats and read him books to make amends.

- Take away TV only if the offense has to do with TV. He won't turn it off; therefore, he doesn't get to watch it anymore. There is nothing to learn from taking the TV away if he has hit his sister. The punishment has to be connected to the crime.

Disciplining Your Child's Friends

The bottom line is that most people don't want you to discipline their child. Everyone has their own philosophy on raising their child, and even your closest friend is likely going about it slightly different than you are. Chances are pretty good, too, that at this age, you are having a play date with the other mother present (very few people with kids under three are simply dropping their kids off for play dates). However, it can be a little sticky when you feel as if your child may be in danger or simply at risk for being hit or pulled at. The best way to deflect it is to speak *for* your child. Get down on your child's level and help vocalize what he might be feeling. In other words, instead of telling the other child "no," say, "Jack, do you want Steven to pull your

MM TIP:
You may have grown up in a family in which a spanking here or a small slap there was perfectly acceptable. Well, there have been a lot of studies that show that children who are physically hurt by their parents, even with a small spanking, are typically the kids who turn around and hurt other kids. It teaches children that someone bigger can hurt someone smaller. So avoid spanking and hitting altogether.

MM TIP:
If your child is sad or angry or upset, let her be. It is important for your child to experience a full range of emotions. Help her get her feelings out by stomping her feet, hitting pillow, punching a stuffed animal. Let her express her anger. And keep in mind that crying is okay and part of this—she is expressing how she is feeling.

hair? Say 'No, Steven, don't pull my hair. That hurts.' " At that point you just have to hope that the other mother isn't brain dead and picks up on your cue—one that hopefully hasn't offended her. If the mother doesn't step in, remove your child from the situation.

Other People Disciplining Your Child

This is also a tricky situation, whether it's your mother, your mother-in-law, your sister, or your best friend. But at the end of the day, it is your child. You need to step in and take over. If it's your mother or mother-in-law, acknowledge what they are doing, thank them, and then say simply, "I know you are a mom, too, but I need you to help me do it my way." If it's your girlfriend, let it go and see if it happens again. If it does, you can either stop the play date (really embarrassing) or the next time you two make plans, suggest going to lunch without the kids.

Praise When Praise Is Due

MM TIP:
Try not to correct your child publicly. Take him aside and explain his behavior, or discipline him however you choose. You don't need to add humiliation on top of an already difficult situation.

Obviously, you want to encourage your children when they have done something great. But too much praise becomes hollow praise. So what's the right amount and what's too much? Here are a few hints:

- Praise a good action, not an object. "Look, you covered the whole picture/carried your jacket to your room/picked up your books." This way you're encouraging an action and may elicit the behavior again.

- Be careful what you call "good," such as "good job" or "good boy," because that means there is a "bad job" and "bad boy." It's much better to be specific about what you are praising.

- Direct the praise toward the child—"you cleaned your room so well"—rather than making it about you, as in, "I like that." Make it less about giving your approval, and more about them knowing they did something great!

The Bad and the Ugly: Dealing With . . .

Okay, so this is all well and good, but how do you deal with the bad behavior when it arises? I can't promise I've covered every behavior (somehow children manage to come up with ones I could never have dreamed of—bless their creativity), but here are some of the biggies.

Tantrums

It's important to understand why tantrums happen in the first place. Your child gets frustrated for any number of reasons having to do with the fact that she has very little control over her environment, and she doesn't have the language skills and the emotional wherewithal to access her feelings. Her fuse gets short, she has a tantrum, and guess what? It works. She gets your attention. Unfortunately, tantrums will go on forever if you give them any credence at all. Now, I'm not saying to abandon your child (as hard as you may try at that moment) and leave her screaming on the floor of the toy store. In fact, you really have to suffer through it, as you need to watch your child to make sure she doesn't hurt herself. But there is also no reasoning with a child when she is in the middle of the tantrum. Trust me on this one. Instead, try this:

- Acknowledge your child's feelings by saying something like, "I see you are really angry, I'll wait to speak with you when you're done." It's very important that you don't belittle your child's feelings and do acknowledge that you understand.

- Then, in the same room as the child, pick up a book or a magazine or fidget with something on the shelf of the toy store, just don't pay attention to the fit.

- Don't interrupt the tantrum; let it run its course.

- When she is at the catch-her-breath stage—you know, that adorable gasping for air thing that kids do after they've been bawling their eyes out for thirty minutes—ask if she needs a hug. Give her a little love and comfort her. But whatever you do, DO NOT BRING UP WHAT IT WAS SHE WAS CRYING ABOUT. It is simply too soon for her to turn off her emotions and be able to handle discussing it. This is kind of like when your husband wants to change the subject after you've had a fight and you have a hard time switching gears.

If you are in a public place, and the tantrum is just too embarrassing, you can remove her. Your child will probably appreciate it, too, as most kids don't like to be embarrassed in public.

When the incident has been over for an hour or two, *then* ask her if it was worth it. Say, "Wow, you made quite a fuss. In the end, did that work how you wanted it to?"

And the most important rule of all: Never but never give in to what she wants because she is having a tantrum. This will only teach her that tantrums get her what she wants.

> MM TIP: If your child manages to hurt herself in the middle of a tantrum—say, banging her head on the floor—stick a pillow under her head and say, "Ouch, I won't let you hurt yourself. I won't let anybody get hurt." And then let her proceed with the tantrum.

Physical Aggression

At some point, all children are going to bite, hit, push, throw, grab, scratch, or pinch. Or do all of the above at the same time. Some are normal acts of assertiveness. And depending on the age of the child, they may be aggressive or even underhanded. Unfortunately, the younger the child, the harder it will be to stop the bad behavior. But the best thing to do is look at how serious the action of your child was, and tailor the response accordingly. Biting is probably the biggest offense:

- Make sure your reaction is big and immediate, with a very surprised and angry look on your face.

- Physically pick up the child and put a two-foot distance between you and your child, holding him out so that he is aware of the distance.

- In your biggest, scariest, nonyelling voice, say sternly, "WE DON'T BITE/HIT/KICK." Again, this needs to be an immediate big reaction.

- Then explain to your child that you (if you were the one he bit) or the friend (if he bit a friend) will not be with someone who bites. Then restate that we don't bite people.

- Consider giving your child something to bite as an alternative such as a teething ring, blanket, or something he can always have with him.

- Then go get ice, and have your child help the victim feel better.

> **MM TIP:** Be sure not to pass judgment on another child or the parent of another child who has bitten your child. Biting is incredibly common with kids this age, and your child could be the next biter. Have sympathy and pity for that parent. Believe me, the parent of the aggressor feels far worse than the parent of the victim.
>
> The same goes for hitting, pushing, and shoving. If you are there at the time (which at this age, you should be), pick up your child and put a two-foot distance between you and him (almost more for the dramatic effect than anything else) and say, very surprised, WE DON'T HIT (shove, pinch, etc.). This is another good time to give an alternative item to your child. You can explain that he can hit the pillow or drum, but not his sister. If that still doesn't work, give your child angry words to use, let him stomp his feet, or act out his aggression in a nonharmful way.

Pulling Hair

Pulling hair is just like biting and warrants a big, surprised reaction, coupled with a "We don't pull hair." In terms of redirecting the behavior, you might want to have a doll around the house with long hair for her to be able to pull if she feels the need. If your child is under fifteen months, chances are that pulling hair is more of an exploratory thing, so tailor your reaction accordingly. But with older children, it's the same reaction. Pull them away from your body. React big. Believe it or not, the best reaction your child could possibly get is if they pull another child's hair and that child screams bloody murder. It will likely scare your child away from ever doing it again. Hopefully.

Spitting Food

Most children spit food because they get a reaction. Someone at the table laughs, whether it be a big brother, or in my case, my husband. Don't react. Spitting is just like throwing food, and it means the child is all done. Then, to redirect the behavior, tell your child that if he needs to spit, he should do it in the bathroom. Chances are you may have a mighty confused toddler standing in the bathroom, but at least you won't have macaroni on your dining room floor.

Banging Heads

This, unfortunately, is very hard to stop. Some kids bang their head against the back of their high chairs; others bang it on hardwood floors over and over again. While it looks a little disturbing, most children grow out of it. In the meantime, try to slip a pillow in when you can or pad the back of the high chair. And also keep in mind that the more attention it gets, the more it usually happens, so try your best to ignore it.

Whining

Most parents have the inclination to say to their child, "Ask me nicely." Well, young toddlers barely know how to speak, never mind understand the difference between tones of voice. Never use that phrase on a toddler; it will simply confuse him. Instead, concentrate on a time when your child is using a pleasant voice that you like. Perhaps he has asked you politely for a cookie. Go over the top in praising that voice. Tell him how good that voice is. Then, when he whines, say, "That is not a voice that I can hear," and put your hands on your ears. Remind him of the voice that he used that made it so easy for you to help him. After he knows how you feel about the voice, ignore his request: "I can't hear that voice." Now, when they are really little, that is hard to do. But as they get older, they will get it. You may also try when they are older to tape record their voice so they can hear how they sound.

Whining is very much like tantrums. Be careful to not give in when a child whines.

Bad Words

Kids are going to say bad words, especially if they are hearing them said at home. The most important thing to do is to get them out of your vocabulary. When your child does say one, ignore it and it will go away. Don't give it too much attention. If it becomes a real problem, say directly to your child, "Are you waiting to see what I will do when you use that language? I don't hear you when you are using those words; they are not appropriate." This is likely a passing phase and if you don't give it attention, it will end.

"I Don't Like You"

This is one of those things that make parents cringe—whether it's being said to another child, an adult, or even to you. In the end, for the child it's about testing his own power, control, and manipulation. But in the end, your child is entitled to feel how he feels—that's life. They're allowed to say that. They will also say "I hate you." Telling them they can't say that means telling them they can't express how they really feel. However, you can suggest that even if they don't like someone, they must still treat them kindly. You can also say that you

MM TIP:
A lot of you will disagree with this advice. I don't blame you. It's not an easy one. I will say, though, that the more I told Jack not to tell his sister he didn't like her, the more he did. The minute I acknowledged his feelings and talked about why he didn't like her, the better things got.

will not let people's feeling be hurt in your house. So they cannot say it in front of the person. You can also explain to your child that "hate" is a very strong word and it is better to use "dislike."

Baby Talk/Play

Many kids—especially around the birth of a sibling—revert to wanting to "play baby." Let them, but commit to it. Put them in a tiny little diaper—that's probably a bit uncomfortable. When she starts to talk, say, "Babies don't talk," and tell her that she can't talk. Do the same with walking and crawling. If she is in baby mode, she has to stay in baby mode. Soon, an exploring toddler will grow tired of the limitations and quickly end the baby time.

Tattling

Disturbingly, Lilia will say, "Jack pushed me," when I know that he didn't. The best thing to do in this situation is to butt out. Don't punish the older child, and don't react to the younger child. You may even throw in an "I don't allow tattling," and your child will quickly learn she gets a negative reaction rather than a positive one. If it continues, chances are your child simply wants a little extra attention. Rather than take her side and punish your innocent child, focus on the "boo-boo." Say, "Are you saying you are hurt? Let's go tend to your bruise."

> **MM TIP:** Toddler-age children don't really "lie." What may seem like a lie to me or you is usually a child trying to get out of trouble or exercising a vivid imagination—but it lacks the maliciousness of, say, a teenager lying. Also, don't set your kids up to lie. In other words, don't ask your two-year-old if she had a poop in her diaper; tell her, "You have a poop, let's go change it." That way, you're not putting her in position of not telling the truth. If she pushed a child, don't ask her if she did, just deal with it.

Mind Your Manners

Most of these things you will only be dealing with toward the end of toddlerdom, and can be tricky for little ones to grasp. But nonetheless, we all try.

Saying You're Sorry

It's almost impossible for children under the age of two to say that they're sorry and truly understand what it means. The result is often a forced and humdrum "I'm sorrrry," or, more annoying, a child capping off something bad they've done with a burst of quick "I'm sorry, I'm sorry, I'm sorry, I'm sorry," in hopes of erasing the past.

The better thing to do is to let your child witness instances in which you need to say you're sorry, and try to explain it to your child. You should also talk through how your child feels after he's done something wrong. If he touches on something that is similar to feeling sorry, you can explain to your child that this is what it feels like to be sorry, and hope he begins to grasp it. This could be when you bump into someone or cut someone off when speaking. Likely you shouldn't even try this until they're at least thirty months or older.

Often, other parents will expect you to force your child to say he's sorry, and honestly, this is about your embarrassment in front of another parent. If your child is not at the stage yet where he can truly say it on his own and mean it, then don't do a, "Sam, say you're sorry" or apologize *for* him ("Sam is really sorry"). But if a mother is sending eye daggers at you, then you may not have a choice but to apologize yourself—"I'm sorry that Sam hit your child"—if you are sorry (hey, maybe the little brat deserved it!). You might also add, "We are working on not hitting. There will be a consequence." Just don't put the words into your child's mouth. It's empty and hollow and does nothing for teaching your child how to use the word and mean it.

Excuse Me

Again, this is one of those things that if your child doesn't grasp the meaning of the words "excuse me," then the words themselves will become your biggest nightmare. Many young children learn those words and think that if they put them on the beginning of any sentence, then it is okay to simply plow right over the conversation that was happening. If your child is old enough, you can:

- Explain to your child what qualifies as an interruption (he's injured, needs help going to the bathroom, or is in danger) and what does not.

- Set up a system with your child in which he squeezes your hand quietly if he needs you in the middle of a conversation. You will squeeze him back to let him know you know he's there. The first time, respond very quickly to him by stopping your other conversation. Then, slowly but surely you can push your response time back and your child will trust that you will get to him.

- When you've noticed that your child hasn't interrupted—for example, if he plays nicely while you were on the phone, praise him for his patience.

Saying "Please" and "Thank You"

While this can easily be one of the first few words you can get your child to say, whether she will grasp the actual meaning is a whole other thing. It's most important that your child see please and thank you in action, rather than simply be taught the words. So you and your other family members need to use these words on a consistent basis, for anything and everything you would want your child to use those words for.

Honestly, as hard as it is culturally to accept, don't force kids to say anything. The more you force them to "use the magic word," the more they may just wait for you to remind them. The best way to get a child to do it is to model it. Make it a habit. Then, when your child does say it, make a big deal out of it.

MM TIP:
Look, this is the best advice, but I will say that I was fairly lax with Jack, and it's still a struggle to get him to "be polite." Although to his credit, he is now. But I really helped Lilia by always saying "thank you, Mommy" if she couldn't, and at two and a half, she's really extremely good about her "pleases," "thank yous," and "excuse mes" (if I do say so myself!). So, while you may not want to force them to say it, a reminder may not hurt.

Hello and Goodbye

While you can't force a child to talk, you can explain social norms and customs prior to social outings. This works for about three-and-a-half-year-olds and beyond. Before that, don't bother. Model the behavior, but don't expect a little salutarian. Explain that you are going to go over to someone's house. Tell your child that it is polite to greet the family. Explain that most people do this with a "hello," but if they don't want to say hello, they must greet in some other way—a handshake, a smile, a wave, or a wink (if your child is coordinated enough!) and that this is part of being a guest. In the same vein, if they don't want to say goodbye and thank you, explain that it's part of a play date. If they still don't want to, then no play date.

> **MM TIP:** Having a child say "please," "thank you," "hello," "goodbye," and "I'm sorry" is incredibly difficult and troubling for parents because we feel as though it's a reflection on us. The second your child doesn't thank another mother for a play date, you feel like the "bad mommy" sign is flashing in neon lights over your head. You have to just remember, it's not about you. It's about your child's learning to be a social creature in the world. Forcing him to recite words won't make him a more polite kid in the long run. Work with him on the meaning of these words and, over time, he will get it and it will stick. If you are truly embarrassed, say to the other adult, "He is learning to say hello/thank you/please/goodbye and we are working on it. It's hard for him right now." And then, throw in a huge thank you from yourself.

Sharing

I remember thinking Jack was a good sharer. He would always share his toys at the park, and happily give one back that he had borrowed. Well, things, it seem, were a bit different on his own turf. I once invited a new potential friend for a play date with Jack when he was two. Jack sat wailing the entire time and refused to let the other boy touch any of his objects (heck, he barely let the kid use one of our sippy cups). I begged him to share. I pleaded. And after about thirty minutes, the other mom packed up her son and left. I couldn't blame her. Jack

MM TIP:
Teaching a child to look someone in the eye goes along with learning to shake hands, which starts somewhere after age five.

MM TIP:
Never force your child to kiss or hug someone. You need to explain that kisses and hugs are reserved for people you really love and are special and they need to be the guardian of their own hugs and kisses. The problem typically arises with Grandma and Grandpa, who want to lay a big wet one on your child, much to your or your child's chagrin. So, before the visit, explain to your child that they really love her and they like it when you kiss and hug. It is your choice, but you have to greet them. Then tell the grandparents that you are teaching about kissing and hugging and being a guardian of her own kisses and hugs, so please ask her, "May I give you a kiss?"

sat victorious, like a king among his subjects, eyeing each toy (and me) skeptically.

Turns out, I wasn't approaching the situation in a positive way. According to many experts, it's important to realize that sharing is not something you impose. If you make your child share a toy, it's not sharing, it's forcing. If your child does share, it's more likely in order to gain parental approval, and it might make him angry and resentful instead.

Developmentally, to be able to share, a child must understand that he has ownership of a thing he is *choosing* to let someone else use it, and it will be returned later. Infants have no understanding of time, so even three minutes may feel like an eternity.

But even at age two, your child is unlikely to be able to truly share. In fact, this is about the time that he begins to develop a sense of self and feel that "things" are an extension of him. While some might happily share, others will scream "mine," and mean it. Around age two and a half or three, he may come to understand the idea of turns and be willing to hand over a toy when he loses interest. Most children won't truly be able to share until closer to three or even four, when the ability to actually understand *how* a child will feel when you snatch a toy will develop.

You can help your toddler learn some of the tenets behind sharing by doing the following:

- When your child shares, praise her for such kind behavior.

- Practice taking turns: She stacks a block, you stack one; she hugs her toy, you hug her toy; she turns a page, you turn a page. This may help her see that taking turns is fun and if she gives something away, it comes back.

- Ask for permission: show respect for her toys and clothes. Ask for permission before you use her markers and don't use them if she says no.

- Be a good sharer yourself: offer your child your muffin, let her wear your hair ribbon, try to use the word "share," as in "I'm so happy to share my dessert with you."

- Don't punish for not sharing: let it be her decision. Respect it; don't make her feel selfish or guilty.

Now that's all well and good, but chances are your child still won't want to share. So when children are toddlers and want the same toy, you might want to try the following:

- First, if they are struggling but not hurting each other, let them try to sort it out themselves. Stay close in case you need to intervene.

- Comment on the situation, nonjudgmentally. Say something like, "I see you both want to play with the same ball."

- Try picking up another toy. This might get one of the children interested in it. Or suggest that one of them might be interested in another toy ("there is a fun truck over there").

- If they still can't sort it out, consider taking the toy away. Don't be punitive; simply say, "I think we should put this toy away now."

- If one child already had the toy, don't tell him to share. Instead, say to the child who has the toy, "When you're finished with that car, I think Jack would like a turn." To the child who is waiting, say, "I know you really want to play with that car. It's hard waiting, but Dennis is using it now. You can play with another toy or wait until he's finished.

(This is based on Magda Gerber's philosophy about sharing. I encourage you to read her book, *Dear Parent: Caring for Infants with Respect*.)

Sharing Among Siblings

If you have more than one child, you may think it's best to have mostly communal toys. But according to many experts, it's better to truly divide up what is whose and not force sharing. If Jack has a toy he doesn't want to share with Lilia, that's okay, but I point out to him that he needs to remember that when Lilia has a toy *she* won't share. If

MM TIP:
When your child is having a play date at home and is over the age of about two and a half, ask her before the other child comes over whether there are any toys she doesn't want to share. Special toys should be put away so that they have some feelings of control and less controversy over certain toys.

MM TIP:
If your child has a lot of trouble sharing, try having play dates at the park so that it is less about a focus on toys and more about just playing.

your siblings have a hard time taking turns with communal toys, consider having a timer and setting it when both want the same toy. Each gets two minutes and when the buzzer rings, they must hand it over. Here are a few more things to remember:

- Don't assume that your older child was the aggressor. Not only might it be wrong, but it immediately puts your older child on the defensive. Instead, say a nonjudgmental, "What happened here?"

- Stay out of it unless there's hitting involved. Otherwise, they'll never learn to work it out themselves.

- Consider a policy of no tattling and that no matter which one "did it," both receive the same "punishment." Not only is it likely to diminish the behavior, but it will diminish tattling.

Eating Behavior

Although I know a two-year-old boy and girl who have better manners than I do, and will sit contentedly with napkins on laps eating quietly for thirty minutes, my sense is this is the exception, not the rule. For the most part, kids don't start to grasp the idea of "table manners"—holding a fork in the correct hand, napkin on lap, and so on—until well after four or five. And while your three-year-old may be holding a spoon by now, most likely she is holding it in one hand and using the other hand to pick up the peas and place them on the spoon.

So about the only expectations you can have—and for this, I'm talking about a three- to five-year-old—is that they don't throw food and they sit at the table with you (proper table manners, using utensils correctly, and chewing with their mouth closed will come much later). But for how long? For a three-year-old, five minutes seem like a lifetime, so think of it as a major accomplishment. Here are a few tips to help:

- Establish a rule that your child has to eat in one sitting. No getting up to go play, and then coming back to the table. Once he's gone, so is the food.

- Have a conversation that is interesting to the child—this shouldn't be too hard as it is really only the first five minutes of the meal. Leave the work talk for when they leave the table or lift their arms to be taken out of the high chair and allowed to play. While they are there, have it focus on fun, innocuous things like, "I saw a Dalmatian when I was on my way to work today." Pick topics your child can identify with.

- Don't expect your child to sit still if you get up and down 100 times to go to the kitchen.

- Don't expect your child to eat broccoli if you won't. Even if you can't stand it, put it on your plate and make it "disappear" once your child has left the table.

- Once a week—or more, preferably—the entire family should all be at the table together. This can be tricky if your child eats early and you work until a bit later. But if your child is still awake, bring him to the table and give him a bowl of fruit or a glass of milk. It is important that everyone gets in the habit of sitting at the table together.

Responsibilities

Traditional chores, in which a child receives an allowance for doing certain things around the house, won't begin until your child truly understands the meaning of money, which is sometime around age six. But before then, it's important to establish that everyone in the family is responsible for certain things: cleaning up books, putting her stuffed animals on the bed after Mommy has made it, placing clothes in the hamper. It's important that you convey to your child

> **MM TIP:** Jen made up a funny clean-up song that she started to sing to Sam when he was about nine months old every time they need to clean up. Now, if Sam hears the song, he stops what he's doing to play the "fun game" of cleaning up. How easily they can be fooled!

that she has possessions and she is responsible for taking care of them. But keep expectations reasonable. A good rule of thumb is that a two-year-old helps *you* to clean up while *you* help a three-year-old to clean up.

Nose Picking, Farting, and Burping

Everyone picks their nose. Everyone. Some pick more. Some pick in private, and many, many people pick their nose in the car, for whatever reason (you will now notice this more than ever before). It's really not something you can stop in your child, but you can say to your child, "When you go to pick your nose, your hands are dirty, so please ask for a Kleenex next time."

All kids think farts are funny—and some thirty-four-year-olds do, too. A small child has little control over his gas, so you have few options. If you ignore it, then your child learns to be ashamed of a bodily function. If you laugh about it, then your child will be the loud-farting frat boy (yuck). The best thing to do is to acknowledge it and say that it's a normal bodily function, everyone does it, and it typically means that he needs to go poo soon. Slowly teach your child to say excuse me when he farts. And whatever you do, don't laugh.

Burping is something you can stop. People can hold in burps, so discourage your child from doing this unless he is in private or has gone into the bathroom. Also make sure you and your husband are modeling correctly and not burping in public—I'd hope not!

Now all that said, if your child is four, give it up—they will fart and burp and find it hilarious. Eventually they *should* grow out of it.

Dealing with the Hard Stuff

Tantrums I can deal with. Lilia's are so extreme, and over such clear things (such as she wants a lollipop the size of her head before dinner), that I can be strong and stand my ground. But the day Lilia grabbed my leg as I was about to head out to work and plaintively pleaded "take me" in her burgeoning two-year-old voice, I about walked in and offered my resignation.

Separation Issues

Virtually all children will go through separation anxiety at some point. We first see it in the form of stranger anxiety at nine months. Whenever there is a leap in cognition, it can be accompanied by separation anxiety. You'll notice it again big time again at around eighteen months. This is because they finally understand that if they can walk away from you, you can walk away from them. It reaches another peak when they start nursery school. If not, then look for it six months later, or when kindergarten starts, or at the first sleepover.

The point is, all children go through some separation anxiety—whether you're a stay-at-home mom or have worked full-time from day one. The degree of the anxiety will be different intensities, depending not just on the situation, but the child. And we do our kids a tremendous disservice if we never leave their side. Separation and the ability to separate are built on trust. A major element of your child overcoming the anxiety is getting them to trust that you are coming back. While it may seem like a short-term fix to distract your child and try to sneak away, you are simply prolonging the inevitable, and you sabotage the trust you may have established.

Instead, it's a process that has to be mastered. It can take from a week to several months, based on your child's temperament and level of development and how you interact with him (how many times you go back into the room, hang at the door, etc.). Most nursery schools don't start children in programs until around age two years and nine months, because this is the earliest age that kids can trust that Mommy is coming back.

Many nursery schools say that kids should cry it out. Often, this has to do with the fact that they don't want Mommy or Daddy hanging around. Crying it out in this case doesn't create trust. Instead, you need to leave and come back—even if it's for just five minutes. Then try it again. Leave, and this time come back after ten minutes. This

MM TIP:
When you are doing a trial separation by leaving your child for just five or ten minutes, leave your purse or car keys so the child knows you have to come back.

MM TIP:
Give your child plenty of extra love and support when she is going through this phase. Thinking *she needs to learn and tough it out* will likely make it harder on her. *Don't* use the words, "I'll miss you." If your child is actually enjoying the time away, she will then have to deal with feelings of guilt because she doesn't miss you back. Instead, say simply, "I love you."

MM TIP:
Most experts agree that
the maximum that a parent
should be away from a
child before he is three
years old is around two to
three nights in a row. While
this isn't always possible or
even reasonable with
business travelers, try to
use it as a guideline,
especially during periods
of intense separation
anxiety. A great escape for
you and your husband
when the baby is five
months old or so (before
separation anxiety kicks in)
is to check into a local
hotel or resort for twenty-
one hours. Leave at 2 P.M.
one day and be home by
11 A.M. the next day. This
is plenty of time for a game
of tennis, a couple's
massage, great sex, a nice
dinner, more great sex, and
a bit of sleeping in. You will
feel totally revived without
sending your kids into a
tizzy.

will help your child realize that Mommy always comes back and Daddy always comes back.

This is one of those topics that I could literally devote five chapters or even five books to. It is a huge issue, and I urge you to get more information on the subject. The pioneer on childhood attachment theory is John Bowlbym and while it is way cerebral and a bit tough to get through, I recommend his book, *Attachment*, if you want to dig in a little deeper.

Death

Talking to your child about death can be one of the most difficult conversations you can have, and you need to choose your words carefully. Preschool-age kids are actually pretty aware of death from cartoons to books to seeing dead bugs or even small animals on the street—and, these days, people on the news. And when it happens in your house to a family member or even a pet, chances are that your child is aware that something is going on, and avoiding the topic will cause your child even more worry. It's also important that your child realize that it is okay for grown-ups to be sad. Here are a few ways to deal with it:

- Don't avoid her questions, and try to answer as directly as possible. If it helps, read her books that deal with death in a safe and friendly way.

- Avoid euphemisms. Using terms like "resting in peace" or "gone away" can be really confusing for a child, since you typically go away to work and she rests every day. You don't want your child to be afraid she won't wake up or you won't come home.

- Keep the explanation simple. Tell her that Uncle Bob's body stopped working, so he can no longer eat, or play, or talk, but that he isn't in pain. Launching into a lengthy discussion of an illness will just confuse your child. Avoid saying that he was sick and died, as your child will certainly worry the next time she is sick.

- Tread lightly on religious matters. Depending on your beliefs, you may choose to explain the death in terms related to God or heaven.

Just be careful to not paint too rosy of a picture, such as, "Sarah was so good that God wanted her with him." Your child will be likely to think: If God wanted to take Sarah, will he take me too? Should I be good so I can be with her in heaven, or bad so I can stay here with Mom and Dad?"

- Be prepared for a variety of reactions, from tantrums to reverting to more babyish behavior, to simply not caring at all (this one can be the toughest on a grieving parent).

- Know that the topic of death will likely be brought up many times in the future.

Ask the Experts

As I mentioned, there have been dozens of books written on the topic of childhood development, and I urge you to explore them on your own. Some methods you may find too harsh, others you may feel require you to learn a second language, and some are simply great reference books to check out on development or bumps along the road. But all have made true believers out of the mothers who have followed them.

The RIE Method

I have to say, some of the most "well adjusted," "kind," and "confident" toddlers I know have been raised using the RIE (Resources for Infant Educators) method. Another regret I have is not taking a RIE class run by Elizabeth Memel in Los Angeles. I figured I was too busy and my child too far along developmentally. Big mistake. Should have just jumped in there.

Developed by Magda Gerber, RIE is a nonprofit organization that has developed and teaches a philosophy in which babies are treated as unique individuals rather than objects from day one. The entire method is based on respect for babies and encourages parents to let children participate in the relationships around them, rather than

MM TIP:
If someone very close to you passes away, you're likely going to need more information on this topic. Check out the following sources:

• *Lifetimes: The Beautiful Way to Explain Death to Children*, by Bryan Mellonie (Bantam Books).

• *Sad Isn't Bad: A Good-Grief Guidebook for Kids Dealing with Loss*, by by Michaelene Mundy (Rebound by Sagebrush).

• *Annie and the Old One*, by Miska Miles (Little, Brown).

MM TIP:
Don't downplay the death of a pet, especially if your child was incredibly attached. If your child fed the goldfish every day but saw Grandma only once a year, chances are the death of the goldfish could prove to be a bigger disruption and more tragic event in your child's life. Go about it with the same sensitivity you would a family member, and allow your child her ample grief.

simply being pawns for the first few years of their lives. This in turn shows the infant that you respect her feelings, emotions, and desires. For example, you don't simply pick up your child; you tell your child, "Mommy is picking you up now." The idea is that you wouldn't come up to another adult and do something without first letting them know what you had planned, so why do that to a child? Once a child is older and is capable of making verbal and even nonverbal reactions, you give your child a choice in what is going on around her—"Do you want the red pajamas or the blue pajamas?"

According to the RIE website, in order to follow the method, you should work to achieve:

- Basic trust in the child to be an initiator, an explorer, and a self-learner.

- An environment for the child that is physically safe, cognitively challenging, and emotionally nurturing.

- Time for uninterrupted play.

- Freedom to explore and interact with other infants.

- Involvement of the child in all care activities to allow the child to become an active participant rather than a passive recipient.

- Sensitive observation of the child in order to understand his/her needs.

- Consistency, clearly defined limits and expectations to develop discipline.

The result, according to RIE, is an infant who is raised to be "competent, confident, curious, attentive, exploring, cooperative, secure, peaceful, focused, self-initiating, resourceful, involved, cheerful, aware, interested, and inner-directed."

Okay, so sign you up, right? I mean what parent wouldn't want to have a two-year-old who was competent, confident, cooperative, peaceful, and all those other adjectives? Hell, I'd settle for just peaceful . . . once a month!

Well, like all good things, there is a bit of a catch. It takes a lot of thinking and a basic retraining of how you speak and interact. We are simply not programmed to act in all the ways that you need to in order to get these results. That's not to say that it can't be done by you and your family and your caregiver. It simply means that you have to be willing to put in the effort. The other thing that is a bit tricky with RIE is that consistency does count, and unfortunately everyone that your child comes in contact with won't be trained in RIE—or agree with its teachings. I remember a friend of mine had just had hip surgery and her boss, a big RIE believer, came in with her eighteen-month-old. The boss insisted that my friend get down on the floor to address the eighteen-month-old, as RIE stresses the importance to be on the same level as the child. My friend nearly buckled over in pain from the experience and to this day thinks her boss is a whack job.

That said, this could be a wonderful method for children who are primarily raised by one caregiver or have a parent at home—as long as everyone is committed to the theory.

Dear Parent: Caring for Infants with Respect, by Magda Gerber (Resources for Infant Educators [RIE])

The Happiest Toddler on the Block

You may already be a fan of Dr. Harvey Karp's from the sleep chapter and his five "S's." Well, once you reach toddlerdom, he's got a whole other theory on the best way to communicate with your child. He stresses the importance of respect, as in RIE, but in a slightly different way. His evolves more from a place of acknowledging your child's feelings and emotions, and encouraging your child to express them. Then, he teaches you how to speak to toddlers in their own language so that communication can begin long before they can actually vocalize what they are feeling. The basic principles include:

- Understanding that toddlers communicate like primitive thinkers or cavemen. Karp divides kids up into developmental groups: the

"Charming Chimp-Child" (twelve to eighteen months), the "Knee-High Neanderthal" (eighteen to twenty-four months), the "Clever Cave-Kid" (twenty-four to thirty-six months), and the "Versatile Villager" (thirty-six to forty-eight months).

- Learning "Toddler-ese," a method of talking to toddlers by using short phrases, lots of repetition, a dramatic tone of voice, and exaggerated body language.

- Using what Karp calls positive discipline such as loss of privileges and time-out.

- Knowing expected milestones and managing expectations accordingly.

I have to say, the DVD of the parents putting this method to use had me convinced. Of course, Jen tried it with Sam, and quite honestly, he started crying harder. But many parents swear by it. I especially like the idea of acknowledging your child's feelings and letting him know that it's okay to be mad/sad/frustrated/annoyed, and all the other emotions kids experience on the hour.

I don't know if I could get past the toddler-ese, as it's basically like an overexaggerated form of baby talk. If I thought asking my eighteen-month-old if I could pick her up seemed funny in public, I certainly was going to have a tough time imitating her tantrums. Some childhood development experts take issue with the same thing, as they think talking to a baby like a baby will impede their language skills in the long run.

The Happiest Toddler on the Block: The New Way to Stop the Daily Battle of Wills and Raise a Secure and Well-Behaved One- to Four-Year-Old, by Dr. Harvey Karp (Bantam)

Books by Louise Bates Ames

I *loved* these books. Nancy Schulman, a woman whose opinion I trust more than just about any others, suggested this series to me. They truly helped me understand my children and myself. Louise Bates Ames gives you a book a year with step-by-step advice on how to handle the problems you may experience with that age group. They are breezy reads that get right to the point. Highlights include:

- *Your One-Year-Old*: From sleep problems to toilet training to picky eating

- *Your Two-Year-Old*: From thumb sucking to toilet training to discipline

- *Your Three-Year-Old*: From table manners to discipline to fear of the dark

Added bonus: If you like the series, she has books for four-, five-, six-, seven-, eight-, and nine-year-olds, plus a version for ten- to fourteen-year-olds lumped together. All are published by Dell.

Dr. Spock

The child-raising expert that your mother probably listened to was Dr. Benjamin Spock, and his books have stood the test of time. Dr. Spock is famous for his number one rule of parenting. "Trust yourself. You know more than you think you do." Don't be scared off by the fact that your mother read this book; newer editions cover such topics as:

- Learning, behavioral, and physical disorders

- Immunizations, vitamins, and nutrition

- Autism

- Raising nonviolent children; teaching tolerance

- International adoption

- Blended families

- Gay and lesbian parenting

- Talking to your child about sex, drugs, and disease

- Dealing with terrorism and disasters

Dr. Spock's Baby and Child Care, by Dr. Benjamin Spock (Pocket)

The *What to Expect* . . . Series

What to Expect When You're Expecting likely got you through your pregnancy. I know I barely got out of bed in the morning without referencing it. Well, the child-raising editions are no less helpful. *What to Expect the First Year* is a basic encyclopedia for parents, and *What to Expect the Toddler Years* continues in the same structure for all things toddler. The 900-page toddler book is divided into four sections:

- Development, milestones, pediatric checkups, parental concerns, and what parents should know and teach toddlers

- Health and safety involving general care, nutrition, home safety, first aid, toilet training, and caring for children with special needs

- The toddler in the family, sibling rivalry, parenting techniques, working parents, child care, adoption, divorce, and death.

- A reference guide with activity suggestions, recipes, home remedies, the symptoms and treatment of common illnesses, and forms for charting growth, health history, and memorable moments.

What to Expect the Toddler Years by Arlene Eisenberg (Workman Publishing Company)

Even though the toddler years can be trying and you will clearly want to read up on anything you can get your hands on to help you through the rough patches, don't spend too much time overanalyzing your little one's every move. It can be a lot of fun, and there are many laughs to be had if you simply sit back and enjoy.

CHAPTER 8

Breaking Up* Is Hard to Do
(*With Old Habits, That Is)

The bad news here is that I don't always practice what I preach. I let Jack have a bottle until he was four years old. Lilia is still sucking away on her pacifier as I write this. I've made the mistakes, used the bribes, all the "bad things" a parent isn't supposed to do. The good news is, for that reason, I have done *a lot* of research in these areas. From blankies to bottles, potty training to pacifier, I've been through the war zone. Here's hoping you won't have to.

Breaking Old Habits

The Mommy Store Is Closed

For most women, weaning off a breast comes pretty early on, and transitioning your child to a bottle is more about dealing with your own pain from engorgement than it is about having a child who refuses a bottle. Then, as time goes on (from about six months to a year), many children simply lose interest in the breast and go to a bottle on their own. That said, other mothers choose to feed for years, and getting a toddler to wean, in this case directly to a cup, can be pretty tough, especially when she is walking up and lifting your shirt.

The only upshot for these moms is that since your child will also be on solid food at this point, the pain of engorgement is far less than a mother who weans at say, three months, because her milk production will have slowed considerably.

Since this is the Modern Mom's book, I'm going to start (for once) with mom, and how to deal with engorgement, before I move on to giving steps to weaning both a baby to a bottle and a toddler to a cup.

Ouch! Engorgement

Okay, so engorgement from weaning kinda sucks, but the good news is, it's pretty short lived. And think of all of the fun cocktails you'll soon be able to enjoy. Start off by gradually weaning your child to the bottle or the cup, depending on age, so that your milk production starts to slow a bit (some tips follow). Then, make sure you have one last feeding session with your baby (and try and take a mental picture, as it is a little sad when you realize it's the end). After that, your breasts will pretty much just start to swell. And swell. And swell. And just about the point that you feel like Pam Anderson, they will likely begin to leak—so make sure your breast pads are handy. And you really just need to tough it out as long as you can. I remember this time being so painful that when we met some friends for dinner and my girlfriend's husband gave me a nice bear hug (no doubt to get closer to that HUGE chest I was sporting that night!) I winced in pain and nearly passed out. In the end, I made it about eighteen hours and had to pump off some of the milk for relief. And strangely, it just tapered off from there. I never got that engorged again, and my milk production just stopped.

> **MM TIP:** Some people recommend leaning over and placing just your nipples in a sink filled with warm water so that some excess milk will run off naturally without having to express/pump. Some mothers who wean off the breast earlier on in their children's lives often bind their breasts with Ace bandages: just a warning to be careful about binding too often or for too long, as some people think it can lead to mastitis.

From Breast to Bottle

Most babies take to the bottle fairly quickly and the bigger issue is keeping them on the breast once you introduce the ease of a free-flowing (albeit silicone) nipple. However, here are some tips:

- Start by eliminating one feeding session at a time if possible, to give your baby a chance to get used to the bottle and the formula. It's best to pump a little milk to mix with the formula to ease the transition.

- Offer the bottle when she's not starving, so she has time to get used to the bottle when she won't get frustrated.

- Keep the nipples slow flowing, so they resemble the flow of your breast.

- Slowly guide the nipple into your baby's mouth, just as you did at first with the breast. Don't force the bottle in.

- Run the nipple under warm water so it resembles the temperature of your nipple.

- Have your husband feed your baby the first few bottles, as she won't be expecting a nipple from him (let's hope!). You may even need to be in a different room.

- When you do feed your baby a bottle, try and hold your baby in a different position than in breast-feeding to avoid confusion.

From Breast to Cup

Some children will naturally be ready for this transition between six and nine months. Some hints that they might be ready include looking around the room or getting distracted during nursing sessions, mouthing the nipple without really sucking, or trying to slide or squirm away before their nursing is complete. If you see this (or if *you're* ready), going from the breast to the cup is very similar to going from the bottle to the cup in the gradual method, so see the next section for specific tips. However, the major difference is the intimacy between you and your child during the breast-feeding sessions. So keep these tips in mind:

- Give your child extra love and support during this time. It's as if they're losing a dear friend (funny, my husband feels the same way about my breasts, but I digress). Come up with some good alone time for just the two of you to substitute for the time you used to breast-feed such as reading a book or taking a walk.

- Expect that your toddler will likely replace breast-feeding with a thumb-sucking habit, a new security blanket, or even a doll. Don't discourage this at this time.

- When it comes to weaning that last breast-feeding session (typically the night one), do it at a time when your child will least miss it: when the grandparents are in town and can put him to bed for a few nights, or when you are on vacation with the child and the surroundings won't remind him of his breast-feeding ritual.

Buh-Bye Bottle

Some doctors will recommend that you start weaning your child off a bottle by age one, which is about the time they switch to whole milk (from formula, if you have stopped breast-feeding). And while this isn't a hard-and-fast rule, and you can certainly keep them on the bottle much longer, it's not an unrealistic or unreasonable goal to try and get them off by age two. That said, there are some definite advantages to getting them off at age one:

- Your child will only get more stubborn and set in his ways. While a one-year-old certainly may have an opinion about what he wants and doesn't want, those fits and tantrums are nothing compared to what you will go through trying to reason with a three- or four-year-old. The battle of the wills is a tough game to play. Believe me. I had to deal with this with Jack. I felt "bad" taking it away at one. Then Lilia was born when Jack was two, and I didn't want to do it to him then. And, of course, once she was on the bottle, I couldn't get him off. So we did it at four, and he got a tortoise in exchange. (Bribery, bad, I know!)

- Too much milk can make for a less-than-hearty eater. Children tend to drink more from a bottle than a cup, causing them to fill up unnecessarily and not be able to eat the healthy meals you're preparing for them. And it might make you think they are "fussy eaters" and limit their diet, when in fact they're just not hungry.

- Infants who drink while lying on their back are at a higher risk for ear infections, and toddlers who continue the habit have continued ear infection risk.

- Bottle mouth can result from milk left on the teeth, which happens more frequently with bottles. As discussed in chapter 6, baby bottle mouth comes from liquid—such as milk or juice—pooling in a child's mouth, especially right before bed and causing intense tooth decay. If it progresses, baby teeth may need to be pulled, which is not only traumatic, but can affect a toddler's developing speech.

There are, however, some cases in which it may be better if your child stays on the bottle. Some children have a very hard time drinking from a cup, and it takes them a little longer to learn. You certainly don't want to dehydrate your child in the meantime. Other children have an intense sucking reflex, and the bottle satisfies this need in a way few things can. It just sucks, but some kids really need to suck. Some children who are forced off the bottle too soon will look to other objects (read: things you don't want them to suck on) to satisfy the void of the bottle. If your child nearly sucked your nipples off while breast-feeding, and is now constantly sucking on a pacifier, a thumb, or anything else she can get her hands on, then chances are she may fall into this category. If you decide to stay with the bottle a little longer, be aware of bottle mouth and brush her teeth after every bottle.

So it's up to you, but if you've decided to wean your child off the bottle, here are a few ways of doing it.

Cold Turkey

Think about how your child reacts to change. If she's fairly easygoing, doesn't panic when things don't go her way, and is fairly proficient with a cup, then a cold turkey method may be for you (er, I mean her).

- Pick a time to quit when no other changes are going on: no travel, no major shift in her schedule, no visitors coming, no new sibling.

- Make sure both you and your child have gotten off on the right foot. She didn't sleep all night? She was up crying? She simply woke up in a bad mood? Pick another day.

- Begin the day with a big announcement that she is now a "big girl," and make comparisons to other big girls she knows. Let her know that today is the day she gets to start drinking all of her beverages out of a cup. (Don't say that she *can't* drink from a bottle; instead, focus on what she *can* drink from.)

- Have her help you get rid of all of the bottles and nipples by throwing them into the recycling bin. (Later, when she's not looking, retrieve them, as you *may* need them later.)

- Give plenty of extra love and attention, as your child could be a bit crankier during this time, and even perhaps start thumb sucking to make up for the absence of the bottle. You are also likely to have more night wakings, and general whininess throughout the day.

At this point, if your child seems fine with the absence of the bottle and is taking to the cup, then pat yourself on the back (and don't brag about it to any of your friends. They will likely shoot you!). If, however, your child is begging for a bottle when you try the first time, here's your backup plan:

- If you feel the need to cave, grab one of the bottles you saved (see, told you so!) and fill it with water. Offer your child water in the bottle, but explain that milk and juice are available only out of a cup now. Also try to limit the bottle to one time period (such as before bed). Chances are that your child will begin to lose interest in the bottle if she's not getting the liquid she wants.

Easy Does It

Most children like routine and have a bit of a tough time with change. For this kind of child, weaning a little bit at a time may be an easier approach.

- Make sure your child is proficient with a cup before proceeding, and pick a time to quit when there are no other changes going on: no travel, no major shift in her schedule, no visitors coming, no new sibling.

- Make drinking from the bottle a "still" activity. Most toddlers begin to find it boring to sit and drink a whole bottle. They like to have a sip here, wander around, have another sip there, drag the bottle across the room, and so on. Make bottle time one in which they have to stay put on your lap or in a chair, thus making it less appealing. The bottle needs to be in your control, not your child's.

- Offer up drinks from a cup and food *before* your child starts to beg for the bottle. In other words, anticipate her needs by satisfying her bottle cravings (which for most moms are like clockwork—morning, midday, and night) with actual meals. This way she may be so full that she doesn't notice she hasn't had a bottle.

- Keep her busy. When you're attempting to wean, make sure to pack her day with lots of fun activities, both at home and out and about. The distraction will hopefully take her mind off the bottle.

- Change up bottle rituals. Taking away a bottle that is part of a bedtime ritual will seem like cold turkey to your little one. Instead, offer milk from a cup before bed. If she's used to a bottle before her nap, try some soothing music and a back rub. Substitute the bottle with a little *you* time.

MM TIP:
Here's another way to wean: some people have success with a strategy that slowly replaces their milk with water. Evening bottles can have three quarters milk and one quarter water mixed together—which may be enough to gross them out—but you can then work every couple of days to add more water and less milk until it's all water.

MM TIP:
Try to wean your child directly to a cup, as opposed to a sippy cup, as then you will likely have to go through the weaning process twice. If you need to use sippy cups for convenience when you are out, it's fine; just try to avoid them at home when possible. Gerber makes some great cups that have a lid with a little opening in it, but still have the normal lip of a cup. They are called Lil Trainer Cups. Another option? Try one of those coffee tumblers with a lip and a lid. That way when your child does the "bottoms up" move with the cup, only a little bit spills out.

- Slowly cut back. Chances are your child has a favorite bottle of the day. Don't eliminate this one first, for heaven's sake. Start with the one she shows the least interest in and get rid of that. Then work backward.

- When you get down to that last bottle to wean—which for most children will be the one before bed—make sure you have a good ritual in place that includes brushing her teeth. If your child doesn't ask for the bottle, count your lucky stars. If she does, offer her a bottle with water in it and stand firm on the "no milk from a bottle" decision. You can always offer up the excuse, "You've just brushed your teeth." Chances are she will lose interest in a bottle with just water in it.

- Avoid having your child "donate" her bottles to another baby that may need them. A child at this age does not understand the concept of sharing, although she does understand resentment—something she could easily develop for other babies who may have "her" bottles. This is especially true if you have another little one on the way soon who will surely be using a bottle.

> **MM TIP:** If your child is old enough, try having him accompany you to a store to pick out fun cups to use. This may make the transition more fun. Buy ones in bright colors that are small so that little hands reach around them easily.

> **MM TIP:** It usually takes a few months to get the hang of using a cup and to stop using it as a toy to fling liquid around the room. You should expect to use water in a cup for at least two and often three months before trying juice and milk.

If All Else Fails

If your child is still having a tough time weaning off a bottle, check out a few of these tried-and-true tricks:

If your child is one who happens to love water and therefore is not losing interest in the bottle once it has only water in it, go out and buy the nipples with much smaller holes. It will make sucking that much harder and should eventually frustrate your child into giving up the bottle.

Cut the tops of the nipples to cause more liquid to come out freely. This can have the opposite effect of the above, thus causing your child to not get the sucking satisfaction and lose interest. Don't cut off too much, as it could be a choking hazard from the ensuing flood.

Dip the nipples of the bottle into something safe but bitter, like grapefruit juice.

Pitching the Pacifier

The good news for all of you who actually have to suffer through weaning your child off of a pacifier is that it's much easier to do than weaning your child off sucking a thumb or a finger. Think about it—you can physically take away a pacifier. Not really the case with a finger.

Of course, that comforting bit of advice doesn't necessarily make the process any easier. In a perfect world, you would wean your child off a pacifier at six months—a time when he is less attached to it and can simply remove it pretty much cold turkey. In fact, a lot of children begin to reject it at that age—much to the delight of their parents—and never look back. This is *really* a great age to get rid of pacifiers, especially as they've been associated with more frequent ear infections in older babies who use them.

Chances are pretty good, however, if you are reading this, the above is *not* your scenario. So keep the following tips in mind:

Begin to limit the use of a pacifier to the crib or the bed only. No pacifiers in the car, walking around the house, or at the mall. Period.

MM SIDE NOTE:
I must admit I'm a bit conflicted on giving this advice. I have to say that I know many happy, healthy well-adjusted kids who sneak a bottle at age five. I know experts would say the sneaking alone isn't good, but heck, we all have bad habits, right? So on this one, trust your gut. But also think about whether you're keeping him on the bottle for *you* or for *him*. It may be that you feel guilty about something, that you don't want him to grow up, or that he just really likes his bottle. Think it through, but remember the three-day rule, and trust that if you do decide to break the habit, you'll all survive.

And I will say that with an almost four-year-old (Jack) and an almost two-year-old (Lilia), I think Jack still misses his bottle, but Lilia basically didn't care at all by the second day. I know you *think* you're doing something "mean" by taking it away, and if it's their only source of comfort, maybe you (and they) aren't ready, but I truly believe if you can do it earlier, it will be easier on everyone.

MM TIP:
It is okay to replace the pacifier with another object of comfort for your child such as a stuffed animal or a blanket, but avoid going out and buying something new for your child as a reward for weaning. As tempting as it is (I did this, and wound up with a tortoise who is going to outlive the next three generations of Buckinghams), it may set up a vicious cycle of bribery in which your child feels justified in being rewarded with objects for each milestone.

Get rid of all of the pacifiers but one, and let your child know that this is the last pacifier. If it gets lost or disappears, that's it. And don't buy any more.

You will always be better off with changing your child's behavior permanently and without resentment if your child rejects the pacifier on her own rather than if you simply take it away. So begin to take steps to make the pacifier physically less appealing:

Let the pacifier get worn out on its own from use.

Rough up the nipple of the pacifier with a little sandpaper to make the texture less appealing.

Cut a slit in the pacifier so that perfect suction isn't achieved—just be careful that no part of the pacifier will break off in your child's mouth. Without the suction, kids quickly lose interest. If she tells you it's broken, just shrug your shoulders and tell her there are no more pacifiers.

Dip the pacifier in a safe but bitter liquid, such as lemon juice or grapefruit juice.

With these methods, your child will quickly lose satisfaction in the sucking process and will likely move on. Like all changes with a child, be prepared for three hard nights in which your child may wake up wanting a pacifier, or will cry out. But after about three nights, you'll likely be in the clear.

If you feel that your child simply has a really strong sucking reflex and are afraid to break her from the binkie, if you limit the use to the bed, you'll likely be okay for a few years letting it slip. And never dis-

MM TIP: As with the bottle, try to avoid using methods in which your child gives her pacifier to the "pacifier fairy" or donates it to another "baby in need." Not only will it likely make your child terrified of fairies (who swoop in and take things they love), but will set up undue resentment toward babies with pacifiers—which may describe a younger sibling.

count the power of her peers. The first time she has a friend/cousin/ relative spend the night and they don't use a binkie, chances are your child will begin to feel the need to self-wean.

Thumb Sucking

Kids who suck their thumbs do it as a means of security and self-soothing. It's a source of comfort for them as they explore the unknown—basically the theme of being a toddler. And while most babies abandon the habit at around a year, others continue it well into the toddler years. In fact, nine out of ten children will suck their thumbs at some point in their early years.

Most parents put a great deal of pressure on their kids to abandon the habit. In reality, this typically makes a child more nervous, and more prone to suck his thumb. So the first thing you need to do is get over *your* embarrassment at his habit. Most parents today *should* realize that this is simply a habit of comfort, not a sign of some emotional of intellectual instability in your child. And those who do shake their head at your child, well, just rest assured that they aren't as well read as you are and have a nice little chuckle about that.

It used to be that people thought thumb sucking interfered with speech development and even tooth alignment. Unless your child is plugging it in for hours upon hours, most experts agree that this shouldn't be a problem until after age five, when changes may actually occur in your child's palate. If left alone, most children will become less interested in thumb sucking at around three years old, especially when their lives rev up with the excitement of preschool. If, however, you find that your child is still a thumb-sucking champ at four, or if her habit interferes at any point with normal activities such as eating, speech development, tooth alignment, or even playing with her hands, then try these tips:

- Keep your child active and engage her hands as much as possible. Try finger painting or any activity that requires your child to hold on (swinging, rocking horse).

MM TIP:
As I mentioned with pacifiers, all habit-breaking techniques—from bottles, pacifiers, thumbs, and so on—should rely on the child's making a decision that is right for her, not being forced into something. The decision can come (rarely) by simply reasoning with your child, (sometimes) by having your child be motivated by an expert, (sadly) from embarrassment by being teased by other children, or (most likely) by just plain being ready, being a more sturdy and confident child, and having made a developmental leap. Just keep in mind that it is better if the child truly wants to change for herself.

MM TIP:
Never put down your child's behavior or call her a baby for sucking her thumb. Instead, praise instances in which she is achieving the desired behavior—not sucking— and go over the top in your praise.

- Put mittens on your child when it is cold and take her outside, or while inside, buy fun costumes with gloves and play dress-up.

- Get your child interested in playing with puppets and putting on puppet shows.

- Engage your child in song and conversation when possible.

- Make sure your child is fed on time and has snacks available at times when she most craves the oral fixation of a thumb.

- For little girls, offer to paint her fingernails, but tell her that a good manicure will be ruined by sucking, so she has to choose between the manicure and her thumb sucking (and be prepared for the fact that she may choose her thumb, and be okay with that).

- If you notice that the situation isn't getting any better, enlist the help of an expert. Just like the way time-outs work for the super-nanny (the theory being that children tend to listen to a stranger better than their parents), take your child to the pediatrician or the pediatric dentist and have her explain that she must quit sucking her thumb or the teeth in her mouth may become crooked. Have the doctor create deadlines for your child, and have your child call the doctor and report in on her progress. Being made accountable to another adult usually does the trick. But still be aware of your child and know what her limitations may be, as you don't want to set your child up to feel like a failure to another adult. This can be really tough on her self-esteem.

- Bring other family members into the mix. Have your child call an aunt or a grandma to report her progress in breaking the habit.

- If all else fails, go back to the doctor or dentist and speak with her about prescribing a bitter ointment or a mouthpiece that stops sucking at night.

Security Blankets and Other Comfort Items

The reason your toddler may choose to carry a comfort item actually makes perfect sense. When you think about it, your child is starting to become independent and doesn't necessarily take Mommy and Daddy everywhere she goes, but she isn't quite ready to go it alone. So the blankie, bear, or ratty old pillowcase becomes that trusted old friend that makes the world seem a bit more manageable. And frankly, adults aren't all that more advanced. I know that I can't stand to be standing at a cocktail party empty-handed, even if it's just a glass of sparkling water. Having a glass in hand makes it a little easier to navigate a cocktail party, especially alone.

The other reason children, especially around two, begin to rely on a comfort object is that new fears surface at that age, whether toward new people (the barber, the mailman, the shoe salesman), the dark, or even the vacuum cleaner (I agree, terrifying). So it should come as no surprise that this age is coupled with an intense need for teddy. Never criticize your child for having a comfort object, but try to take the following steps to make the object less important, and hopefully, make the transition off of it easier when the time comes:

- Limit the use of the blanket or teddy bear if possible. If your child hasn't started to carry it around the house, nip that one in the bud. Have her special teddy reserved for bedtime only. If she's already carrying it around the house, or out and about, start to create limits: The blanket can come in the car, but can't go to the playground. Couple the limits with reasonable explanations that look out for the security item: "Blankie might get dirty or lost." If she still insists, don't stress too much, she'll wean herself when she's ready.

- Wash the item regularly so that she doesn't become attached to the disgusting smell it is likely to take on. Once that happens, you will never be able to wash it (yuck!).

- Consider buying (or making—blankets, for instance, can be ripped in half) a duplicate. God forbid teddy gets lost or left behind; this can be traumatic for a two-year-old. Likewise, when it gets dirty, or an ear falls off, a duplicate allows you to substitute for repairs without your child's noticing (never let your child know there are two teddies). Some theories say that if it gets lost, then that is the time to deal with getting over the security item, but the problem is that you can't always guarantee it will go missing at an opportune moment. It's much better to be in control of when the object is weaned than have your child lose her favorite teddy the week her new baby brother arrives.

• Try to cut down on stress for your child when possible. Reliance on a security item can stem from a child feeling forced to achieve too much or grow up too fast. Be cognizant of your child's development and let her pick a pace that's right for her.

Chances are that your toddler will outgrow her security item any time between two and five years of age—with a few tendencies to reach back for it at stressful times. Don't *you* stress over the item if it's around until age five; it is completely normal and healthy as long as your child seems to be thriving, active, and developing socially. If, however, you notice that your child is becoming obsessive about her object, or spends more time with it than with toys, books, or other children, start to look for other issues that may be developing. These can range from stress at school or day care, an unhappy home situation, or, more seriously, a medical condition. If this is the case, consult your pediatrician.

Have a Seat: The Fine Art of Potty Training

Here's the thing. Like all habits good and bad, you can't create lasting behavior by forcing something on a child. And although *you* are no doubt ready (at this point you have likely changed 4,325 diapers, give or take a dozen or so), you need to look for signs that *your child* is ready and interested in being toilet trained, and encourage his behavior.

Some children begin to exhibit signs as early as fifteen months (rare); for other children, it can be as late as four years. For many children, being toilet trained comes in waves: good to go at two, a baby comes along, and they revert for nine months. Whatever your child's pace, the best thing to do is to simply encourage actions, create situations that make the toilet seem appealing, and, likewise, make diapers less appealing (if they don't begin to feel downright uncomfortable on their own). From there, you have to let your child go at his own pace and become the master of his own porcelain throne.

Are We There Yet? Signs Your Child Might Be Ready

Always remember, there is no good or bad to potty training, but rather ready and not ready. Before your child can have success at toilet training, he needs to fit the following descriptions:

- He can walk.

- He is aware of when he is going to the bathroom and you can either pick up on signals (a grunt, moving to a corner to squat) or he can tell you, even if just with a word, "pee-pee" or "poo-poo."

- He can hold his bladder. If you start to notice that your child wakes up from naps with a dry diaper, or you change a diaper every two hours and find that it is dry, chances are your child is beginning to "hold it." This typically can begin after around twenty months.

- He can pull his pants up and down.

- He is interested in wearing underwear instead of diapers.

- He has regular times that he goes poo—after breakfast, at a certain point in the afternoon. However, like some adults, some children are never regular, so rely less on this point.

- He expresses interest in the potty and may even follow family members into the bathroom.

MM TIP:
Somewhere between 18 months and two years, a child may have a false start. They may show an interest in wearing big girl pants, or going to the potty, get off to a great start for two days, and then just as rapidly change their minds and go back to diapers for another six months. This is typical, so don't worry, and try again when she's ready.

MM TIP:
Keep a potty in the back of your car. Some kids don't like foreign toilets, and with the portable toilets being small, and, well, portable, it can save you a few accidents.

MM TIP:
For little boys learning to stand and pee, paint a target with nail polish in the bottom of the portable toilet for him to aim.

- He understands that the feeling he is having in his tummy will lead to going to the toilet.

- He shows an interest in putting things where they belong.

Ready, Aim, Pee

If all systems are a go, then try some of these tried-and-true potty-training tips:

- Make sure the timing is right in the household. If you are about to move, expecting another child momentarily, or switching day care, or if he is sick, postpone for a little while.

- Set out several child-sized potties and let your child know they are there, and he has several places he can get to quickly.

- Take your child to the bathroom with you all the time. Let your child see you (or a member of the family of the same sex) using the big potty so that he understands the process (imitation works wonders). Let him see what is in there, and then let him flush.

- Put the potty in place even before the child seems ready. Let him sit there (even while clothed) to get used to how it feels. Let him put his toys in it (before he is peeing in it). Let him feel ownership over it.

- Talk about how fun the potty can be. Explain how fun it will be for him to wear underwear/pee in the toilet/go just like Mommy and Daddy. Just be careful not to put down diapers, as this could result in rebellion.

> MM TIP: Mastering the toilet is tough enough, let alone trying to have little boys stand, aim, and fire. Getting boys to sit first is typically the best way to proceed. Then, once he is proficient with the skill, have his dad or other male figure introduce him to the act of standing to pee.

> **MM TIP:** Add food coloring to the toilet that will change color when he pees in it (red plus yellow urine will turn orange, blue plus yellow urine will turn green.) Also try Cheerios for little boys as an object to hit, but beware, this could cause him to not want to eat his breakfast!

- Some pediatricians recommend letting children decorate their potties with stickers, so that it becomes that much more special and "theirs."

- Decide on your terminology and have the entire family be consistent with it. Some experts urge you to use the clinical terms like *urine* and *feces* or *bowel movement*. Personally, I think it's tough enough to get a two-year-old to the potty, let alone to utter the words "bowel movement." So in our house we go pee and poo.

- Move away from the changing table and into the bathroom. If you are changing his diapers in the bathroom, he will begin to understand the connection between the toilet and going to the bathroom. Dump bowel movements from his diaper into the toilet (so that he can see).

- Swap snaps and zippers for elastic waistbands. Come on, one objective at a time—there will be plenty of time to learn how to button. Easy access is a must.

- Let your child flush the toilet. Not only will he find it fun, he will get used to the sound.

- Buy underwear that he gets to pick out. Getting to wear Superman skivvies can be a powerful motivator for a little one.

- If your backyard is fairly private and it's a warm day, consider letting your child run around bottomless and pull out the potty if he starts to go. This is a great way for your child to become visually familiar with what is going on with his body.

- Point out to your child when he is making a bowel movement. This is typically pretty easy to recognize, as your child will grunt or

MM TIP:
Peeing in the potty starts first. It's not unusual for children to want to pee in the potty and still poo in their diaper. Children view poo differently than we do. They see it as an extension of their body. As gross as it sounds, they are used to having it up cozy next to their body. We're telling them to get rid of it. They do, and we clap our hands, cheer, and we flush it away. This can be sad and traumatic to children. Also, some children don't like the feeling of the space between their body and the toilet water or the splash of the water. It is certainly within the range of typical behavior to have a diaper to poop in up to four years old. Consult with your doctor or child development specialist if you find this is your situation.

MM TIP:
Look for signs that your child needs to go to the bathroom—when he is tugging at his pants or fidgeting. Also, anticipate his needs by escorting him to the bathroom after mealtime, a bottle, or before a ride in the car.

squat. Simply say, "See, when you are pushing like that, you are making a poop. Soon, you will be able to do that in the potty." Then change his diaper.

- When possible, let your child wear real underwear at home instead of diapers or pull-ups. He can feel the wetness better, and it is less comfortable to run around in wet underwear than it is a wet diaper. This will be a good motivator for him.

- Offer a special toy or book for use only when your child is on the potty.

- Don't force your child to stay on the potty. You don't want the bathroom to feel like prison. Five minutes is a good rule of thumb. If he hasn't gone by then, let him leave the bathroom and try again later.

- Offer lots of praise and cheers when your child succeeds, but don't go so over the top that it seems hollow, or worse, makes your child feel like a failure when he has an accident (no pressure here!). Avoid using terms like "good pee" or "good poo," as that then implies a bad pee or poo (in the diaper in this case). Instead focus on the action: "You made a pee in the toilet!"

- If your child will pee in the toilet but refuses to poo (and therefore ends up going in her pants), say to her, "It's not okay to go poo in your pants. It's okay to go in a diaper or the potty, so I am going to let you choose." If they don't choose the potty or can't say the potty, then put them in a diaper. Then, when you have the urge to go poo yourself, tell your child you have the feeling in your belly that you have to make a poo and have her follow you into the bathroom to see how it's done.

MM TIP: Don't be surprised to find a child who runs and hides to make a poo in his diaper. They are getting the aspect of privacy—which is good—and that's why they are hiding. Encourage them to go into the bathroom for that privacy.

At Night

Getting your child through the day dry is one thing (why do I feel like I'm writing a deodorant commercial right now?), but making it through the night is quite another. Your child should not be expected to hold his bladder for ten to twelve hours at this point, so expecting it is incredibly premature. (Look, try it, but don't be freaked if it doesn't work.) By around age four, you can begin the transition out of nighttime diapers and take these special precautions:

- Limit the intake of liquids after 5 P.M. and during or after dinner. Bottles at bed sabotage night dryness. (Be careful *not* to do this during the day, as you don't want to risk dehydration. On the contrary, giving your child lots of liquids during the day creates many opportunities for him to use the restroom.)

- Make sure your child has gone to the bathroom before he gets into bed.

- Do a fun "potty-drill" with your child that helps him outline the steps to the bathroom at night, and leave on enough lights for him to find his way.

- Consider using pull-ups that allow your child to try on his own, but cut down on the mess for you when accidents occur.

- Create a special incentive by letting your child pick out special sheets or pajamas to wear and try to keep dry.

- Make sure you buy a liquidproof mattress pad to keep your mattress dry.

MM TIP: Many children wet their bed—either regularly or occasionally—as late as age eight. Chances are, your child is more embarrassed than anyone else (one friend's six-year-old son dreads sleepovers and stops drinking liquid on his own after 4 P.M. when he is having a sleepover in fear that he might wet the bed). Give your child encouragement and support during this time, and never scold.

MM TIP:
When your child has an accident, which he will—many times, never scold. Simply comment on the accident matter-of-factly: "You had an accident, let's go change you." Be careful not to say "It's okay," as this could discount your child's own feelings of embarrassment. At the same time, you don't want to add to his shame.

MM TIP:
Never let your child wear underwear over a diaper. Underpants are a reward for mastering the toilet. By letting them wear them *with* a diaper, you sabotage a major reason to move away from diapers.

MM TIP:
Make your child's bed with a waterproof pad, then a fitted sheet, then another waterproof pad and another fitted sheet. That way, if there is a middle of the night accident, you will simply have to strip off a layer rather than fidget with remaking the bed.

Bathroom Hygiene

You may have mastered the toilet, but you're sadly only halfway there. With many children, potty training signals independence, something that translates into wiping and washing their hands on their own as well. But if your child doesn't wipe properly, you could be stuck with smell, or worse, infection. The same is true with bathroom hands. Here are the tricks you must pass along to your child:

- Teach girls to wipe from front to back to avoid urinary tract infections.

- Show children how to wipe gently so as not to irritate their skin, but firmly enough to get rid of waste.

- Try Kan-dos wipes, which are wet like baby wipes. They sit nicely on the toilet, and make wiping easier (a little moistness cleans better than dry toilet paper), and it is less likely to crumble and get little hands dirty.

- Show a child how to wipe a doll by putting jam on the doll and making sure they wipe until the tissue is clean.

- Make sure both you and your child wash your hands after every visit to the potty. Even if you're doing the wiping—which will likely be the case in the beginning—by including the washing ritual at the end, your child will get the picture that going to the bathroom and washing hands go, well, hand in hand.

- Some kids wipe better if they get off the toilet and squat. The wipe is more important than the position they do it in.

- Most nursery schools will not (and should not) wipe a four-year-old. Keep this in mind as a goal.

- Wiping is hard, and bad wiping is the reason kids this age need to bathe every night.

Okay, I don't know about you, but I need a break. . . .

CHAPTER 9

The Play Dating Game and Beyond

Sure, you knew feeding a baby might be tricky, and everyone knows you'll be tired with an infant, but playing with him? Heck, anyone can *play* with a baby, right? Wrong. In those first few weeks with Jack I felt somewhat stymied. Should I talk to him? What should I say? Should I read him the newspaper? God no, that's too depressing even for me. Play with him? Of course, but how? He couldn't hold anything, didn't know how to play a game, and seemed to fall asleep whenever I broke out a toy. And given that we were awake for seeming eternities (see chapter 5), there was an awful lot of awkward silence between us. So what do you actually *do* with a baby and then, later, a child?

Well, first, recognize that your baby does *not* need you to play with her every moment. She should absolutely be in a safe place, but assuming that is the case, you can leave her on her own a bit so that she can explore her environment on her own. Playing with infants and children is wonderful, but they also need some peace and quiet, just as you do. As she grows, you should help her explore and learn, but not run in with a new toy the second she seems tired of the old one. If you allow her no frustration with a task, then how will she learn to overcome frustration and solve problems creatively herself? As we discussed in chapter 7, try to wait before rushing in, and let them learn at their own pace. You are their guide and at times their playmate, but, as I've said, you are not their savior.

But when you are feeling up to a little entertainment, here are some of my favorite toys, activities, and "when all else fails" ideas for having something to do.

Best Toys and Activities at Any Age

Ah, toys. They're supposed to be fun, right? Well, when they overtake your house, start quacking at 3 A.M., and make you feel as though your paycheck goes directly to the local toy store, you might wonder. And while many are inexpensive, you don't want to be wasting money on toys that never see the light of day or break just when the going gets good. So here's a guide to some of the favorites around.

Birth to Three Months

At this age, chances are your baby needs very few (if any) actual toys. They're probably happy just looking around. Lights, colors, shadows, and patterns will all intrigue them (Jen's son Sam had a thing for ceiling fans; go figure). Their hands and people's faces are new enough. Try an eighteen-inch cotton scarf with many colors. Consider hanging it on a clothesline and as the baby gets older, he can manipulate a scarf how he prefers by pushing, pulling, twirling. (This is a great alternative to mobiles, which—although moving—are less changeable.) Scarves do not pose a choking risk unless tied (so don't do that!). Remember, infant play is about them exploring their own body, and their surroundings visually and aurally. A pinwheel, leaves on a tree, even just watching you do your thing is great stimulation.

Okay, so that's all well and good, but I know very few parents who can completely resist buying their babies toys. So when you do:

Look for toys with bright colors and high-contrast patterns, as those will be easiest for your baby to see. This is why many infant toys are red with black and white patterns. Also, remember that at this age babies are somewhat nearsighted.

Look for toys that move in and out of her sight line, like a mobile.

Consider toys that play music or a wind chime that she can sometimes even ring herself.

Think about a soft book with patterns that are easy to see.

Try sensory toys that make a noise when touched. Not only will the sound interest the baby, but over the next few months she'll learn that her hand can control the noise. But beware; the noise might drive *you* crazy.

MM ACTIVITIES:

- At this age, the best thing to do is create a continuous dialogue. Treat her as if she understands. Narrating what you're doing, from "I'm going to give you a bottle now" to "We're going into the other room to change your diaper," is great stimulus.
- Play soft music, but keep in mind that babies like a strong, methodical beat (it's all about repetition and mimicking the beat they are used to in the womb, which is surprisingly fast). While many parents opt for classical, reggae music has a solid, steady beat that has natural buoyancy. Reggae cycles at around sixty to seventy beats per minute, and while that may seem fast to you, it's actually a perfect rhythm to complement the natural rocking a baby felt inside the womb. Bob Marley's *Buffalo Soldier* is close to a perfect sixty beats per minute.
- At this point, the activities are really about you. Go to the zoo or museum if you want to, but know this isn't doing a lot to enrich your child at this point. Personally, I'd indulge in a little shopping with your child since they will still sleep through the experience in a stroller. Later, you won't have that luxury.

MM TIP:

At this age, infants look to the right 80 percent of the time; so put a mobile, mirror, or other toy on the right crib rail. Some research shows that this has to do with how their brain develops.

MM FAVES:

- Gymini Total Playground by Tiny Love: This playmat plays music, has toys, a mirror, and seems like heaven to an infant.

- Lamaze Clutch Cube: This multisensory cube will grow with them in the months to come.

- Peek Rattle and Teether by Infantino: Name says it all, no?

- *My Quiet Book* by Babystyle: This is a great book for you to read to them at bedtime.

Baby Massage

One activity you can pretty much start with an infant is baby massage. While I'm not a big fan of spa treatments for infants (what? You think highlighting Lilia's hair at two is too much?), massage is a great relaxing time for you and your baby. According to Alison Lister, a fabulous Los Angeles–based masseuse and creator of some of the cutest baby products I've seen (www.rosemarybaby.com), massaging your baby is an excellent way to build the bond between you and your child. It also offers health and relaxation benefits for both of you. The optimal time for massage is after your baby's bath and before bed, but not just after eating.

According to Lister, you will need:

- Warm baby oil or talc-free powder

- Towels

- Your warm and loving hands

- Short fingernails

- No rings or bracelets

Sample basic massage:

- Start with your baby on his back.

- Place a small amount of warm oil or powder in your hands and rub them together.

- Start with the feet and slide your hands gently up the body and down again several times.

- Hold one foot in your hands, thumb in the arch of the foot, and massage gently. Don't forget to give some attention to those little toes.

- Holding the foot with one hand, use your other hand to work slowly up the leg with your fingertips.

- Repeat on the opposite leg.

- Move your touch to the tummy.

- Place one flat hand underneath on your baby's back and the other on his tummy and make small gentle circles with your palm (or for the itty-bittys, your fingertips) in a circular, clockwise motion.

- Move your hands to the chest and gently stroke your fingertips from the center out.

- Move down the arm to the hand.

- Place your thumb in the palm and massage gently, paying extra attention to each little finger.

- Hold your baby's hand with one of your hands, and with the other massage up the arm with your fingertips.

- Repeat on the opposite hand and arm.

- Move to stand behind your baby's head.

- Move your hands under the head and gently massage the neck and base of the skull.

- Lightly place your fingertips on your baby's forehead and move them from the center outward.

- Massage the jaw.

- Stroke the ears.

- Turn your baby onto his tummy.

- Place a small amount of warm oil or powder in your hands and rub them together.

- Massage his back from the head to the bottom.

- Gently stoke the back in a downward motion working from the spine outward on either side.

- Place one hand on your baby's back just above her tiny little bottom and rock gently. This is highly relaxing and a great movement to send your little one off to a peaceful slumber!

Some things to keep in mind:

- Always massage with a gentle touch with an infant. Start with the lightest and as you work you can move deeper.

- Test your oil to make sure it is warm and soothing, not hot.

- Slow massage movements are relaxing and are excellent before bedtime.

- When massaging the torso, your heavier movements should be down, toward the feet.

- When massaging the limbs, your heavier movements should be toward the heart to increase circulation.

- When massaging the tummy, it is important to only move clockwise, as this motion aids in digestion.

- Ears are great to massage, but never cover the ears completely and release them suddenly, as this can damage delicate ear tissue.

- Make sure you massage your baby on a secure surface, and keep a guiding hand on him at all times.

- Babies can wriggle and squirm during massage. Don't worry. Just go with the flow. If your baby wants to roll over on her tummy, start on her back, and vice-versa.

- The optimal duration for massage is ten to thirty minutes at least once a day. You may have to build up to this as your baby adjusts to this kind of relaxation. Don't worry, she'll love it!

MM TIP:
Remember that all your baby's toys will end up in his mouth, and so paper-covered blocks or toys will get ruined. Make sure all your toys for this age are chewable.

Four to Twelve Months

Good news: At this point your baby can actually reach for things, and probably move them from one hand to another and even play with her feet. Most of the toys that you bought before are ones she'll actually start responding to now:

- Musical instruments that are easy to hold

- Wiffle balls he can stick his fingers through and grasp

- Stacking and building toys

- Toy telephones

- Soft puppets

MM ACTIVITIES:

- If you haven't already, this is a great time to try Itsy Bitsy Spider and Peek-a-Boo. If you don't know how to do these, I'm afraid I can't really help you.
- Although I think children are a bit young to appreciate the zoo at this age (they can't see a thing from those strollers), many young children love aquariums. Big fish tanks, with all the colors and movement, are very appealing.
- Around six to ten months you'll see a change in that if you hide an object under a blanket or pillow, your baby will be able to find it. Try it every couple of weeks to see when the change takes place. He now understands "object permanence" and will realize that when an object goes out of his sight, it's not just "gone."

MM TIP: Remember to encourage solitary play. Put some (safe) things in the crib such as toys, a baby mirror, or a scarf to encourage them to spend some time playing alone. If you're concerned that toys in the crib will prevent them from sleeping, you can put them in after your child falls asleep. Don't fall into the trap of always carrying or entertaining your baby; it's a habit he'll get used to pretty quickly.

MM TIP:
Trust the manufacturer's suggested age. Sure, yours might be a little genius, but even if he's "advanced," a toy that's too old for him may cause a lot of frustration or be unsafe. Sure, try it if you must, but be prepared to pack it up for later.

MM FAVES:
- Skwish Classic from Manhattan Toys: This toy is hard to describe but is fun to hold, twist, and explore.

- Little Softy books (www.onestepahead.com): These small tactile books are great to carry around and play with.

- Mini Orchestra (www.onestepahead.com): These small instruments let children explore music in a fun way.

- Classical Stacker by Fisher Price: You'll find you remember this classic toy, but with new music and lights, this one does you one better.

Twelve to Eighteen Months

Ha ha. You were just dying for your baby to walk, right? And you were *so* proud when he did it before your friend's baby. And now you're wondering what you've gotten yourself into. Or what he's getting into. He's probably going a mile a minute and eager to explore with his new mobility. He'll also be a bit more coordinated with his hands and feet at this point. Some ideas:

- *Climbing gyms/centers.* Your guy wants to move around but you can't go to the park all day, so (space allowing) try to bring a bit of the park home. Crawl spaces or inflatable houses are great.

- *Balls.* They're round, they bounce, they come in lots of sizes, but beyond that you may wonder where the fascination lies. Trust me, boys or girls all dig balls. Jen bought a little inflatable swimming pool and filled it with balls, and Sam loved to dive in and out of it all day long.

> **MM TIP:** Remember, they'll be putting them in their mouth, so don't get small balls that are choking hazards or foam ones that they can bite pieces off. A good rule of thumb: If you can get your mouth around it, it's too small.

MM TIP:
Remember to disinfect and clean toys regularly, especially after play dates. These things have been in their mouths and are headed right back there. This is especially true of ball pits, otherwise known as germ pits.

- *Push/pull toys.* Although you may be able to use them earlier, this age seems to be when kids truly love them. They can lean their weight against the toy for added support. Some function as activity centers, with lights, levers, and music. Typically, kids push them at first and pull them as they get older.

- *Ride-on cars.* At this age they can't really pedal, so look for ones with long poles at the back that you can push easily. Although electric ones can be fun, they are pricey, have to be charged frequently, and do nothing to advance their motor development. Just make sure that if your child is still dealing with balance issues there is a strap to hold her in.

Picture books. Around this time, your toddler will probably really begin to get into books. Look for ones with a variety of pictures, but words that repeat often. It's also a good idea to buy the durable cardboard books without covers that rip, as much of the fun early on comes from roughly turning the pages.

> **MM TIP:** Keep reading. Even if he isn't sitting there and prefers to be running around, he's probably listening. Children like the magic of words and your energy and intonation can create a great habit and love of reading.

MM ACTIVITIES:

- Create a mini-fort with pillows and blankets.
- Try puppet shows. But use smaller handheld puppets; big ones may scare them.
- Sing fun songs they can *begin* to mime, like "Wheels on the Bus," "Twinkle Twinkle Little Star," and "Where Is Thumbkin?"
- Look for a local kiddy space or gym class to take your child to; it will have some of these activities and many more.

Eighteen to Twenty-four Months

At this point, she is getting into everything, putting teething biscuits in the VCR tape slot, shutting doors and drawers (often on her fingers), pulling every available pot or pan out from the cupboard. Well, that's how she is going to learn. So look for toys that have interlocking parts, that mimic real life, and that help build handling skills.

Some ideas:

Nesting toys. Although this is when they may start stacking, don't expect it to be in the right order.

MM FAVE:
Sandra Boynton books such as *But Not the Hippopotamus* and *Barnyard Dance* (Little Simon, Board division)

MM FAVES:
- Quatro Large by Lego: Larger than regular Legos, these are great for building.

- Ambi Teddy Carousel by Brio: This easy-to-push spinning toy tends to mesmerize toddlers.

- Learning Band Walker by LeapFrog: This push toy has learning parts, enter-taining parts, and everything a toddler could want.

- Baby Symphony Cube by International Playthings: Your child can discover music and the power of his touch.

MM TIP:
Allow your child to play *his* way. Don't direct the play or show him the "right" way to play with a toy. If he wants to kiss the toy guitar or use it as a drum, let him do it (unless, of course, he's hurting someone). Also, be careful not to distract your child from what he's enjoying or overwhelm him with too many toys. If he is happy with his toy train, no reason to start vrooming the car (unless you are bored).

MM TIP:
Remember to leave a cupboard or drawer filled with "safe" pots and pans and unbreakable containers so that your child can discover them on his own and play with them as he likes.

MM FAVES:
• Nesting Action Vehicles by Fisher Price: These are two-in-one toys in that they are cars that roll and stack. If your child doesn't like them, you will.

• Building Block Choo Choo by Babystyle: This pull-along train also teaches stacking.

• Jungle Safari Tent and Tunnel by Pacific Play Tents: Here's a fun but safe exploring tent thingy. That's a technical term.

• Wooden food set (www.rightstart.com): These fun-looking fruits and veggies are also great for learning to cut because they are sectioned and stick together with Velcro, yet come with a wooden "knife" to separate.

- Blocks of different sizes
- Paints
- Plastic tea set, food, and kitchen items
- Puzzles with big knobs to make grabbing easier
- Train sets (yes, for girls too)
- Playhouses
- Washable crayons and paper

MM ACTIVITIES:

- At this point, a trip to the zoo might be fun (finally); but plan on putting your child on your shoulders much of the time, as they won't be able to see much from a low stroller.
- Try making play dough: In a large bowl, mix 2 cups of white flour and ¼ cup cream of tartar. Stir in 2 cups of water, 2 tablespoons of vegetable oil, and whatever food coloring you like. Pour the mixture into a medium saucepan and simmer over medium heat, stirring constantly until it won't stir anymore. Cool, knead, and play! Try using some of your kitchen tools like a garlic press, potato masher, or others as toys. Store in plastic containers.
- Try painting with shaving cream. It's a fun way to make a manageable mess.
- Paint the house: Fill a small bucket with a handle with water and let your child "paint" the outside of the house (or wash the car or his bike). Use a two-inch fat painter's brush.
- Water the plants. Watering cans are a big hit at this age. Start with outside plants if you have hardwood floors.
- Make pasta necklaces by stringing pasta on a piece of fat yarn. Be sure to mold one end into a point with tape, and tie a piece macaroni at the end so it doesn't fall off. Try painting it as well.

continued

A FEW NOTES ON PAINTS

- Go for fat brushes with big handles.
- Until age three, skip the watercolors and instead, try making your own paints by combining tempera paint with liquid starch by Vanno. It doubles your paint supply and makes the paint less runny.
- Buy plastic containers with different color lids and a hole in which to put the brush. Match the top to the color to help your toddler find the "right" place to put the red, yellow, or blue brush.
- Try placing the paint colors in an egg carton rather than plastic reusable containers. That way when you're done, you just toss it.
- If the paint is so drippy it gets all over the place, add a bit of cornstarch to thicken it up. Add the cornstarch only to the paint you're using, though, as it will make the rest too thick for use later.
- Add a few drops of liquid detergent to paint so that it will wash out more easily. But beware, for some reason, blue paint never truly comes out.
- Try using an old raincoat as a smock. Cut the arms off and put it on backward.

A FEW NOTES ON COLORING

- Many experts believe that you should give your child blank paper over coloring books when possible, and here's why. Not only might it stifle their creativity, but children can't color within the lines until about age four. The lines will only set them up for frustration and some feelings of failure.
- Look for "fat" crayons. Ask for kindergarten-size ones. These will be easier for your child to handle.

MM TIP:
I *love* Color Wonder Paper and Markers. The markers are designed so that they don't show up or color unless they are on the special paper. These are brilliant, especially when traveling or going to someone else's house where "sorry about your couch" doesn't really cut it.

MM TIP:
Instead of commenting on the "quality" of your toddler's painting, talk about the use of different colors, or comment about the process: "You covered the whole page!"

continued

- If you're coloring with your child, don't draw elaborate pictures that they can't hope to achieve. Instead, doodle and scribble as they do.
- Consider covering your play table with paper. Inevitably your toddler will color off of his paper, and this way you won't mess up the table and can change out the paper when it gets too grungy. Many school supply stores sell large rolls of butcher paper with a cutter. Or at least use oversize paper. You can also use a trash bag or old shower curtain as a cover.

Twenty-four to Thirty-six Months

Now's a good time to find toys that help channel your toddler's ever increasing energy and (as they near three) their thirst for more challenges. In addition to the above, try:

- Instruments
- Child-size household products—such as vacuum cleaners, pots and pans, small brooms—you can enlist their help for real!
- Big construction toys
- Puzzles
- Simple games such as Bingo

MM TIP: Skip the 500, 100, or even 50 pieces. At the most, puzzles should have 12 pieces. Look for ones with big pieces and simple pictures they can follow.

MM TIP: Although they are hard to categorize, I'm a *huge* fan of the LeapFrog toys. From the learning drum to the portable Leapster, they are engaging and educational toys that both of my children have loved. While I'm not a big fan of forcing education at young ages, these help teach your child in a fun, engaging way.

MM TIP: At this age your child isn't really able to play board games with rules, but is interested in games with the opportunity for completion and success. That's why a game like bingo may be a big hit—he can cover the whole row.

- Memory games

- Books that are slightly more grown up than board books, as they are now able to treat books respectfully and learn to love them

MM ACTIVITIES:

- Learn letters and coordination: You draw letters with chalk outside. Call out a letter and have your child jump to it! Or consider getting magnetic letters for your fridge or alphabet and number cookie cutters as a way to begin to expose your children to letters and numbers.
- Color mixing: Get clear glasses, fill with water, and let your child add food coloring to make different colors. Beware. Food coloring can be a mess! So either be prepared or wear some gloves or use tempera paint instead.
- Teach your child how plants drink: Use white carnations, put food coloring in the water and watch the flowers turn a different color.
- Plant a seed: Avocados and lima beans grow fast! Or try carrots, tomatoes, or green beans, which he may enjoy eating when ready.
- Practice cutting (thirty-six months and older): Allow your child to use a child's scissors to cut fringe along the bottom of a piece of paper. Don't bother drawing lines, as this will be too hard to follow and sets them up for failure. Many boys may not be able to do this until closer to age three and a half.
- Clean a carrot: Kids love to use a vegetable peeler (assisted, of course). Let them peel the carrot down until it wiggles. And they can eat the peelings if they peel it that far.
- Paint flowerpots or shiny stones: Use them for gifts or to plant seeds.
- Take pictures: Give your child a disposable camera. Let him take pictures. Develop them and put in an album (yes, even if they're all of his thumb). If you have a small, easy digital camera, kids enjoy the instant gratification. If you have a Polaroid camera, they'll love to see it "spit out" the picture.

MM TIP:

Although she probably won't be playing board games until three and a half or four, when you do start, don't let her win all the time. Although it's natural to want to let your child "win," you'd be doing her a disservice. If she wins all the time with you, she'll be awfully disappointed once she plays with anyone else and will be more of a "sore loser." Some subtle confidence building is okay, but trust me, you don't want to wind up with a sore loser.

MM FAVES:

- Board games: Candy Land, Chutes and Ladders, I Spy

- Little Tykes Vacuum Cleaner

- Cozy Coupe II by Little Tikes

- Books: *Stop That Pickle, If You Give a Mouse a Cookie, Chicka Chicka Boom Boom*

To TV or Not TV

Okay, you'll tell yourself that you will *not* be one of those parents who park their kid in front of the TV just to get a break. Your child will be different. Your child will be better. And if you can stick to that, more power to you. After all, the research supports you in your quest toward abstinence. One study from the American Academy of Pediatrics (AAP) showed that watching videos as a toddler may lead to attention deficit hyperactivity disorder in later life, and a study for the University of Washington found that TV viewing before the age of three was linked to poorer reading and math skills at six and seven. And if that's not enough, the AAP study showed that quick scene shifts become "normal" to a baby and may overstimulate her brain, causing permanent changes in neural pathways. To that end, the AAP recommends that children over two watch no more than an hour or two of TV a day and under two watch no TV at all.

Having said that, I bought the entire Baby Einstein video series faster than you could say, "Where's the remote?" There were days when the choice was (in my mind anyway) a shower and twenty minutes of "educational videos," or sticking with a no TV rule. And darn it, I wanted to smell nice. So if you're going to let them watch something, there are ways to alleviate your guilt.

MM TIP:
Always watch any DVD you buy for your child before you show it to him. You'd be amazed at how scary or inappropriate some "classics" are. Your child may love them, or they might scare the heck out of him.

- Watch DVDs, videos, or recorded TV. That way you can control not only the content, but keep out commercials. (If you don't have Tivo or a DVR, run, do not walk to get it.)

- Designate times that TV is and isn't allowed. Be consistent about this. Otherwise, set a daily time limit and keep count.

- Don't set your family room up around a TV. Put the TV somewhere less comfortable or in a cabinet, so that it's out of sight and out of mind.

- Look for slower-paced programs (*Blues Clues*, *Dora the Explorer*, and *Teletubbies* are all good options).

- Avoid scary themes.

- Give your children a five-minute warning when a program is going to end and the TV will be turned off.

- Find ways to broaden the learning. If a show focused on numbers, try counting steps or reading books about numbers later.

- Don't, under any circumstances, put a TV in your child's bedroom.

Play: Is It All It's Cracked Up to Be?

I remember when I was about seven months pregnant with Jack meeting a woman in a maternity store near me who asked what school and classes I had my baby enrolled in. Given that I was barely sure whether I was taking a Lamaze class for myself, I chirpily told her none. The woman looked at me as if I had told her my child-raising philosophy involved dark closets and beatings. She told me that I was already way behind for the best preschool in our neighborhood, and that there was no *way* I'd get into the to-die-for fancy baby group. Jack was a fetus and he was already behind.

Well, New York is a bit more aggressive than the rest of the country, and Jack and I enrolled in a lovely Mommy & Me class that turned out to be just fine, thank you. But it did raise the question of when he should start playing, who he should be playing with, and what the heck I should be doing to plan for this all. You'll worry that your child has no friends, then you'll feel he has too many when you spend all of your time at birthday parties. You'll think he has too many toys, and then you'll wonder why all of your friends' babies seem to have better and far more educational ones. Play, I'm afraid, is far more work than it looks!

Picking the Right Playgroup and Classes

Newborn

Many experts would say that you shouldn't enroll your child in *any* classes until he is at least six months old. By taking your child to classes with other infants (let alone toddlers) you are exposing him to

MM TIP:
If you're a movie buff like me, chances are you're pretty anxious to whisk your child off to the next big-screen animated feature (finally you'll feel justified for shelling out $10 to see a talking fish!). Put on the brakes. Until your child is four or five (depending on his maturity), it will be pretty tough for him to sit through a full-length animated feature. It's also a good idea to check out the film first, talk to other parents who have seen the film, or read extensive reviews. My friend's son nearly passed out at age four at the shark in *Finding Nemo*.

MM TIP:
Aim for a group with five to seven parents. That way if some are sick (or sleeping, or the other numerous reasons you won't be able to go) the group won't be too small. Any more and the babies might feel overwhelmed.

MM TIP:
You may find yourself in a playgroup with parents of very different child-raising philosophies. While that might be okay for some, for others it might be reason enough to find a new group.

MM TIP:
Although there are many regional classes, Gymboree (www.gymboree.com), My Gym (www.my-gym.com), and Music Together (www.musictogether.com) are great ones to check out nationally. You may want to see if there is an RIE class in your area if you are into the RIE method (see page 235), although these are more limited nationally.

many germs and possible illnesses. And truth is, your baby gets enough exercise during the day and doesn't *need* other children as regularly as he will when he gets older. But, although your baby isn't ready to get out and meet new people, *you* might well benefit from a new mom's support group that talks about child-rearing issues. Classes can also show you some ways to interact with your baby and point out what your baby might be capable of at different ages. Try to find a class that's nearby and has children within a few months of age of your child. Not only will that allow you to be going through many of the same issues, but as your children get older, they'll be good playmates!

Six Months

While I'm an advocate of classes for socialization (for both you and your child), try to keep from overscheduling your child. Children need their downtime, and you also run the risk of turning your child off a sport or activity he might have enjoyed if you had waited another year.

That said, at about six months, you might want to look for a class that has activities, like padded ramps, big balls, slides, swings, and music. But remember, your child might be overwhelmed by the action and may want to take it all in the first few times. If he isn't crawling yet, look for a class that also has some singing or out-of-the-action areas where you two can sit and look at toys or books.

You can also consider swim classes. But don't let the name fool you. This isn't about "teaching" your baby as much as socialization and getting you and your baby used to the water. The AAP recom-

MM TIP: Just because your child may "know" how to swim doesn't mean he should ever be left alone in the water. According to the Consumer Product Safety Commission, 75 percent of backyard-pool drowning victims are between twelve and thirty-five months of age, so keep a watchful eye.

mends you hold off on swim lessons until age four, as they feel children younger than four generally don't have the motor and cognitive skills needed to learn to swim. Having said that, Jack and Lilia both started learning at two through lessons and with Marcus and I, and they are both great swimmers with few tears in the water. On the other hand, I have friends who held off until four, and their kids refuse to even get their hair wet.

Eighteen Months

At eighteen months you may want to consider Mommy & Me class held at a school or religious center. Not only will this be a great way to get your child familiar with school, but also it will give *you* a chance to check out and evaluate some programs near you (see below for picking a preschool). Also at eighteen months, your child might really like a music class. Look for one that gives her a chance to develop her motor skills—through playing musical instruments, free dance, and singing songs.

> **MM TIP:** Don't be alarmed if your baby (like mine) doesn't want to sit through circle time. Many babies will want to get up and explore. They probably won't be able to sit through a five-minute circle time until about age two, and probably won't be able to do fifteen minutes until they head to kindergarten. But just because they're running around doesn't mean they're not paying attention or listening.

Twenty-four Months

Dance classes or gymnastic classes are great around age two. At about two, she can join movement or "pre-dance." These tend to be fun and are great for burning off energy, but are not truly formal dance instruction. Hold off on formal training until your child can really focus for about thirty minutes, have real coordination, and wait her turn, which will happen around age four or five. You do not want her to feel as if she is not performing well or is inadequate. She should be having fun!

MM TIP:
At the end of the day, the best way to get your child comfortable is for you to spend as much time as possible in the pool with them.

MM TIP:
Hold off on formal musical training until age five, which is when the brain is truly ready to start learning in this way. For some instruments, like the guitar, you may want to wait until even later, as children's small hands have a hard time manipulating the strings. Also, remember that formal lessons can take away some creative expression.

MM TIP:
Look for sports your child is interested in, not the ones *you* think he should be interested in (or the ones in which your best friend's child is interested). Also, sit through an entire class with your child before signing up to see if both you and she are still into it. Marcus took Jack to "the" soccer class, and after watching the coach yell at the kids and send one home for not focusing, we realized that it wasn't right for Jack.

MM TIP:
If your child wants to quit a class that he showed interest in, tell him that you signed up for whatever number of classes (four seems reasonable) and that he needs to finish the commitment. After that, he can stop.

Thirty-six Months

In addition to preschool (discussed on page 289) at about thirty-six months, you might want to consider a team sport such as soccer. At this age the game should *not* be about winning but should be about learning skills, spending time with other children, and beginning to appreciate the value of a team. Team sports and classes for which you leave your child shouldn't begin until about age five.

> **MM TIP:** As he gets older, consider having your child work toward expertise in one team sport (such as soccer) and one individual sport (such as tennis). This will allow him both to have his own achievements and to know the value of being part of a team.

Play Dating

You'd have thought that the queen was coming for Jack's first play date. The house had to be spotless. We had every snack an eighteen-month-old might even *think* he may want. We bought two of virtually every favorite toy so that no one would feel left out. The room was babyproofed well enough for a child living in a bubble. Well, as it happened, Jack's new friend had missed his nap, stayed for about thirty minutes during which the two boys virtually ignored each other, and our new friend left crying because he tripped and banged his head on one of the new toys. So rather than plan a play date more grand than your wedding, think instead about when, who, and how to make the most of the time. First, recognize that *how* your child plays will change over time. And if you understand these stages of play, you may be setting your child, and yourself, up for more "successful" play dates.

Observational Play

Up until about eighteen months, toddlers will play with similar toys near each other in the same room, but they probably won't really play *together*. At this stage, they are trying figure out social behaviors and how to get the attention of other children. As they pass a year, they might get interest in a toy the other is around or imitate each others' sounds, but they probably won't do much jointly.

Parallel Play

Parallel play is important and one of the first relationships your child may have outside of her family. Around eighteen months, you may notice that your child seems more attracted to other children. Although they may not play together, they will likely be interested in what the other is doing. They'll play on the same side of the room but not actually *together*. And even if your child doesn't seem very interested in the other child, chances are she is watching and learning from the other child.

Imaginary Play

Starting around age two, you may notice some pretend play, although they will also still be participating in parallel play. This allows your child to try out new ideas, experience life from a different perspective, and role play in new ways. Around age three, he might have an imaginary friend or imaginary powers. If this happens, not only should you not worry, but you should encourage it! Research by Dr. Jerome Singer at Yale University found that preschoolers with imaginary friends had bigger imaginations and vocabularies and generally got along better with classmates (real ones, that is).

Cooperative Play

Around age three, children begin to learn to new social skills such as sharing, obeying rules, and taking turns, but don't expect this to really take hold until age four or older. Chances are there will still be a lot of parallel and imaginary play. In fact, a child may grab another child's toy simply as a way of (awkwardly) showing he wants to play together. Although collaborative play can be wonderful, it can also be hard on a child who is used to having what he wants when he wants it.

Play Date Ideas

Although a play date will change depending upon the age of the children, here are a few things to keep in mind (and please take a moment to read about sharing in chapter 7, as this will save you some grief):

- Ask your child if there are toys he wants to put away that are special to him and he is unable to share. Respect his wishes and put them somewhere the other child won't happen upon them.

- Make sure you have a safe, clean area for the kids to play. If you're going to be outside, spread a blanket or towel large enough for your child and her friend to sit.

- Bring out a few toys that lend themselves to sharing, such as blocks, art supplies, dress-up clothes, and so on. Avoid "star" toys that children are likely to fight for.

- Limit the play date to an hour or two.

- Don't leave your children alone until you know extremely well how they play together. And even then, be sure to be within close range.

- Have light beverages and snacks for the adult. Lemonade or iced tea and fruit are plenty.

- Ask the parent before you bring out any snacks for the children. The other parent may have different food preferences or schedules. Don't bring out juice boxes or cookies, as they might not be welcome.

- Look for snacks that allow them some independence and don't need you to help out. Also remember to check whether any of the children have any food allergies. Snack time is a great break for the kids if they are getting irritated or tired. Some good snacks for play dates (after eighteen months):

- Sliced apples

- Goldfish crackers

- Bread and butter sandwiches

- Yogurt (in a tube that they can do themselves, or drinkable ones with a straw)

- Applesauce

- String cheese

- Fruit juice popsicle

- Cheerios

MM TIP:
It's awfully embarrassing when a friend's or acquaintance's child wants to have a play date and your child isn't interested. Try telling your friend that you are trying to help your child achieve some independence, and she really isn't interested in play dates right now. Similarly, if a child declines your play date invitation more than two times in a row without a reciprocal invitation, it's better to redirect your and your child's interests.

Nannies Versus Mommies

If you're a mom who works outside of the home or you can't be available for play dates during the day, you'll quickly find that there is a play date pecking order and you're at the bottom of it. Mommies tend to have play dates with other mommies (and *occasionally* daddies). Nannies tend to have play dates with nannies. It's not so much a class thing as a similarity thing. This is the mommies' and nannies' "play time," too. It's their chance for a little adult stimulation. However, this can be quite tricky if you are one of a few working mommies who finds her child with a woeful lack of play dates. If this is the case, I encourage you to find a nice mommy with whom you can have a few play dates on the weekends. Explain the situation and ask her if she would have a play date with your nanny. Offer to do it at your house so that she isn't entertaining. Typically, she'll oblige.

Birthday Parties

Think of the birthday party as the uber-play date. Many moms start planning the first one right after labor. I didn't, and perhaps I should have. I have to admit I blew it there. I hired a man to be Elmo. I think he had come from a gig as a stripping cop. Once Elmo showed his head, Jack burst into tears. Party over.

The truth is, parties can be as elaborate as you want or as simple as you choose. But there are a few things to remember:

- Parties should last two hours, maximum. You want it to be over before *they* want it to be over. Serve the cake after ninety minutes. Trust me, not only will a longer affair overstimulate your child, but with as many parties as you'll be going to, you won't want to spend more time.

- Parties should be planned around naps, depending upon the age of your child. Although there's no time that guarantees everyone will come, 11 A.M. to 1 P.M. is often a good time, as many kids can come early or late.

- If you're inviting a lot of people, consider RSVPs for "Regrets only." And think about e-mail RSVPs as sometimes people remember when it's too late in the day (or too early) to call.

- Don't forget to put your name on the RSVP line on the invitation. Many parents may know your child's name but not yours.

- Clearly state whether siblings are welcome or not. Although I think it is nicer to include them, remember that this can double the size of your party.

- If you're looking for a smaller party, plan it on a weekday. Parents (and children) are more likely to have commitments they can't get out of.

- Don't hand out invitations in class (Mommy & Me or preschool) unless you are inviting everyone.

- Decide whether you want to have the party at your home or another space. The advantage of your home is that your child might feel more comfortable and you don't have to lug gifts. But you do have to clean up and run the risk of ten two-year-olds destroying your furniture or, say, your cat. Also, your child may not *want* to share his toys, and may feel more comfortable on neutral territory. The advantage of outside spaces or indoor play spaces are that they have more "fun things" to do than you probably do; they do the cleanup and setup; and all you really have to provide (usually) is the cake and paper goods. The downside is they can be quite expensive.

Party Ideas

Before we get started, it's really important to think about whether this is a party you are doing that your child will enjoy or one you are doing to keep up with the Joneses. I'll admit it, I threw one that kept up with the Joneses, their cousins, and everyone else within a forty-mile radius. It was great fun, but it was way over the top (you'd have thought I'd have learned with Elmo, but nooooo). Anyway, there was more stuff to do than any child could process in two hours. The fact that neither Jack nor Lilia threw a fit is a huge shocker. But the very next weekend we went to a party with cupcake decorating, bubble blowers, pin the tail on the donkey, and only four kids, and Jack had an even better time than at his own. Plus, now I wonder what I'll do for the kid's next party. At this rate, we're going to need elephants, a trapeze artist, and Beyonce performing live by age ten. The moral is, small kids, small party. Honor your child's temperament. If you think he'd enjoy a small affair with his favorite foods and one activity and you're looking to impress your friends, throw him his party, and then throw a separate adult one in which you toast him!

Here are some things to think about as you start planning:

Age One

- At age one, the party is definitely about *you*, not your child. Your child won't remember a big shindig, and is more than likely to get overwhelmed by crowds and spend much of it in tears (Elmo or not). If you choose to simply buy a cake and invite a friend (or not) and sing happy birthday and take a picture (as we did for Lilia), that's really plenty.

- If you want to have a bigger party, consider having it at a park. That way it feels more spacious and less overwhelming. Parents and kids can come and go as they please.

Age Two

- Chances are at this age you can still get away with the same as above. But if you're looking for something bigger, consider a performer who sings songs, brings musical instruments, and makes balloon animals. Remember to check references on anyone you hire. Look for someone with enthusiasm and lots of activities. Wit and humor will be lost on this crowd.

- Try to limit the number of children at the party to the age of your child plus one. (If you have a two-year-old, invite three kids.) Try to keep the children's ages within a few years of each other so older kids don't get bored.

- Consider cupcakes instead of a cake. Two-year-olds can handle these much better than a fork. It's a bit easier to clean up, can be very festive, and if you let them decorate their own, you've got a fun activity for all.

Age Three or Four

MM TIP:
Up until age four or five, your child won't care if there are more children at his friend's party than his own. He won't need to keep up with the Joneses, so think about whether you really need to.

- Although again, you do not need to do anything fancy, chances are your child may want some kind of party.

- If your child is in school, either:

  - Invite the whole class. (Look, I know parties are expensive, but I'm a big fan of including everyone. I just hate for anyone's feelings to be hurt.)

  - Invite all the boys or all the girls.

  - Invite the same number of children as your child's new age plus one.

- If you don't want to throw a party, suggest a special outing to your child instead. We went to Sea World one year when Jack's birthday was over spring break and most of his friends were away. We had a great time, ate cake in the hotel, and the "party" lasted all weekend.

Some Fun Party Activities

- *Bouncy houses.* What a good sample sale is to women, a bouncy house is to toddlers. They just can't resist them! A bouncy makes a party. Consider having it arrive a bit early or stay a bit later than the party so that your child can have some special time in it. Also look for one that has steps that let them climb in (duh) and a flap/door that closes on its own so children don't fall out!

- *Bring in the puppies.* Lots of companies will bring seven or eight puppies for your children to pet. Big hit. Huge. Great for two- to three-year-olds.

- *Bubble blowing.* Get lots of different bubble blowers and have fun.

- *Wild animal show.* Consider it a more sophisticated version of puppies. Many companies will bring everything from a boa to a ferret to a hissing cockroach. Great for ages three to four.

- *Magicians or puppet shows.* Local companies can provide these, but I strongly encourage you to try to see their act in advance. Like a comedian, some are huge hits, others are duds.

- *Sugar cookie or cupcake decorating.* Have the cookies or cupcakes already made and cooled, and then let the kids have fun with the icing and sprinkles.

- *Ice cream sundae making.* Set out a big table with all of the fixings, and let each child build his own.

- *Frame making.* Buy inexpensive frames and stickers and let the children decorate them. It's even more fun if you take Polaroids or digital pictures you can print at home.

- *Scavenger hunt.* Think Easter, but get rid of the eggs. Hide little toys or candies around your yard.

- *Decorate bird houses with stickers and designs.* My friend Katie had this as the activity and then gave birdseed as the favor (see goodie bags below). Totally adorable!

MM TIP:
Bouncy houses aren't good for children under two, and it's better to have children of the same age in at once. If you have a lot of older children, consider giving them a special fifteen minutes alone to be as rough as they want—then out!

MM TIP:
Maybe it was watching that scary clown in Stephen King's *It* or a bad experience with Bozo, but personally, I'm just not a big fan of clowns. If you have one, consider having him put on his makeup in front of the children (my friend Julie had her clown do this, and it was so smart). If he starts out "normal" but then turns into a freakish-looking creature, somehow it's okay. Consider having him put clown faces (or at least clown noses) on children who are interested to further remove any fear.

MM TIP:
I'm not a huge fan of piñatas. Bats and small children? Just not the best combo. If your child is desperate for one, as Jack was, consider doing it the next day, or well after the party with one or two friends. Also, you don't have to fill it with candy. Try small toys. Just nothing sharp as you don't want it to wound someone as it comes flying out.

- *Decorate hats.* A friend used an Alice in Wonderland theme with top hats and straw hats kids could paint, glue cards on, and put stickers and feathers on. Just avoid the hot glue gun. Ouch.

- *Old standby classics.* Pin the tail on the donkey or hide and seek.

- *Field day.* Create fun field games in your backyard or basement that include potato sack races, three-legged races, and egg-on-spoon races (skip the latter if you're doing it indoors).

- *Watch planes take off.* We went to a terrific party for a two-year-old airplane aficionado at a location where you could watch planes take off and land. It was inexpensive and fun for the kids. They handed out earplugs as everyone arrived, which was supersmart.

- *Consider going on a public bus.* Sounds crazy, I know, but let them put the money in, give them a special "bus hat," and they go somewhere, turn around, and come back! Obviously, this is a lot more fun for kids who don't live in a city in which they usually take the bus with their parents.

- *Get a fire engine to come to your house.* Many local fire houses will drive over a fire engine and let the kids climb or even take a ride.

- *Let them wash your car.* A party you and they will enjoy!

MM TIP: Bowling makes for a great party, but not until children are five or six. Until then, they can't really pick up the balls. An exception is if your bowling alley has bumpers they can put up that keep the balls from going in the gutter. In this case, you can try it with four-year-olds.

Goodie Bags

We've gotten goodie bags nicer than the gift we've brought. Heck, truth be told, we've *given* goodie bags nicer than the gifts we received. For Jack's fourth and Lilia's second birthday (we combined them), I went to three different Targets to hunt down the exact same Play-doh, cars, and candies I felt were "musts" for the party. While goodie bags do not need to reach epic proportions (hey, just because I give advice doesn't mean I always take it), there are a few things to keep in mind:

- Goodie bags should be the same. Even though you may *think* you've cleverly figured out what your children's friends want and love, if they see each other's goodie bag, what they'll suddenly *love* is what the other child has. The exception to this is by age. If you have three- and one-year-olds at the same party, you may want to adjust the gift to be age specific.

- It's nice to have the goodie bags match the theme of the party. If the party is zoo themed, look for beanie animals or figurines. If you hired a magician, find a simple magic trick for the bags.

- Don't include candy. Many parents really restrict sweets, and after cake or cupcakes, they may not appreciate another injection of sugar.

MM TIP:
www.birthdaypartyideas.com has lots of, well, good ideas, and www.birthdaydirect.com has lots of great party supplies.

MM TIP:
Although personalizing party favors is a wonderful way to make children feel special, it can be a huge pain! Also, if you have any last-minute guests you won't have a favor for them, and any no-shows will stick out like a sore thumb.

Some Goodie Bag Ideas

One-year-olds
- Tube of bouncy balls (big enough that they aren't a choking hazard)
- Puppets
- Shovel and pail
- Little stuffed animals
- Bath toys

Two-year-olds
- Bubble blowers
- Mini-Play-doh tubs
- Make your own play dough (page 270) and add a cookie cutter
- A mix CD of your child's favorite songs

MM TIP:
To help commemorate your child's birthday, try writing a letter about the year they've just had. Put them all in a box. What a great gift for when they are older!

MM TIP
To avoid getting candle wax on your cake as your two-year-old attempts to blow out the candles, try sticking the candles in marshmallows or gumdrops if you don't have candleholders.

- Face paint
- Puzzles
- Books

Three-year-olds

- Safari hats with binoculars and a stuffed animal
- Rub-on tattoos
- Kites
- www.orientaltradingcompany.com has a variety of fairly inexpensive goodie bags and fun things to stuff in them (although some can break, so maybe buy one and make sure you like it)
- Toy trains
- Disposable cameras
- Paper and crayons

Gift Tips

- If you've ever seen three-year-old open gifts, you'll understand why your friend Annie never sent a thank-you note. Cards get lost faster than you can say "Lego! My favorite." Instead, consider stickers with your child's name (or family name) on them. www.tinaj.com and www.snapfish.com make great ones. Stick it onto the gift. Another option is to print a stack of four by six photos of your child or children and use that as the card (attach with tape!) You can also print out pictures onto mailing labels on your own.

- Try to avoid having your child open gifts in front of his friends. Not only will this add chaos, but your child may not be ready to share his gift and the giver may be bummed he's not leaving with it. Instead, either open after the party with one friend or alone with your child.

- If you receive a lot of gifts, consider opening three or four, then doling out two every other day until they run out (but give your child warning the day before they'll run out).

- Consider having no gifts at all, and let your child know the party is his present. Or do as one noble mom in LA did and ask parents to bring an unwrapped book. The mom and her son then donated the books to a local school that was desperately in need.

- Save yourself some money. If you didn't follow the above advice on elaborate parties, and kids are bringing presents, you really don't have to buy something spectacular. Don't go overboard on present buying; maybe just give him one.

- When he's three or four, consider having your child pick one or two gifts he was given, or at the least old toys, to donate to charity for children who don't have as much as you do. It doesn't matter what toy, or even if it's because he received two of something, it is the thought that counts. If you think that won't fly, before the party, have your child look around his room and have him donate some (okay, one) toys to make room for the new ones.

- Although your child won't be able to write thank-you notes himself at this age, consider having him draw a small picture or letter on a few to let him know that thanking people is important. Get in the habit of thanking and appreciating.

Picking a Preschool

Okay, we're getting to the end of my guide, and I'm confident that with your newfound tricks, tips, and own innate genius you're going to be just fine. Except about preschool. You've heard of Bridezilla? Think Mommyzilla—the suddenly unrecognizable woman who will stop at nothing to get her child into the school of "her dreams." Because just when you thought you'd figured out the tricky things—found a class you liked, gotten your child to loosen his death grip on most toys, and even found a few children (and parents) you'd call friends—it comes

MM TIP:
Although it's hard to know a "bad" preschool, if they have a lax sick child policy (i.e., the child doesn't have to wait twenty-four hours after a fever to come back) or the school has no curriculum and relies heavily on TV or videos, you may want to rethink it as an option. Also, too rigid of a curriculum may not allow your child to explore.

time to figure out preschool. And this is no playground. I am sorry to say this truly could be its own book, so I am just going to give you *some* of the highlights so you don't feel like I'm leaving you in the lurch at your moment of need. But this is a serious subject, and perhaps one I'll take on big time next time.

But you can't wait until then. While I don't want to panic you, you *should* look and ask around about local preschools as early as age one. Some schools base admission (in part) on when an application was filed. Most won't allow you to apply before birth, but you can soon after. As I said, don't panic. Sometimes enrolling in a Mommy & Me or volunteering in the school is another way to help gain admission.

Some preschools will admit children at age two and a half, although many will not accept them until age three. Although children don't *have* to go to preschool, studies have shown that children who do attend preschool are more easily able to adjust to kindergarten. It's also important for your child to learn to trust someone other than the mommy (or primary caregiver). Typically, you need to apply a year before that date, unless the school bases admission on when the application was filed. Best to fill one out early, and you can always withdraw it later.

The best reasons to be looking for a preschool are if you feel your child isn't stimulated enough at home (or at day care) and you feel she is ready to broaden her social horizons. But picking the "right" school for you and your child isn't easy. It's easy to get seduced by "the" preschool, but the most important thing is determining what you want most for your child and the environment that will be best for him. When I first moved to Los Angeles, I was in a panic because Jack was two and a half and I had missed the application for most preschools. Every mother I spoke to seemed to recommend the same impossible-to-get-into school. I finagled an interview and thought I might even be able to secure a place (a boy with a similar birthday to Jack's had just moved out of town). But upon visiting the school I found it was a forty-minute drive from my house and, in my opinion, too sterile an environment. The teachers did not seem friendly, and one parent told me that if your child was crying, the teachers would tell your child they were going to call you, but then wouldn't. "The" school or not, it was not a place I wanted to send my child. Instead, we found a nice school near our house where Jack (and I) happily settled in.

Look back to my list for choosing a good day care center (page 76), as many of the same rules apply, but you will want a preschool that offers a bit more structure than you might be looking for in day care. And while you should certainly ask for recommendations from neighbors, friends, and relatives, remember that a good preschool for their children might not be the right preschool for yours.

Here are some things to think about:

MM TIP:
Although you may think you're sending your child to preschool to learn his ABCs and times tables, think again. You may do better to look for a school that fosters self-esteem, confidence, independence skills, and socialization. A child who doesn't know the alphabet at four can be taught. A child who isn't well socialized may have further to go.

The most important thing is that your child is in a place where she is safe and well supervised. There is no such thing as "the best" school. Every one will have things you like about it and things that you don't.

Although you certainly want a school that is licensed, most licensing requirements are less about quality and more about meeting health and safety requirements. So look for schools that are accredited by an outside organization. The National Association for the Education of Young Children is the biggest and probably best. You can find a list of schools near you at www.naeyc.org.

Ask whether the school has an open house night or tours. You should ask about everything from philosophies to activities and schedules to fees, hours, and discipline.

Check the teacher-to-child ratios (1:5 is best for two- to three-year-olds, 1:7 is best for three- to four-year-olds)

Meet the director and try to determine her philosophy. She's the person who will be hiring the teachers. If you don't subscribe to her theories, you're likely to be unsatisfied. Ask what their discipline and separation policies are and see if they fit with your ideas.

Watch the teachers with the kids. Are they friendly and encouraging? Do they look bored and tired? Look for a school with a combination of veteran teachers who have been with the school awhile and some younger teachers with new methods and possibly more energy.

- Think about convenience. You may be spending a lot of time there. And if the program is only three hours long and the drive is forty minutes, by the time you drop your child off, you'll have to turn around and go back for pickup. Also, if the school is far away, chances are many of the children she'll be having play dates with will live far away, too.

- Check references. Ask parents *why* they like it. Ask the school for a list of some parents to talk to about the school. Consider calling your state's Better Business Bureau to check if any complaints against teachers or the school have been filed.

> **MM TIP:** Trust your gut. If a school doesn't feel right to you, it doesn't matter how "popular" it is—don't go. On the other hand, if *no* school feels right, question *your* gut. It's like finding the right shoe that fits. When you know, you'll know.

Getting Your Child Ready for Preschool

Some children head off to preschool with nary a wave. Others have a meltdown. Others, like Jack, are fine for the first few months and then suddenly don't want to go a few months in (when the novelty of it has worn off). Although much has to do with separation anxiety (which we discussed in chapter 7) and some to do with the school itself, once he's enrolled and ready to go, here are a few ways to help get him ready:

- Take a tour of the school with your child. Focus on some fun things they have at the school that you do not have at home.

- Find a special backpack for her to bring.

- Explain that school is like "work" and very important. But don't say things that aren't true, like "This will be the best day ever," as it might not be.

- Don't belittle any fears. Try to help him by giving information about what the day will be like.

> MM TIP: Separation at preschool is a *big* issue. I can't tell you that one school's philosophy is better than another, but personally, I think the idea of leaving your child and never looking back doesn't work. Although different schools have different separation policies, I'm a fan of schools that allow you to stay with your child until they are ready to go. I refer you back to chapter 7, and the great resource we suggested there. But one thing: don't sneak out without your child noticing. Separation is about building trust that you will come back. Sneaking and trust don't usually go hand in hand.

- Try to arrange play dates with children who will be in his class either before or soon after school begins. This is important. The more play dates he has, the more likely he is to feel socially comfortable.

- Read and look at books about going to school.

- Put your child's first name and last initial on everything you are bringing to school.

- Get there early the first few days. It may be easier for your child to enter a playground/classroom that isn't filled with children already.

- Opt for clothing that's easy to take on and off to facilitate going to the bathroom.

- Ask her silly questions about school to get her to open up like, "Did you fly on an airplane today at school?" or "Were those silly ladybugs trying to take all the paint?" so she can laugh and potentially open up. If it still doesn't work, ask your child's teacher what they will do on certain days so that you can be specific and ask, "How was music today?", not just "How was school?"

- Celebrate the first day of school with a fun activity he can look forward to (such as baking a cake or going to a favorite restaurant). Take a picture to mark the achievement.

MM TIP:
Do not buy a backpack with your child's name printed on it. Although it is not a common occurrence, a stranger could call your child by his name and thereby seem familiar and safe.

MM TIP: If you have lots of time to volunteer at your child's school, great! But if you have to be selective, be sure to pick things that your child will see you doing at school so that he knows you're involved with the school and like it too!

Okay, so that's it. No more writing in the car waiting to pick up my son, and no more hoping my daughter will sleep an extra hour for her nap. For now, I'm off to be a mom (as are you). Here's the good news: your child is going to grow up in spite of you or despite you. Hopefully, this book will help to make the process just a little bit easier. So have fun, relax, and remember: being a Modern Mom isn't about being perfect, perky, or in the best preschool. It's about unconditional love, clear limits, and (every so often) looking good doing it.

XO

Bibliography

Bates Ames, Louise, PhD, and Francis L. Ilg, MD. *Your Two-Year-Old: Terrible or Tender*. New York: Dell Publishing, 1976.

Bates Ames, Louise, PhD, and Francis L. Ilg, MD. *Your Three-Year-Old: Friend or Enemy*. New York: Dell Publishing, 1985.

Behan, Eileen. *Meals That Heal for Babies, Toddlers, and Children*. New York: Pocket Books, 1996.

DeBroff, Stacy M. *The Mom Book*. New York: The Free Press, 2002.

Douglas, Ann. *The Mother of All Toddler Books*. New York: Wiley Publishing, Inc., 2004.

Ferber, Richard, MD. *Solve Your Child's Sleep Problems*. New York: Fireside Books, 1985.

Gaskin, Ina May. *Ina May's Guide to Childbirth*. New York: Bantam Books, 2004.

Gerber, Magda. *Dear Parent: Caring for Infants with Respect*. Los Angeles: Resources for Infant Educators, 2002.

Goer, Henci, and Rhonda Wheeler. *The Thinking Woman's Guide to a Better Birth*. New York: Perigee Books, 1999.

Greenberg, Gary, and Jeannie Hayden. *Be Prepared: A Practical Handbook for New Dads*. New York: Simon & Schuster, 2004.

Greene, Alan, MD. *From First Kicks to First Steps: Nurturing Your Baby's Development from Pregnancy Through the First Year of Life*. New York: McGraw-Hill, 2004.

Hogg, Tracy, and Melinda Blau. *Secrets of the Baby Whisperer for Toddlers*. New York: Ballantine Books, 2002.

Iovine, Vicki. *The Girlfriends' Guide to Surviving the First Year of Motherhood*. New York: Perigee Books, 1997.

Karp, Harvey, MD. *The Happiest Baby on the Block: The New Way to Calm Crying and Help Your Baby Sleep Longer*. New York: Bantam Books, 2002.

Karp, Harvey, MD. *The Happiest Toddler on the Block: The New Way to Stop Tantrums and Raise a Happy, Secure Child*. New York: Bantam Books, 2004.

Kuffner, Trish. *The Toddler's Busy Book*. Minnetonka, MN: The Meadowbrook Press, 1999.

Lothrop, Hannah. *Breastfeeding Naturally: A New Approach for Today's Mother*. Tucson: Fisher Books, 1999.

McCutcheon, Susan. *Natural Childbirth the Bradley Way*, Revised Edition. New York: Plume Books, 1996.

Mindel, Jodi A. *Sleeping Through the Night: How Infants, Toddlers, and Their Parents Can Get a Good Night's Sleep*. New York: HarperCollins, 1997.

Murkoff, Heidi, Arlene Eisenberg, and Sandee Hathaway, BSN. *What to Expect When You're Expecting*. New York: Workman Publishing, 2002.

Murkoff, Heidi, Arlene Eisenberg, and Sandee Hathaway, BSN. *What to Expect the First Year*. New York: Workman Publishing, 2003.

Murkoff, Heidi, Arlene Eisenberg, and Sandee Hathaway, BSN. *What to Expect the Toddler Years*. New York: Workman Publishing, 1996.

Sears, Martha and William Sears, MD. *The Birth Book: Everything You Need to Know to Have a Safe and Satisfying Birth*. New York: Little Brown, 1994.

Spock, Benjamin, MD, and Steven J. Parker, MD. *Dr. Spock's Baby and Child Care*. New York: Pocket Books, 1998.

Van Der Zande, Irene. *1,2,3 . . . The Toddler Years*. Santa Cruz: Santa Cruz Toddler Care Center, 1995.

Waldstein, Laurie, and Leslie Zinberg. *The Pink and Blue Baby Pages: Practical Tips and Advice for New Parents*. Lincolnwood, IL: Contemporary Books, 1995.

Weissbluth, Marc, M.D., *Healthy Sleep Habits, Happy Child*, Revised Edition. New York: Fawcett Books, 1999.

Williams, Jan. *Household Detective: Protecting Your Child from Toxins at Home*. Los Angeles: Children's Health Environmental Coalition, 2003.

Acknowledgments

Many thanks to Judith Regan and Cassie Jones. They humor me, let me do books I want, and tolerate my ideas. Thank you.

Rebecca McQuigg now knows more about motherhood than any single gal should. She researched, combed, and listened to my endless whining. She managed my life so I could manage this book. Kristin Bennett will be the best mom ever—with or without this book. What she didn't know by gut she researched. Despina Georgiou found information the CIA might have hidden. Don't ask me how, she just did. Ditto Catherine Stellin who gave advice and criss-crossed the country so I could do a few more days of pickup at preschool.

Andrea Stanford has three kids and a job, and still combed through this manuscript to make it better. There must be two of her; I can't explain it otherwise.

I may not have a mom, but there are some women in my life I couldn't get by without. Joni Evans is a friend, mentor, agent, and ultimate sounding board. Nancy Schulman offers the best advice on parenting there is, and Kate White manages to support me in more ways than anyone could ever ask or expect while being the perfect mom and businesswoman—What did I do to deserve such amazing role models? You each play such a vital role in my life. And you may not even know it.

And speaking of people I can't live without. . . . Linda and Mitch Hart redefined what parents are and what they do. How did I get so lucky?

Tim and Sarah Geary were such good friends they forgave oversights in the first book. At least I don't make the same mistake twice. Thank you for your friendship.

Ellen Sassa had comfort, warmth, and great tips. Truly a modern mom and friend.

Kary McHoul Gatens, Ann Lewis Roberts, and Lisa Berger are smart, gorgeous, and great friends. Thank you for your advice and never wavering on what MG and I could be. To Michelle Edwards, a great friend, mom, and wife. To everyone at E!: Ted Harbert, Deana Delshad Schwartz, Renee Simon, Salaam Coleman Smith, and David Kelleher, thank you for believing in the show. And the ultimate modern girls Eva La Rue, Jess Zaino, and Claudia Jordan are really the kind of girlfriends anyone is lucky to have.

Michael Rubel, Richard Lovett, Bryan Lourd, and Lee Gabler continue to let me pursue things for my heart, not for dollars. That's a gift.

Ben Sherwood and Jessica Guff tolerate my urge to be on TV. And Karen Sherwood tells me I was good even if I wasn't. Those are friends.

Thanks for the support of my friends and moms with great advice: Barbara Coulon, Deborah Fine, Amanda Freeman, Danyelle Freeman, Debbie Hutman, Andrea Hutton, Nina Kotick, Andy McNicol, Dana Oliver, Dawn Ostroff, Clare Ramsey, Andrea Simon, Stephanie Sourapas, Katie Tarses, Melissa Thomas, Tiffany Ward, Vicki Waller, Alison Zager, Andrea Orbeck and everyone at Youth Intelligence.

Leah Albright, Olivia Sinaguinan, Emma Cunningham, and Doris Miranda made my home run smoothly, so I could bring home some bacon.

Jo Boorman showed me that not only are mothers-in-law not monsters, but one of the best friends to have. I feel so grateful to have her in my and my children's life. Ditto Pippa, a sister-in-law and true friend. Their advice and love are spectacular.

Dad, Beth, Paul: If anyone asks, I'm the perfect mother.

Julie, Mark, and Luke Rowen: Everything else may be bronze but our friendship is gold. Awww. You're inspirations, we love you, and you're stuck with us.

And to Jen Furmaniak again. I said it at the beginning, but without her there wouldn't have been a book. A great writer, partner, and friend.

Michael, I love you. Don't work so hard.

To Marcus, Jack, and Lilia; It seems silly that writing a book about motherhood took moments away from you when all I ever want are more of them. I feel so incredibly lucky to call you my loves.

Mommy, I wish you could be here for my motherhood; but I feel lucky to have been there for yours. I love you.

Jen Furmaniak's Acknowledgments

Everyone has ideas. Many of us even dream about acting on our ideas. But Jane manages to put her ideas into action at warp speed, and pull them off successfully, stylishly, and with the greatest of ease. That's not to say that writing this book was easy—you should have seen us pecking away at our laptops between kids' naps and e-mailing at 2 a.m. on several occasions—but without Jane, I would probably still be daydreaming about writing a book "someday." So for her recruitment, trust, encouragement, and partnership, I am grateful. But most of all, I'm honored to know her and call her a dear friend.

Many modern moms—sisters, cousins, friends, relatives, friends of friends—pitched in and shared their grisly stories and solutions from the front lines. You know who you are, and this book is all the better because of you. Thank you.

To my son, Sam: You inspire me to be a better Modern Mom. You have enriched my life immeasurably, and taught me patience, playfulness, and unconditional love in a way I didn't think possible. Thank you for sharing me with this book and for taking long naps when I needed to write. I promise I'm yours for park afternoons from now on.

To my husband, Ben: I couldn't do any of this—writing a book, raising an amazing child—without you. To call myself a Modern Mom is a gross exaggeration without giving credit to you for your love, support, and partnership. You're an amazing husband, a fantastic father, and my life.

To Dad: You've never doubted me and always encouraged me. Your belief in me is unwavering and I wouldn't be where I am today without it. I love you.

And to my mom: The original Modern Mom. It took becoming one to truly understand how selflessly, gracefully, and patiently you pulled off motherhood. Thank you for your tolerance, advice, and teaching me the art of multitasking. Motherhood is all the sweeter because I'm sharing it with you.

Index

accidents, responding to, 211
acetaminophen, 34, 178, 180
  see also Tylenol
acid reflux, 107, 109, 110
adenoids, 179
aggression, physical, 217, 220–21
air vents, 77
alcohol, breast-feeding and, 101
allergies, allergens, 34, 101, 105, 174
  breast milk and, 94, 95
  to solid foods, 114, 116–17
aloe, 183
Ambi Teddy Carousel, 269
American Academy of Pediatrics
  (AAP), 22, 72, 95, 188
  on sleep issues, 144, 155
  on swimming, 276–77
  on TV watching, 274
  on vitamins, 129
American Association of Pediatrics,
  173
American Association of Poison
  Control Centers, 184
American Dental Association, 173
American Red Cross, 74, 123, 184

Ames, Louise Bates, 238–39
anemia, 72, 118, 129
anesthesia, epidural, 47–48
Angelcare Movement Sensor with
  Sound Monitor, 18
anger, in response to child's crying,
  141
animals, stuffed, 11, 250, 253–54
Annie and the Old One (Miles), 236
announcements, 50, 60
antibacterial gel, 85
antibiotics, 179, 181
antidepressants, 71
anxiety, separation, 146, 148–49, 152,
  233–34
aplastic anemia, 72
appetite, loss of, 173, 179
appointments, doctor, scheduling of,
  45
aprons, 115
Aquaphor diaper rash cream, 16
aquariums, 267
Armsreach, 13
aspirin, 178
asthma, 189

25

autism, vaccinations and, 187–88
Avent, 119
Axion, 39

Babies 'R Us, 20
Baby Bjorn, 27, 28
Baby Bliss, 110
"baby blues," 70
Baby Carrier Original, 28
babycenter.com, 48
Baby Gap, 37
babyish behavior, reverting to, 81, 235
babymoon, 78–91
   babyproofing during, 88–89
   introducing new siblings and,
      79–81
   pets and, 82–83
   reality check during, 90–91
   visitors and, 84–87
baby powder, 16
babyproofing, 88–89, 212–13
baby-sitting, baby-sitters, 90, 130
Baby's Quiet Sounds Video Monitor, 18
Babystyle, 13, 263, 270
Babystyle.com, 6, 32
Baby Symphony Cube, 269
baby talk/play, as behavioral problem,
   224
back, sleeping on, 140, 144
back pain, 67–68
bacteria, 25, 103, 106, 177, 181, 187
   cavities and, 171
bad words, 223
baking soda, as laundry booster, 38
balls, 268
Balmex, 29
banana, 124
Banana Boat sunscreen, 33, 35
Band-Aids, 35, 183
baskets:
   Moses, 12–13, 140, 151
   with partitioned inserts, 14–15
Bassinet (by Pottery Barn Kids), 14
bassinets, 12, 13, 31, 80, 140

bath products, 24, 161
bathrooms:
   breast-feeding in, 98
   congestion relief and, 181
   see also toilet training
baths, bathing, 146, 160–66
   in bathtubs, 162–63
   daily requirements for, 24, 90, 160,
      260
   fear of, 165–66
   frequency of, 24, 25, 160
   little kid activities and, 165
   Sitz, 66
   sponge, 24, 161–62
   switching to a big tub for, 164–65
   time for, 164
Bebe Sounds, 18
bedding:
   humidifier use and, 25
   shopping for, 11–12
   see also sheets
beds, 12
   futons vs., 12
   portable, 14, 31
   putting babies in, 140
   switching to, 151–52
   toddler, 151
   twin, 10–11, 12, 151
   wetting of, 259
bedtimes, 147–48, 150, 151
beer, nonalcoholic, 97
bee stings, 186
behavioral problems, 217, 219–24
Benadryl, 33, 34, 186
berry stains, removal of, 39
bibs, 115
bingo, 272
Birth Book, The (Sears and Sears), 46
birthday parties, 281–89
biting, 220–21
Biz detergent, 39
BlackBerry, 60, 61
bladder, 65, 255
blankets, 32, 36, 62
   security, 244, 250, 253–54
   stroller, 12

blisters, 183
blood, bleeding, 176
    cord, banking of, 71–74
    after delivery, 64
    hepatitis B and, 189
    from nose, 186
    oxytocin and, 97
    after sex, 69
    stain removal for, 39
blood vessels, broken, 67
board games, 272, 273
Boden (bodenusa.com), 37
bonding, breast-feeding and, 95, 98
boo-boo bunny, 185
books:
    children's, 81, 150, 263, 269, 273
    about labor and delivery, 46–47
    about sleep, 156–59
booster seats:
    car, 27
    for table use, 20, 23
bottle holders, 32
bottles, baby, 32, 33, 103–6, 118
    breast milk in, 103–4, 111
    do's and don'ts for, 106, 171
    leaking of, 31
    while lying down, 179
    night feedings and, 104, 140, 147,
        157–58
    sneaking of, 249
    transitioning and weaning from,
        118, 119, 244–49
    transitioning to, 241, 243
bouncy seats, 20–21, 163
Boynton, Sandra, 269
boys:
    circumcised, 16, 161, 162, 168–69
    leaking diapers of, 15
    toilet training for, 256–57, 258
Bradley, Robert, 48
Bradley method, 46, 48
brain:
    colors and, 10
    infections and, 189, 190, 191
bras, 62, 102, 103
Braun, Betsy Brown, 155

bread, 121, 128
breast cancer, 95
breast-feeding, 62, 67, 85, 86,
    92–104, 140, 178
    advantages of, 94–95
    alternating sides in, 96
    bonding and, 95, 98
    colic and, 111
    diarrhea and, 181
    diet for, 100–101
    engorgement and, 241, 242
    feeding on demand and, 99–100
    finger test and, 100
    hormones and, 69
    latching and learning the ropes for,
        95–99, 103
    length of time for, 95
    problem eaters and, 100
    pumping and, 103–4, 111
    refusing solid foods and, 117
    schedule for, 98, 99
    sleep and, 98, 146, 147
    sore nipples and, 93, 99, 102–3
    support for, 97
    vitamin D and, 129
    weaning off, 241–44
breast milk:
    amount of, 97–98, 99, 115, 121
    congestion relief and, 181
    duration and storage of, 104
    eye care and, 166
    in solid food, 114
breast pads, 102, 242
breasts, leaking of, 64, 102
breathing problems, 16, 98, 176
    monitors for detection of, 144
breathing techniques, 48
bribery, 245, 250
Brio, 269
Britax, 26, 27
"broken" rules, acknowledging of, 212
bruises, 185
bubble baths, 164
Buffalo Soldier (Marley), 263
Bugaboo, 30
Building Block Choo Choo, 270

Bumper Jumper, 22
bumps, 185
burns, 183–85
burp cloths, 32, 99
burping, 107–9, 232
burp pads, 14
business travel, 234
butter stains, removal of, 39

cabbage, in bras, 102
cabinets, babyproofing of, 89
caffeine, 101
calcium, 105
call list, compiling of, 60
calories, breast-feeding and, 95, 101
cameras, 61, 273
cancer, 128, 189
    breast-feeding and, 95
carpooling, booster seats and, 27
car seats, 25–28
    infant, 25–26
    snap-and-go stroller as, 28, 29
    toddler, 26–27
Carter's, 17
car trunks, items to keep in, 33
cats, 13, 82–83
cavities, 171
CD players, electric clocks with, 19
cell phones, 62
cereal, 113, 114, 115, 121, 128
cesarean births (c-sections), 47, 62,
    65, 68
chairs, 18–19
changing pads, 14, 32
changing tables, 10, 14–17
chapping, 67
Cheerios, 33, 120
chemical burns, 184
chemicals, in detergents, 37–38
chemotherapy, 72
chickenpox vaccination, 189
childbirth, see labor and delivery
Children's Health Environmental
    Coalition (CHEC), 38

chocolate stains, removal of, 39
choices:
    limiting of, 125–26, 212
    toilet training and, 258
chori.org/siblingcordblood/home.ht
    ml, 73–74
circumcision, 16, 168–69
    bathing and, 161, 162
citrus fruits, 101
Classical Stacker, 267
cleaning:
    of high chairs, 23
    of humidifiers, 25
    see also washing
climbing gyms/centers, 268
clocks, electric, with CD players, 19
clothes, 35–42
    buying guide for, 36–37
    changes of, 32, 33
    going-home, 62
    for hospital stay, 61, 62
    size of, 36, 38
    stain removal guide for, 39–42
    transition, 91
    washing of, 37–38, 75
colds, 98, 177
colic, 107, 109–11, 140
college tuition, saving for, 59
colored pencil stains, removal of, 39
coloring, 271–72
colors:
    in children's painting, 271
    fabric softeners and, 38
    selection of, 10, 19
    of socks, 37
Color Wonder Paper and Markers, 271
colostrum, 97
Combi, 29
comfort items, 253–54
communication, 210–13, 237–38, 263
congestion, 179, 180–81
consistency, 212, 215, 236
constipation, 105
Consumer Product Safety
    Commission, 10, 276
Continental Burping, 14

convulsions, 175
cookies, 125
cooperative play, 279–80
cord blood banking, 71–74
Cord Blood Registry, 73
cords, babyproofing of, 88, 89
cornstarch, 16
corn syrup, 125
cortisone, 16
cosleepers, 12, 13, 140, 151
cotton squares vs. balls, 15
cotton swabs and tissues, 16
coughing, 172, 177
CPR, 123, 144, 184
crackers, 124
cradle cap, 163, 167
crawling, 121, 147, 160
crayons, 271
   soap, 165
   stain removal for, 39, 40
cribs, 9–12, 107
   putting Moses baskets in, 13
   temporary, 14
   transitioning from, 151
   travel, 31
   see also cosleepers
crying, 107, 175
   breast-feeding and, 99–100
   change of venue and, 109
   manipulative, 138, 148–49
   pain and, 149
   of parent, 111
   response time to, 142–43
   sleep practices and, 139–40, 141,
      147, 148–49, 153, 156–57
   see also colic
cups:
   sippy, 118–19, 248
   transitioning to, 243–44, 248
curtains, 10, 19
cuts, 182–83

dairy products:
   breast-feeding and, 101

   limiting of, 180, 182
   see also milk; yogurt
Danish study, of MMR vaccine, 188
dark, fear of, 9, 154
day care:
   child's staying home from, 81
   security items and, 254
   selection of, 76–77
   separation anxiety and, 233–34
   toilet training and, 260
   for two-and-a half year olds, 209
days off, for caregivers, 76
Dear Parent (Gerber), 229, 237
death, talking about, 234–35
decoration, of nurseries, 6, 9–10
defecation, *see* pooing
dehydration, 67, 176, 245, 259
delivery, *see* labor and delivery
Deluxe Zoo Mobile, 19
dentists, 171, 173, 252
depression, postpartum (PPD), 70–71
Desitin, 16, 29
desserts, 126
detergents, 37–38
   in stain removal, 39, 40, 41
developmental stages, 207–9
development mini-milestones, what
      to expect and when in, 194–205
diabetes, Type I, 95
Diaper Bag Essentials, 32
diaper bags, 31–33
Diaper Genie, 19
diaper pads, *see* changing pads
diaper pails, 19
diaper rash cream/ointment, 16
diapers, 32, 33
   bathing and, 161, 162
   cloth, 11
   disposable, 6, 11, 15, 19
   dry, 255
   leaking of, 15
   shopping for, 6
   size of, 15
   toilet training and, 255, 257, 258
   wet, breast-feeding and, 97
diarrhea, 16, 115, 172, 177, 181–82

diet, for breast-feeding, 100–101
digestion, 94, 104
    immature, 110
dining out, 131–33
diphtheria, 190
direction, taking, 216
dirt, stain removal for, 39
discipline, 214–18
    for child's friends, 217–18
    consequences of actions and,
        215–16
    by other people, 218
    praise and, 218
    saying "yes" instead of "no" and,
        214–15
    time-outs and, 216–17, 238
divorce, child custody and, 58
docinfo.org, 44
doctors, 252
    when to call, 175–76
    see also pediatricians
dogs, 82–83
doors, 89
double strollers, 30
doulas, 49
Doulas of North America (DONA), 49
DPT (diphtheria, pertussis, and
        tetanus) vaccination, 190
drapery cords, babyproofing of, 89
Dr. Brown's bottles, 106
Dreft, 38
drinks, 118–20
    pouring of, 119
    sippy cups and, 118–19
    see also juice; milk
drooling, 172
drugs:
    antibiotics, 179, 181
    antidepressants, 71
    colic and, 110
    epidurals, 47–48, 67
    fever-reducing, 178
    measuring of, 178
    for medicine cabinet, 34
    for post-delivery pain, 66
    see also specific drugs

Drugstore.com, 6, 174
DuoGlider Stroller, 30
DVDs, 274

ear care, 169
eardrops, 179
ear infections, 95, 173, 177, 179, 190
Earth's Best, 113
eating behavior, *see* manners, table
eczema, 189
Eisenberg, Arlene, 240
electrical burns, 184
electric clocks with CD players, 19
electric pumps, 103
electronics, babyproofing of, 89
e-mailing, of birth announcement,
        60
emergency rooms, 76
    when to go to, 175–76, 184
encephalitis, 189, 190
enemas, 63
engorgement, 241, 242
environment, 236, 261
    babyproofing of, 88–89, 212–13
epidurals, 47–48
    side effects of, 67
epiglottitis, 189
episiotomies, 63–64
Evenflo, 22
excuse me, saying, 225–26
executors, selection of, 53–54
exercise:
    breast-feeding and, 101
    Kegel, 65, 69
ExerSaucer Active Learning Center,
        22
exersaucers, 21–22
expectations, 236
    measuring of, 212
    reasonable, 220, 238
eyes:
    broken blood vessels in, 67
    care of, 166
    glassy, 176

fabrics:
    for high chairs, 23
    selection of, 6, 11, 31
    washable, 6, 31
fabric softeners, 38
facial swelling, 67
Family Cord Blood Services, 73
farting, 232
fear:
    of baths, 165–66
    of child's illness, 174–75
    comfort items and, 253
    of dark, 9, 154
    development of concept of, 9
    separation anxiety, 146, 148–49,
        152, 233–34
Federal Motor Vehicle Safety
        Standards, 26
feeding, 5, 92–133
    bottle, *see* bottles, baby
    burping and, 107–8
    colic and, 109–11
    hiccups while, 187
    at night, 104, 140, 141–42, 147,
        157–58
    reading during, 81
    see also breast feeding; breast
        milk
feelings and emotions:
    expressing of, 215, 217, 223, 237
    validation of, 211
Ferber, Richard, 156–58
Ferberizing, 156–58
fever, 35, 173–80, 190
fights, 135
financial future, planning of,
        59–60
finger feeding, 120–21, 133
First Teeth Baby Toothpaste with
        Infra-Dent Finger Toothbrush
        kit, 171
fish, 121, 128
Fisher Price, 18, 21, 23, 267, 270
flat head (plagiocephaly), 144–45
fluid intake, increase in, 178, 181
focusing, 211

food:
    amount of, 115, 121, 128
    to avoid, 116–17, 122
    baby, making your own, 118
    breast-feeding and, 100–101
    choice of, 125–26
    dining out and, 131–33
    drinks, 118–20
    family dinners and, 129–31
    headaches and, 67
    healthy eating habits and, 123–26
    for hospital stay, 62
    introducing solid, 113–23
    for one year and beyond, 123–29
    picky eaters and, 124, 126–27, 245
    playing with, 125
    refusing, 117, 124
    shopping for, 129
    from six to ten months, 113–15
    snacks, 123, 125, 280–81
    spitting of, 222
    suggested, 115, 121
    sweets, 124
    table manners and, 130–31, 132
    teeth and, 119, 120, 123, 171, 245
    from ten to twelve months,
        120–21
    throwing of, 215–16
    visitors and, 85
food dye stains, removal of, 39
Forever Mine, 11
formula, 104–5, 166, 178, 244
    allergic reactions to, 94, 105, 107
    amount of, 105, 115, 121
    choosing of, 105
    microwaving of, 106
    premeasured, 32
    saving on, 95
    in solid food, 114
    spit-up and, 108
    stain removal for, 39
    storage of, 106
    vitamin D-fortified, 129
freezing:
    of breast milk, 104
    of meals, 130

friends:
    disciplining children of, 217–18
    drop-by visits from, 84–86
    with toddlers, 86
fruit, 128, 181
    as baby food, 113, 114, 115, 121
    breast-feeding and, 101
    stain removal for, 39
fruit juice, *see* juice
futons, 12

gag reflex, 174
games, 272, 273
garlic, breast-feeding and, 100–101
gas, 101, 107–10, 117
Gaskin, Ina May, 46
gastrointestinal problems, 95
gates, baby, 151, 152
gear guide, 7–9
genetic immunodeficiencies, 72
Gerber, Magda, 229, 235, 237
Gerber cereals, 113
Gerber "puffs," 120
Gerber's Lil Trainer Cup, 119, 248
gifts, 8, 81
    birthday, 288–89
    cord blood banking as, 73
    for siblings, 81
    thank-you notes for, 50
glue stains, removal of, 39
Goer, Henci, 46
goodbye, saying, 227
goodie bags, 286–88
gowns, infant, 17, 26
Graco, 22, 26, 27, 30, 31
grains, as baby food, 113
"grandma hold," 110
grandparents, 80, 218, 227, 244
grass stain, removal of, 39
Gripe Water, 110
grocery shopping, 129
guardians, legal, 55–58
guests, overnight, 86–87
guilt, 233, 249

gym bags, 32
Gymboree (gymboree.com), 276
Gymini 3D Activity Gym, 21
Gymini Total Playground, 263

habit breaking, 241–60
    bottle feeding and, 118, 119, 244–49
    breast-feeding and, 241–44
    decision making and, 252
    pacifiers and, 100, 249–52
Haemophilus influenzae, 189
hair, 168
    falling out in clumps of, 67
    pulling of, 218, 221–22
    washing of, 24, 163, 168
haircuts, 168
hands, washing of, 24, 76, 80, 85, 121,
    182, 260
hangings, 9, 19
Hanna Andersson, 37
Happiest Baby on the Block, The (Karp),
    158–59
Happiest Toddler on the Block, The
    (Karp), 237–38
hats, 37, 62
    sun, 32, 37
head:
    bald spot on, 145
    banging of, 220, 222
    flat (plagiocephaly), 144–45
    injuries to, 185, 211, 220
headaches, 67
Head-to-Toe baby wash, 24
Healthy Care Booster Seat, 23
Healthy Sleep Habits, Healthy Child
    (Weissbluth), 158
heat burns, 183–84
heavy objects, babyproofing of, 89
Heimlich maneuver, 123
hello, saying, 227
hemorrhoids, 66
hepatitis B vaccination, 189
Hib vaccination, 189
hiccups, 110, 187

high blood pressure, 95
high chairs, 20, 23
    in restaurants, 132, 133
hitting, 221
holidays, for caregivers, 76
homemadebaby.com, 113
hormones, 68, 69, 97
    in milk, 126
hospitals:
    drop-by visitors at, 84–86
    packing for stay in, 60–62
    sibling visits to, 80
houseguests, overnight, 86–87
Household Detective, 38
Huggies diapers, 15
Huggies holder, 32
Huggies Supreme Care wipes, 16
hugs, 227
humidifiers, 25, 181
humiliation, avoiding, 218
husbands or partners, 80, 90
    bottle feeding and, 103, 104
    drop-by visitors and, 85
    fighting with, 135
    labor and delivery and, 48, 49
    refusing solid food and, 117
    sleep and, 135
hydrocortisone, 16
hydrogen peroxide, 34
    in stain removal, 40, 41
hygiene, bathroom, 260
Hyland's Homeopathic Teething
        Tablets, 174

ibuprofen, 34
ice, for pain, 66, 185, 186, 221
ice cream stains, removal of, 41
"I don't like you," 223–24
imaginary play, 279
immune system, 72, 189
    breast milk and, 94
immunize.com, 188
Ina May's Guide to Childbirth (Gaskin),
        46

independence, 253
    communication and, 212–13
    play dates and, 280, 281
    pouring and, 119
    sleep issues and, 146–47, 148, 150
infant carriers, 27–28
infant car seats, 25–26
infant gowns, 17, 36
Infantino, 263
infant seats, 14, 20–21
infant swings, 20–21
infant tubs, 23, 24
infections, 95, 177, 183, 189, 190
    breast, 103
    ear, 95, 173, 177, 179, 190
    fevers in fighting of, 178
    urinary tract, 260
    vaginal, 164
ingrown nails, avoiding, 17
injections, for babies, 45
    see also vaccinations
ink stain, removal of, 41
insurance, medical, 76
intelligence, 95
International Playthings, 269
IPV (inactive polio vaccine), 190
iron, 129
    in formula, 105
irritability, 180, 190
itchiness, 67

jackets, 32
Janie and Jack (janieandjack.com),
        37
jogger, the, 29, 30
Johnson's, 24
juice, 120, 171, 178, 180, 181,
        246–47
    stain removal for, 39
    water vs., 120
juice boxes, 120
jumpers, 22
Jungle Safari Tent and Tunnel, 270
"just one more," 154

Karp, Harvey, 158–59, 237–38
Kegel exercises, 65, 69
keys, places for, 29, 31
kiddy stands, 30
kisses, 227
Kolcraft, 29

labor and delivery, 45–49, 60–70
    bizarre side effects after, 66–68
    books about, 46–47
    breakthrough pain during, 48
    doulas and, 49
    epidurals for, 47–48
    hemorrhoids after, 66
    natural techniques for, 48
    packing for hospital stays and,
        60–62
    pain after, 65–66, 68
    peeing and pooing after, 64–65
    pooing during, 63
    sex after, 68–70
    tears and episiotomies during,
        63–64
    water births and, 49
Laclede (laclede.com), 171
lactation consultants, 97, 103–4
lactic acid, 101
lactose intolerance, 105
Lamaze, Ferdinand, 48
Lamaze Clutch Cube, 263
Lamaze method, 48
Lansinoh, 62, 102, 103
lap pads, 11, 12, 14
latching techniques, 96–97
laundry baskets, as Moses baskets, 13
laundry booster, 38
lawyers, consulting of, 52–53
laxative-inducing fruits, 101
laxatives, 65
layette, creation of, 35–37
leaders, children as, 213
LeapFrog toys, 269, 272
Learning Band Walker, 269
legal guardians, appointing of, 55–58

legal issues, nannies and, 75
Lego, 269
lemon juice, in stain removal, 40, 42
Le Sportsac, 32
letter of medical consent, 76
leukemia, 72, 95
Lifetimes (Mellonie), 235
light:
    sensitivity to, 177
    sleep and, 137, 138
    see also night-lights
Lily Padz, 102
limits and boundaries, establishing,
        212, 214–17, 236
linens, shopping for, 11–12
Link-a-doos Top Take-along Swing,
        21
lip gloss, 91
Lister, Alison, 264
lists, 75, 130
Little Softy books, 267
liver damage, 189
living trusts, 58
lotions, 24
love, 227, 233, 244
lying, 224

Maclaren, 29
Maderma, 68
Magic Toddler Spout, 119
makeup, 91
Manhattan Toys, 267
manners, 225–32
    excuse me, 225–26
    hello and goodbye, 227
    nose picking, farting, and burping,
        232
    responsibilities and, 231–32
    saying please and thank you, 226,
        227
    saying your sorry, 225
    sharing and, 227–30
    table, 130–31, 132, 230–31
Marathon, 26, 27

margarine stains, removal of, 39
marker stains, removal of, 41
Marley, Bob, 263
masks, 80
massage:
    baby, 264–66
    during labor, 49
mastitis, 103
mattresses:
    for cribs, 11
    liquidproof, 259
    waterproof covers for, 64
mattress pads, 11
measles, *see* MMR
meats, 128
    as baby food, 113, 114, 115, 121
    nitrates and nitrites in, 128
Medela, 103
medical care:
    get help when it's practical and,
        176–77
    immediate need for, 175–76
medical consent, letters of, 76
medicine cabinet, home, shopping
        for, 33–35
Mellonie, Bryan, 235
meltdowns, 220
Memel, Elizabeth, 235
memories, preserving, 50–51
meningitis, 189, 190
menstruation, 104
metabolic storage disorders, 72
microwaving, of formula, 106
Midwives Alliance of North America,
        46
Miles, Miska, 235
milk, 114, 128, 129, 244, 246–47
    stain removal for, 41
    whole vs. skim, 126
    see also breast milk
Mindell, Jodi, 138
mini-bags, supplies in, 33
mini-milestones, 193–205
Mini Orchestra, 267
MMR (measles, mumps, and rubella)
        vaccination, 187–90

mobiles, 19, 31, 263
moisturizer, 62
molds, 25
Mommy & Me classes, 275, 277
Mommy's Helper, 32
monitors, 17–18, 144
monsters, 154
Moses baskets, 12–13, 140, 151
Mother's Milk homeopathic pills, 97
Mother's Milk tea, 97
Motrin, 34, 178
movement monitors, 18
movies, 71, 98, 274, 275
mucus, green and yellow, 177
mumps, *see* MMR
Mundy, Michaelene, 235
Murkoff, Heidi, 46
museum visits, 263
music, 19, 99, 263, 267
    singing of, 269
    training in, 277
music boxes, 31
Music Together, 276
mustard stains, removal of, 41
My Gym, 276
Mylicon, 110
My Quiet Book, 263

nail care, 17, 169–70
nail clippers, 17, 170
nannies, 74–76, 281
naps:
    of child, 137, 145, 146, 147, 149,
        150, 153, 155–56, 158
    of mother, 85, 86
    transitioning from, 149
National Marrow Donor Program,
        74
natural birth techniques, 46–47, 48
Natural Childbirth, The Bradley Way
        (McCutcheon), 46–47
nearsightedness, 9
neck, stiff, 176
Nesting Action Vehicles, 270

nicotine, breast-feeding and, 101
nightgowns:
    for hospital stay, 61, 62
    infant, 17, 36
night-lights, 6, 9, 31, 149
nightmares, 154–55
night terrors, 155
900–MHz long range monitors, 17
911, calling, 183, 184
nitrates, 128
nitrites, 128
noise, sleep and, 137, 138, 140
nose:
    care of, 169
    congestion and, 180–81
    picking of, 232
    runny, 172, 177, 179, 181
nose aspirator, baby, 16–17
nosebleeds, 186
notepads, at changing tables, 14
nurseries, shopping for, 6, 9–19
    changing tables, 14–17
    cribs, beds, and planning ahead
        and, 10–11
    decorating themes and, 6, 9–10
    linens, 11–12
    monitors, 17–18
    Moses baskets, cosleepers, and
        bassinets, 12–13
    other essentials, 18–19
nursery schools, see day care;
        preschool, preschoolers

obesity, 95, 125, 126
object permanence, 267
observational play, 278–79
Ocean Wonders Aquarium Bouncer,
    21
onesies, 17, 36, 37
Orajel, 174
ottomans, 18
outlets, babyproofing of, 88
ovarian cancer, 95
overnight houseguests, 86–87

overstimulation, colic and, 109,
    110–11
oxytocin, 97

Pacific Play Tents, 270
pacifiers, 33, 100, 111–13, 147, 159
    breaking the habit of, 100, 249–52
    ear infections and, 179
    medicine administered with, 178
packing, for hospital stay, 60–62
Pack N Play Playard, 31
pain:
    back, 67–68
    crying and, 149
    after delivery, 65–66, 68
    ear, 179
    of engorgement, 241, 242
    ice for, 66, 185, 186, 221
    of labor and delivery, 47–49
    as punishment, 217
    sex and, 69
    teething and, 149, 172, 173–74
    of vaccines, 192, 193
painting, paint:
    lead-based, 10
    for nurseries, 9, 10
    playing and, 165, 270, 271
    stain removal for, 41
pajamas, 17, 150, 259
    footie, 36
    for hospital stay, 62
Pampers Premium, 15
panties, for hospital stay, 62
parallel play, 279
parks, play dates in, 229
pasta necklaces, 270
pastas, 121, 127, 128
PCV (Prevnar) vaccination, 190
pear juice, 65
peas, frozen, as ice pack, 66, 185
Pedialyte, 34, 182
pediatricians, 34, 66, 90, 128, 145,
        166, 173, 184
    feeding issues and, 105, 106, 130

mini-milestones and, 193

potty training and, 257

selection of, 44–45

peeing, 176, 256–57

after delivery, 64–65

Pook Rattle and Toother, 268

Peg Perego, 23

pencil stain, removal of, 39, 41

penis, circumcision and, 16, 161, 162, 168–69

permission, asking for, 228

pertussis (whooping cough), 190

petroleum jelly, 16

petroleum ointment, 16

pets, 82–83

death of, 235

pharmacies, twenty-four hour, 176

phone cords, babyproofing of, 89

photos, 155, 273

physical aggression, 217, 220–21

picture books, 269

pillows, 11, 62

breast-feeding, 99

c-sections and, 68

donut, 66

head banging and, 220, 222

placemats, 89

plagiocephaly (flat head), 144–45

plastic surgery, 182

play dates, 217–18, 268, 278–89

cooperative play and, 279–80

ideas for, 280–81

imaginary play and, 279

nannies vs. mommies for, 281

observational play and, 278–79

parallel play and, 279

sharing and, 229

see also birthday parties

play dough, 270

playgroups and classes, 275–78

playing, 150, 236, 261–94

in baths, 165

from birth to three months, 262–66

from eighteen to twenty-four months, 269–72

with food, 125

from four to twelve months, 266–67

solitary, 261, 267

from twelve to eighteen months, 268–69

from twenty-four to thirty-six months, 272–73

playmats, 21, 263

playpens/travel cribs, 31

please, saying, 226, 227

pneumonia, 16, 189, 190, 191

Poison Control Center, 184

polio, 190

Polo (polo.com), 37

pooing:

after delivery, 64–65

on the delivery table, 63

solid food and, 115

toilet training and, 255, 257–58

portable toilets, 256

postpartum depression (PPD), 70–71

Pottery Barn Kids, 14, 15, 126

potty training, *see* toilet training

pouring, 119

praise, 218, 228, 258

predictability, maintaining, 211

pregnancy, 43, 46, 104, 151

see also labor and delivery

premature babies, breast-feeding of, 95

preschool, preschoolers, 289–94

diseases and germs of, 80

getting your child ready for, 292–94

see also day care

Prima Pappa, 23

Prince Lionheart, 15

Prozac, 71

prune juice, 65

pumping, of breast milk, 103–4, 111

Pump in Style Advanced Breast Pump, 103

punishment, 150, 151, 214, 217

Purell, 85

pushing, 221

push/pull toys, 268
puzzles, 272

Quatro Large, 269
Quicken Willmaker kits, 54

raisins, as snacks, 123
rashes, 38, 172, 177, 190
    diaper, 16
reading, 263, 269, 274
    to toddlers, 81, 150
    see also books
redcross.org, 123, 184
redirecting behavior, 214–15
reggae music, 263
religion, 234–35
respect, 210, 235–36, 237
respiratory problems, 95
    see also breathing problems
responsibilities, 231–32
restaurants, dining out in, 131–33
rewards, 150, 152, 245, 250, 259
rice, 121, 128
ride-on cars, 268
RIE (Resources for Infant Educators)
        method, 235–37, 276
Right Start, 32
rocking, 138, 158
rompers, 36
Roundabout, 26
rubella, *see* MMR
rules of the road, learning of, 211–12
rust stains, removal of, 42

Sad Isn't Bad (Mundy), 235
Safe Glow 2 Receiver Monitor, 17
Safety First, 17
safety issues:
    bathing and, 162–63, 164
    for beds, 151
    for bouncy seats, 21
    for changing tables, 14
    cribs and, 10
    food, 116–17, 122
    for walkers, 22
    for windows, 89
salad, dry, 130
sanitary pads, 64, 66
savings account, 59
savior (controller), avoiding the role
        of, 210–11
Schulman, Nancy, 238
Scotch tape, removing splinters with,
        34
screaming, 139–40
screens, babyproofing of, 89
Sears, Bill, 139
Sears, Martha and William, 46
seats:
    booster, 20, 23, 27
    car, *see* car seats
    infant, 14, 20–21
security blankets, 244, 250, 253–54
self-discipline, 214
Self Help Law Center, 54
separation anxiety, 146, 148–49, 152,
        233–34
sex, 64
    breast-feeding and, 94
    after childbirth, 68–70, 104
    hepatitis B and, 189
shades, blackout, 19
shame, toilet training and, 258
shampoo, 24, 163, 165, 167, 168
sharing, 227–30
sharp edges, babyproofing of, 89
shaving cream, 165, 270
sheets, 11, 12, 259
shhh sounds, 159
Shields, Brooke, 70
shopping, 5–42, 263
    for bath products, 24
    for car seats, 25–27
    for diaper bags and supplies, 31–33
    for exersaucers, 21–22
    gear guide for, 7–9

grocery, 129
for high chairs, 23
for home medicine cabinets, 33–35
for humidifiers, 25
for infant carriers, 27–28
for infant seats and swings, 20–21
for infant tubs, 23–24
for jumpers, 22
for nurseries, 6, 9–19
for playmats, 21
for playpens/travel cribs, 31
after receiving gifts, 8
for strollers, 28–30
for toys, 22–23
for walkers, 22
shoving, 221
showers, daily, 90
Sibling Donor Cord Blood Program,
  73–74
siblings:
  new, 79–81
  sharing among, 229–30
sickle cell anemia, 72
side sleeping, 140, 145, 159
silverware, 131, 132
single mothers, sleep and, 143
sippy cups, 118–19, 248
sitting up, 147
Sitz baths, 66
skin, dry, 16, 25, 62, 176
  see also rashes
Skwish Classic, 267
sleep, 134–59, 176
  bedtime routines for, 146–50, 152,
    156
  bedtimes and, 147–48, 150, 151
  big boy/girl beds and, 151–53
  from birth to three months, 136–45
  body position for, 140, 144, 159
  books about, 156–59
  breast-feeding and, 98, 146, 147
  discerning between day and night
    and, 98, 137–38, 143, 158
  establishing independence and,
    146–47, 148, 150
  fears and, 154–55

formula and, 104
identifying signs of fatigue and, 136
nighttime resistance and, 150
from nine to twelve months,
  148–49
one-year-old patterns of, 149–50
putting your baby or child down
  awake and, 138–39, 148,
  152–53, 156
REM vs. non-REM, 153
response time to crying and, 142–43
schedule for, 141–42, 148, 150
screaming and, 139–40
separation anxiety and, 146,
  148–49, 152
staying with child until, 152–53
teething and, 149
terrible twos and, 153–56
three-day rule and, 143
from three to nine months, 145–48
travel and, 146–47
what the experts say about, 156–59
Sleeping Through the Night (Mindell),
  138
smoking, 101, 111, 144
snacks, 125
  for play dates, 280–81
  raisins as, 123
snap-and-go strollers, 28–29, 30
snowsuits, 37
Snug Ride, 26
soap, 24, 25
soccer, 278
socialization, 276
socks, 36, 37, 62
Solve Your Child's Sleep Problems
  (Ferber), 156–58
Soothies (soothies.com), 103
sore throats, 180
sorry, saying you're, 225
soy, as allergen, 101, 105
spanking, 214, 217
spices, 101
spine, 191
spitting, 107–10, 222
splinters, 34, 186

Spock, Benjamin, 141, 239–40
sponge baths, 24, 161–62
sports, team, 278
stain removal guide, 39–42
stairs:
    babyproofing of, 89
    climbing, 6
    walkers and, 22
standing up, 147
stem cells, 72
steroids, avoiding, 16
stickers, stain removal for, 42
stimulation:
    avoiding vs. encouraging, 9–10
    colic and, 109, 110–11
    colors and, 10
    from mobiles, 19
stomach sleeping, 140, 144, 159
Streptococcus pneumoniae, 190
stress, cutting down on, 254
strollers, 28–30
    blankets for, 12
    children's protests about, 28
    tying toys to, 33
sucking, 159
    pain while, 179
    see also pacifiers
sudden infant death syndrome
        (SIDS), 140, 143–44
Summer Infant, 18
sunburn, 184
sunscreen, 32, 33, 35
support:
    for breast-feeding, 97
    for child, 233, 244
    postpartum, 71
Sure Comfort Deluxe Newborn-to-
        Toddler Tub, 23
swaddling, 159
sweaters, 33, 36, 37
Sweet Dreams Monitor, 18
sweets, 124
    healthful alternatives to, 127–28
    treats and desserts, 126
swimming, 276–77
swimming pools, babyproofing of, 89

swinging, 159
swings, infant, 20–21
Symphony-in-Motion geometric
        shapes, 19

tablecloths, 89
table manners, 130–31, 132, 230–31
tantrums, 81, 215, 219–20, 232, 235
Target, 12, 37, 89, 91
Target.com, 6, 37
tattling, 224
TB test, 191
teaching, 206–40
    bad behavior and, 219–24
    communication and, 210–13,
        237–38
    about death, 234–35
    developmental stages and, 207–9
    discipline and, 214–18
    expert views on, 235–40
    of manners, 225–32
    RIE method and, 235–37
    separation issues and, 233–34
tears, during labor and delivery,
        63–64
teaspoons, size of, 178
teddy bears, 253–54
teenagers, 224
    sleep problems of, 158
teeth, 172
    care of, 170–71
    food and, 119, 120, 123, 171, 245
    raisins and, 123
    sippy cups and, 119
teething, 110, 149, 172–74, 181
    pain relief from, 173–74
temperatures, 176, 177–78
tetanus, 190
thalassemia, 72
thank you, saying, 226, 227
thank-you notes, 50
thermometers:
    digital, 35
    rectal, 177–78

thimerosal, 187–88
Thinking Woman's Guide to a Better Birth, The (Goer and Wheeler), 46
throats, sore, 180
thumb sucking, 112, 244, 246
    breaking the habit of, 251–52
time-outs, 216–17, 238
Tiny Love, 19, 21, 263
tips, for waiters, 133
tobacco, *see* smoking
toddlers:
    caregiver ratio to, 77
    car seats for, 26–27
    diseases and germs of, 80
    feeding of, 123–29
    friends with, 86
    regression of, 81
    sleep issues and, 149–56
tofu, 121, 128
toilet training, 254–60
    bathroom hygiene and, 260
    for boys, 256–57, 258
    clothes and, 37, 255
    at night, 259
    signs of readiness for, 254–56
    terminology and, 257
    tips for, 256–58
tomato stains, removal of, 42
towels, 24, 33
toys, 32, 132
    bath, 166
    from birth to three months, 262–63
    cleaning and disinfecting of, 268
    color of, 10
    from eighteen to twenty-four months, 269–72
    from four to twelve months, 266–67
    on playmats, 21
    sharing of, 229–30
    shopping for, 22–23
    throwing, 216
    tied to strollers, 33
    from twelve to eighteen months, 268–69

    from twenty-four to thirty-six months, 272–73
Toys 'R Us, 220
transitioning, 118, 119, 159
travel:
    business, 234
    with nannies, 75
    sleep routines and, 146–47
travel cribs/playpens, 31
treats, 126
trust, 210, 236
trusts, 54, 58
tuberculosis, 191
tubs, infant, 23–24
Tucks wipes, 66
Turbobooster, 27
turns, taking, 228
TV watching, 212, 216, 217, 274–75
two-piece outfits, 36
two-way monitors, 18
Tylenol, 33, 34, 149, 173, 174, 177, 178, 192

umbilical cord:
    blood banking and, 71–74
    stump of, 24, 161, 162, 167
umbrella strollers, 29
underwear:
    of child, 255–59
    for hospital stay, 62
Universal Car Seat Carrier, 29
urinary tract infections, 260
urination, *see* peeing
uterine cancer, 95
uterus, breast-feeding and, 95, 97

vaccinations, 187–93
    autism and, 187–88
    month by month, 191–92
    preparation for, 192–93
    types of, 189–91
vaginal infections, 164

Vaseline, 177, 185
vegetables, 124, 128
   as baby food, 113, 114, 115, 118, 121
   breast-feeding and, 101
   disguising of, 127
   nitrates in, 118
ventilation, 6
ViaCord (viacord.com), 73
video cameras, 61
video monitors, 18
videos, 86, 274
vinegar, white:
   as fabric softener, 38
   for humidifier cleaning, 25
   in stain removal, 40, 41, 42
visitors, 84–87
vitamin D, 129
vitamin E oil, 68
vitamins, 129
vomiting, 110, 157, 176, 185

waiters, 132, 133
walkers, 22
walks, taking, 91
wallpaper, 9
washcloths, color of, 183
washing:
   of clothes, 37–38, 75
   daily, 24
   of hands, 24, 76, 80, 85, 121, 182,
      260
   stain removal guide and, 39–42
water:
   bottle of, 32, 33, 246, 248, 249
   distilled, 25, 106
   filtered, 106
   in formula, 106

   juice vs., 120
   parent's drinking of, 67, 98, 99
water births, 49
WD-40, 39, 42
weaning, 241–52
   off bottle, 118, 244–49
   off breast, 118, 241–44
   off pacifiers, 100, 249–52
weight, sleep and, 136, 140, 142
weight loss, breast-feeding and, 95
Weissbluth, Marc, 158
What to Expect the First Year, 240
What to Expect the Toddler Years
     (Eisenberg), 240
What to Expect When You're Expecting
     (Murkoff), 46, 240
Wheeler, Rhonda, 46
whining, 222–23
white zinc oxide, 16
wills, writing of, 51–55, 58
windows, babyproofing of, 89
wipes, 32, 33, 121, 210
   shopping for, 6, 15, 16
   for spit-up, 107
   Tucks, 66
   warmers for, 15
working mothers, nannies and,
     74–76

yogurt, 114, 115, 121, 124

zinc oxide stains, removal of, 42
Ziploc bags, 32, 33
Zoloft, 71
zoos, visits to, 263, 267, 270